FLIGHT
ATTENDANT

FLIGHT

ATTENDANT

FROM CAREER PLANNING TO PROFESSIONAL SERVICE

ALICE MUSBACH &
BARBARA DAVIS

FOREWORD BY EDWARD E. CARLSON,
CHAIRMAN, UAL, INC.

CROWN PUBLISHERS, INC.
NEW YORK

Library of Congress Cataloging in Publication Data
Musbach, Alice.
Flight attendant.
1. Air lines—Flight attendants. 2. Aeronautics,
Commercial—Vocational guidance. I. Davis, Barbara,
joint author. II. Title.
HD8039.A43M87   387.7'42   79-22889
ISBN: 0-517-540681 (cloth)
        0-517-54069X (paper)

Design by Deborah B. Kerner

10 9 8 7 6 5 4 3 2 1
First edition

*Dedicated to the corps of professionals
who have contributed to more than
fifty years of flight attendant service*

CONTENTS

CONTENTS

SECTION III *The Flight Attendant as a Professional* **67**

APPENDIXES

ACKNOWLEDGMENTS

This book was written by more than just two flight attendants. We may have put the thoughts and words together, but without the patience, support, and encouragement of the following people, *Flight Attendant* might never have "gotten off the ground":

Both sets of Moms and Dads and family members, whose interest and help was unending; Don Leach, who guided us in the right direction; personnel in training departments, public relations and inflight services divisions of many U.S. airlines across the country, who supplied us with information and contacts throughout the industry; instructors from other colleges and vocational schools, who also see the need for this book; flight attendants, past and present, with whom we work and share this life-style and whose professionalism spirited the way for the book; Anne Zeeman, who opened the door for us at Crown Publishers; and family, friends, and neighbors for their devotion and the grace to let us "put them on hold" in order to finish the book.

A very special thanks to our editor, Marian Behrman, for her faith and confidence in us, and her ability to find whatever answers we needed.

FOREWORD

by Edward E. Carlson
Chairman, UAL, Inc.

Passenger safety and comfort were key considerations when the first stewardesses were employed by a predecessor of United Airlines nearly a half century ago. Today, monitoring passenger safety and comfort remain the primary duties of more than 54,000 flight attendants working for airlines around the world. But like the airline industry itself, the flight attendant profession has matured and become more sophisticated in the decades since the 1930s. Indeed, the days when people like Ellen Church, the first stewardess, dispensed chicken dinners to passengers seem far removed from the world of today's flight attendants.

Although the media tends to glamorize the flight attendant profession, the image they project is not totally accurate. Today's flight attendant must acquire a variety of technical, psychological, and social skills as well as display a thorough knowledge of first aid and emergency procedures.

In their book, *Flight Attendant,* authors Alice Musbach and Barbara Davis, both United Airlines flight attendants, provide an in-depth look at the flight attendant profession—its challenges, its satisfactions, and the marvelous opportunity it offers for travel.

FOREWORD

The flight attendant profession is a worthy career goal, and one I heartily endorse for people seeking a rewarding and fulfilling career. The impact of the flight attendant on the airline industry cannot be minimized. I hope after reading this book, you'll gain an appreciation of the flight attendant's profession and an awareness of the rich and immense possibilities it holds.

INTRODUCTION

What does it mean to be a flight attendant? Obviously, different things to different people. How do we see the profession? As an opportunity to glimpse many aspects of life that some people may never even imagine. We have the chance to meet a great variety of people, the ability to work as effective team members, and the pleasure of taking pride in the work we do. A simple "thank you" from a passenger at the end of a trip works wonders, especially when you've flown six flights in one fifteen-hour day. And knowing you've comforted a grieving passenger, calmed another's anxieties, or befriended a child traveling alone is a gratifying confirmation of your professionalism. Flying also affords us a captive audience filled with the famous, the not-so-famous, the young and the old, the first-time riders and the seasoned travelers. These passengers not only take with them an impression of the airline through our service to them, but they in turn touch our lives through a sharing experience on board the aircraft.

Most people think that being a flight attendant provides the opportunity for adventure, intrigue, and memorable travel experiences—they're right. It's there for the taking—and for our part, we've only just begun to scratch the surface of our travels. While Barbara was off skiing her way across the Alps of Switzerland and Austria, Alice seized the opportunity to live in an East African village. And sailing around the Galápagos

Islands was just as exhilarating for Alice as Barbara's under-water explorations off the coasts of Hawaii and the Virgin Islands were for her. Who could resist the delight of sampling fine foods throughout France, Great Britain, and Spain as Barbara did, or exploring the jungles and waterways of the Amazon and witnessing a revolution in Afghanistan as Alice has? It's the combination, then, of our travels and the people we meet that brings personal gratification and rewards.

The desire to share our enthusiasm for and knowledge of the flight attendant profession prompted us to accept teaching positions with the California Community College system. As instructors in airline career programs, we're excited to bring an updated, complete version of the flight attendant profession to many classrooms across the country. It has been our ambition to make real the world of the flight attendant so that those outside the profession can understand what it is that we do on our job, and how we manage to get it all done and continue to smile. This book, then, is an attempt to broaden the scope of our teaching so that this information is available to everyone.

From its conception in 1930, when women were first allowed to serve as stewardesses, the position of flight attendant has grown into a highly respected corps of professionals over 50,000 strong. The airline industry itself has grown significantly as a result of increasing passenger travel, as well as advancements in technology. Today's flight attendant enters a dramatic and constantly changing new world. The purpose of this book is to reveal how these changes result in a new image, job scope, and life-style for the man or woman entering the career of flight attendant today.

Since it is unrealistic to pursue a career until you have investigated the job market and the basic eligibility requirements, Section I encourages readers to examine their personal career goals in relation to the requirements of the profession. The airlines discussed in the book are those carriers whose principal centers of operation are located in the United States. The scope of flying includes domestic, international, charter, intrastate, and regional flights. You will discover that flight attendant life-styles vary from one airline to another. Once you have decided which airline(s) to pursue, the book guides you in attaining the position by describing current airline hiring practices.

Section II takes the candidate through the entire training experience and helps him or her prepare for the responsibilities that lie ahead. Emphasis is placed on the standards of performance that are taught in training and will be monitored throughout a flight attendant's career.

Section III can be regarded as the complete handbook for the professional flight attendant. It offers a comprehensive description of flight attendants' duties and responsibilities, emphasizing the teamwork and professionalism required. Subjects include aircraft structure, inflight duties, safety and emergency procedures, appearance standards, and the variety of services provided for passengers.

Since, in a service industry, enthusiasm and a sense of personal commitment are essential for success, interaction between the flight attendant, fellow employees, and passengers is emphasized throughout the book.

It is our intention to direct the volume to a variety of readers. It serves as a valuable guide to the prospective flight attendant and is an excellent text for students enrolled in airline career programs. Even the present flight attendant will find much to enrich his or her experience, as well as an opportunity to view the profession in its entirety. Teachers, too, will find the volume a comprehensive and authoritative companion to every phase of classroom discussion.

It is hoped that *Flight Attendant* will provide a stimulating approach to the profession, as well as an enjoyable, realistic portrayal of the flight attendant in the airline world today.

SECTION I

CAREER PLANNING

"I wanted to join a profession that was really moving with the times."

BONITA BEACH KENT, FLIGHT ATTENDANT, AIR CALIFORNIA

"I knew that I had to find a job that was extraordinary, prestigious, and demanding."

JEANNA ROBINETTE, FLIGHT ATTENDANT, TRANSAMERICA AIRLINES

"Remember that interviewers have been in your situation and are now where you would like to be someday—so relax, see them as people just like you, and trust their judgment."

CELESTE EVANS, FLIGHT ATTENDANT, PAN AMERICAN WORLD
AIRWAYS

"To my knowledge, there has never been a career where so much of one company's success is dependent upon its employees' abilities to work with the public."

JAN SHEPHERD, FLIGHT ATTENDANT, REPUBLIC AIRLINES

"I never knew for sure that I wanted to be a flight attendant until I started being interviewed and became intrigued with the job."

SHERIL VRADENBURG, FLIGHT ATTENDANT, FRONTIER AIRLINES

ESTABLISHING A CAREER GOAL

From the perspective of choosing a career, the flight attendant position is now one of the most sought-after professions in this country. Flight attendants today are independent, better educated, older, and more experienced than ever before. Their maturity and sense of responsibility have helped them create a positive image in the public eye and develop a self-awareness and pride in themselves. Today's flight attendants strive for better working conditions because they are seeking a permanent career more than temporary employment.

The picture of today's professional flight attendant takes in a wide variety of ages, backgrounds, and life-styles. The average age is late twenties to mid-thirties. Average educational experience is three-plus years of college. Average seniority is ten years with a very low attrition rate (around 4 percent). Approximately one half are married, while many are single, divorced, widowed, parents, and even grandparents!

Flight attendants today work with a purpose. They desire to be self-supporting and, fortunately, today's salaries make that feasible. They own homes, rent apartments, commute from distant cities, and have outside business interests and hobbies. Many flight attendants take advantage of their days off to take a temporary leave of absence to pursue educational interests. Any flight attendant has the opportunity to seek advancement to a management position, but the flight attendant profession itself is certainly a worthwhile lifetime career.

3

ADVANTAGES AND DISADVANTAGES

Although the profession of flight attendant is challenging, exciting, and interesting, anyone considering it as a career will want to know as much about the job as possible. Only then can you make a realistic decision about entering the field. The drawbacks are few but they are worth your consideration. Although some of them may occur in other professions, others are unique. Consider the fact that there are long hours of service in one day; there may be several days or weeks away from home, multiple trip segments, short flight times and fast services, smoke-filled cabins, an occasionally difficult passenger, the possibility of holiday duty and being "on-call," and physically demanding work. All of the above can have an impact on your home life, as well as influence your physical health and mental stability. Armed with a positive attitude, though, you can put these disadvantages in their proper perspective and realize that the benefits of being a flight attendant far surpass any negative aspects of the job.

The flight attendant profession offers opportunities that, individually, may be found in other fields of endeavor but, collectively, distinguish one of today's most desirable careers. One of the first advantages is that it can be pursued as a lifelong vocation. It is a job that offers independence, travel, new environments, and the opportunity to meet and interrelate with people from all walks of life. The flexibility of hours and working days, coupled with nonroutine schedules, allows you the advantage of arranging time to suit yourself in your personal and professional life.

As a flight attendant you have a chance to exercise common sense and good judgment when faced with unusual and unpredictable situations. It is a job in which problems can be left behind at the end of each trip and each day starts anew. The time off allows you to pursue a multitude of activities and/or other careers, as long as your participation in them does not interfere with your performance. As a flight attendant, you are also provided with an education that can't be obtained from any book. You are more aware of current events, not only because of the people you meet but because you are often in the very place where news is happening. There is no doubt

4

that being a flight attendant can be stimulating and educational, as well as providing a rich opportunity for growth.

Now that you have had a very brief overview of the flight attendant profession, let's consider it in relation to your individual requirements.

WHO AM I?

Each of us has certain ingredients that make us unique as individuals. Discovery of your own characteristics can only be done through self-assessment. Remember, you and only you can choose an appropriate career based on an analysis of your values, accomplishments, interests, attitudes, and aspirations.

Your values play a major role in the career selection process and will help define what is most important to you. For example, you might prefer a job with regular work hours as opposed to one with frequent schedule changes; or consider working in one specific locale versus extensive travel. Then again, do you prefer working alone or with a variety of people? The career you choose is one that satisfies these feelings and has an effect on your ultimate life-style.

Reflect back on your personal, educational, and work histories to determine your likes/dislikes, successes/failures, aptitudes, and skills. By analyzing your interests in school, church, community functions, home environment, and military service, you begin to discern certain patterns to the activities that bring you personal satisfaction. These same components should be kept in mind when searching for a suitable profession. Only when you like what you are doing can you be happy in your work. However, you first have to determine what it is that you *want* to do. This can be accomplished by developing a self-inventory.

A self-inventory is a tool for evaluating your potential in a specific occupation. Listed on the following page is a sampling of questions, the answers to which may reveal "who you are." Write down your immediate responses. Not only will you get a clearer picture of yourself, but you will have a valuable reference tool to be used later in your career search.

What are my assets?

What situations make me uncomfortable?

How do I get along with others?

Do I recognize my weaknesses and attempt to correct them?

How am I perceived by my family? friends? business associates?

Do I see myself as an introvert or an extrovert?

Do I seize the opportunity to assume a leadership role?

What would I expect a job to do for me?

How do I demonstrate my dependability?

Am I a spectator or a participant?

Do I communicate effectively in written skills? conversational techniques? body language?

What would I like to be doing five years from now?

In what ways have I expressed my creativity?

Am I people-oriented? How?

Can I mix well in any social situation?

How do I relate my educational experience to my career aspirations?

How do I respond when faced with unfamiliar situations?

Do I function better as a member of a team or by myself in my work performance?

Am I self-motivated?

Do I keep informed of current events?

Can I accept constructive criticism?

What are my achievements?

What do I value most in a job?

What are my favorite leisure-time activities?

Do I assume additional responsibilities without being asked?

What accomplishments have brought me the most satisfaction?

In what volunteer work have I participated?

What are my special talents and skills?

What things do I enjoy doing the most?

What are my hobbies?

In what community service organizations have I participated?

What honors/awards have I won in school or the military?

To me SUCCESS is _____ .

By putting time and thought into discovering what you are all about, you are beginning to collect the materials needed to pursue the job you want.

CORRELATING YOUR PROFILE WITH THE JOB REQUIREMENTS

We will assume at this point that your interests lie with the flight attendant profession. In order to test your decision, you must be able to match your capabilities and assets with those required of a flight attendant. In the course of just one day a flight attendant assumes many different roles: psychiatrist, nurse, aeronautics expert, geographical genius, babysitter, sympathetic listener, tactful arbitrator, intelligent decision-maker, tour guide, and gourmet chef. The profession also requires an enormous amount of patience, empathy, maturity, and endless energy. Add confidence and a genuine smile, and you have the makings of a successful flight attendant.

Can you imagine yourself taking tickets (making sure each passenger is on the right flight), hanging coats, taking drink orders, passing out menus, monitoring carry-on baggage, serving beverages to the cockpit crew, ordering extra meals, settling seat duplications, and remaining calm at the same time —all before the airplane leaves the gate? There are times when flight attendants must call upon every personal resource available to get through difficult situations, but then that's what makes them unique.

While doing your self-evaluation did you come up with attributes similar to those of a flight attendant? Can you assume leadership responsibilities on the spur of the moment? Do you show kindness and understanding to a fellow human being, no matter what walk of life he represents? Could you react quickly to a sudden change of pace in emergency situations? Can you organize your work habits in a timely fashion? Do you know how to handle stress and display calmness at the same time? Can you find the patience to endure lengthy delays and still maintain a sense of humor? Do you know how to tell the difference between a sincere plea for help and a play for attention? Have you ever tried to swallow your anger and ambivalence under the attack of a misdirected accusation? Can you be an effective team member and still display your individuality? If you come up with positive answers to these soul-searching questions, then your first instincts about wanting to be a flight attendant were correct.

CAREER PREPARATION

Now that you have defined your career ambitions, let's consider some of the different activities that would help prepare you for the profession. In addition to the basic requirement of a high school diploma, most airlines prefer at least two years of college (Chapter 2 gives further details). Any courses in the following areas would be most helpful: public speaking, dramatics, modeling, debating, and group dynamics—i.e., any subjects to help you develop self-confidence and learn to assert yourself when confronting strangers. Holding elected offices in clubs and organizations cultivates your leadership and communication skills. A good solid background in geography, health and first aid, foreign languages (if required), and a working knowledge of mathematics are a must for the flight attendant. Subjects dealing with sociology and psychology are highly recommended. In addition, participation in sports activities not only keeps you in good physical condition and develops coordination but teaches you how to be a member of a team. The more you understand about yourself and others, the easier it will be to handle public situations without offending other people or sacrificing your own dignity. Overall, try to achieve a well-balanced academic and social background.

Any jobs in which you have had public contact would add to your qualifications. For example, experience as a teacher, nurse, salesperson, or receptionist would be invaluable when applying to the airlines. Participation in volunteer activities affiliated with hospitals, charities, and churches emphasizes your willingness to give of your time and service to others. The only way to learn how to deal with the public is to work with people. Avail yourself of any part-time or full-time work in which you are challenged by the demands of the public.

Depending on the area in which you live, there may be programs available that offer information on airline careers. The most reputable are those offered as part of an accredited course of study, such as in the community college system, where the student pays little or nothing at all for a thorough, comprehensive overview of the flight attendant profession. These courses can be found by exploring college catalogs or visiting the campuses. It is best to avoid those places advertising "guaranteed employment" at a high cost to the student. The most you can get out of any informational course is just that—facts that will help you decide if this is the right career for you.

ESTABLISHING ACTION OBJECTIVES TO START YOUR CAREER CAMPAIGN

A job-hunting technique that has proven most successful is the use of "action objectives," which define the "when" and the "how" of your strategy. These objectives should be stated in writing in a logical sequence of activities. It is a slow process, each one building on the previous one. The following is an example. We suggest you use it only as a guideline, since each person's goals will be stated in individual terms.

Goal: To obtain employment as a flight attendant with a U. S.-based carrier.

Action Objective: On a continual basis, read newspaper and magazine articles pertaining to the airline industry as a whole.

Action Objective: As of __(date)__ investigate the type of airline that would best suit personal objectives and life-style by writing and/or calling individual airlines for information, reading pamphlets and books, and interviewing airline personnel.

Action Objective: By __(date)__ complete a résumé for possible distribution.

Action Objective: By __(date)__ construct a letter to airlines requesting information on basic eligibility requirements and interview procedures. Also, request an application form.

Action Objective: Have all application forms completed and ready to send by __(date)__ .

Action Objective: Prior to __(date)__ prepare for interviews by participating in practice workshops conducted at a local college.

Action Objective: During the months of _____ to _____ interview with specific airlines for the flight attendant position.

Action Objective: After each interview session, follow up with a thank-you note to the employment representative who conducted the interview.

Action Objective: Immediately following an interview, evaluate the experience for future reference.

You have now completed the most time-consuming and thought-provoking phase of the job search. A successful career campaign depends on a positive attitude and a commitment to a definite course of action. You now have the tools to proceed with a strategy based on knowledge of yourself and an awareness of available career choices. When you are sure the goals you have selected are the best ones for you, you will have confidence to pursue your occupational objectives. Gather your mental and physical energies together and maintain a high level of enthusiasm. The more positive you are in your endeavors, the more motivation there will be to keep going. No one is saying the task is an easy one. As a matter of fact, you may encounter roadblocks along the way, but if you view them as learning experiences, you will avoid frustration. Setbacks may be just a test of your convictions and an opportunity to reevaluate the direction and purpose you have given your life. Positive thinking breeds positive action. It is time to turn your ambitions into reality by choosing the airline that would best meet your needs.

2

SELECTING AN AIRLINE TO SUIT YOUR LIFE-STYLE

What if this advertisement appeared in your local newspaper?

Seeking enthusiastic, mature individuals who can meet the challenging demands of the airline industry as a PROFESSIONAL FLIGHT ATTENDANT. Must be 5'2" to 6'0" tall. Weight in proportion to height. Two years public contact work or college preferred. Willing to work long and irregular hours, weekends, and holidays. Excellent travel and work benefits. Interested? Contact our Personnel Dept. at F.L.Y. Airlines, 555–1212, for more information on qualifications and application procedures.

What an opportunity! A chance to fly for F.L.Y. Airlines! "All I have to do is pick up the phone and call." BUT WAIT. Have you thought about the type of employee that F.L.Y. is seeking? Do you know what kind of benefits will be provided to you as a flight attendant? Now is the time to put all your resources to work to accumulate and evaluate information from all airline choices available. You will want to eliminate automatically some airlines from your list of potential employers, because either you do not meet the basic eligibility requirements, or the promised company benefits and working conditions do not meet with your expectations. ACCUMULATE, EVALUATE, ELIMINATE—this is the key. Take the time to thor-

11

oughly investigate F.L.Y. in comparison with other airlines to be certain that this is the company for you.

SELECTION CRITERIA

Today's flight attendants are viewing their profession as a "way of life" that encompasses not only their occupational opportunities but also their personal lives. Essentially, your life-style is determined by the type of airline you select.

In order to determine what airline best suits your needs, consider the following criteria:

Location   Flight attendant bases/domiciles, routes flown in system.

Size   Number of cities served, number of employees, financial stability of airline.

Types of Flying   Domestic, international, charter, regional, intrastate.

Aircraft Flown   Propeller, narrow-body jet, wide-body jet.

Special Skills Required   Foreign language, first aid, swimming.

Training   Number of weeks, location, facilities available, expenses paid by airline.

Salary   Hourly rate of pay, starting salary, meal/hotel expenses, overtime pay, increments based on merit and/or seniority.

Uniforms   Payment, summer/winter, duration, style.

Scheduling   Assigned/bid, based on seniority, monthly/quarterly/trip to trip, reserve system.

Benefits   Vacation, travel, insurance, sick leave, credit union, retirement.

Growth Potential   Individual opportunities for advancement, company's forecast for expansion.

Image   Commercial advertising, reputation.

To help in your selection process, you should begin to contact airlines for this data. The easiest way is to call or write the personnel department requesting information on the flight attendant career. They will most likely send you a qualification fact sheet and/or a brochure about their company. If they are not accepting applications for the flight attendant position, you will be so advised at this time. Another effective method of obtaining information about a particular airline is to talk directly to one of its employees—a flight attendant would be an excellent source.

TYPES OF FLYING OPERATIONS

Most U.S.-based air carriers are certified by the government to engage in air transportation on specific routes on a scheduled, nonscheduled, or limited service basis. Although air carriers are classified by their scope of operations for economic reasons, it would be more appropriate for you to examine them from the standpoint of the type of flying offered and the way in which that might affect your life-style. When soliciting information, consider that an airline may offer more than one type of flying to its flight attendants.

The flight attendant position has many similarities in job function and benefits from one airline to the next. However, there is enough difference to produce a measurable effect on your life-style. Compare your self-profile with what you have read thus far on the flight attendant profession. Narrow down your field of choices to several types of flying for a more concentrated job campaign.

DOMESTIC

Airline Characteristics
  Flies within boundaries of continental U.S.
  Offers scheduled service to business and pleasure passengers; occasional charter and military service
  Serves medium-sized to major cities
  Medium- to long-range routes

Service and Equipment
  Multiple classes of service (first, coach, economy)
  Variety of food/beverage services
  Inflight movie/audio entertainment
  Narrow-body and wide-body jets

13

FLIGHT ATTENDANT

Domiciles
   Number up to 11
   Located in principal U.S. cities
   Transfer opportunities

Scopes of Operation
   Flight attendants aware of schedules for given time frame
   Flight attendants away from home 1–3 days
   Travel through 1–5 time zones
   One or multiple segments per day
   Trip duration ranges from ½ hour to 10 hours

Special Features
   Training: Room and board provided by company; 4–6
      weeks in duration
   Uniforms: Initially purchased by flight attendant; replaced
      by company
   Expenses: Meals, hotel, ground transportation all paid by
      company
   Advancement: Possible promotion to inflight manage-
      ment, instructor, other departments

INTERNATIONAL

Airline Characteristics
   Flies between U.S. and foreign countries and U.S. and U.S.
      territories
   Offers scheduled service to business, pleasure, diplomatic,
      and military passengers
   Serves medium-sized to major cities
   Long-range routes

Service and Equipment
   Multiple classes of service
   One to several food/beverage services
   Inflight entertainment
   Inflight duty-free shopping
   Narrow-body and wide-body jets

Domiciles
   Number up to 11

Located in principal U.S. cities and foreign countries
Transfer opportunities

Scopes of Operation
Flight attendants aware of schedules for given time frame
Flight attendants away from home 1 day to 2 weeks
Travel through multiple time zones
One or multiple segments per day
Trip duration ranges from 1–14 hours
Special requirements: foreign language, visas, water survival skills

Special Features
Training: Room and board provided by company; 4–6½ weeks in duration
Uniforms: Initially purchased by flight attendant; replaced by company
Expenses: Meals, hotel, ground transportation all paid by company
Advancement: Possible promotion to supervisor, instructor, purser, service manager, other departments

REGIONAL

Airline Characteristics
Flies within specific territory or region
Offers scheduled service to business and pleasure passengers
Serves smaller communities; feeds traffic to major cities
Short- to medium-range routes

Service and Equipment
One class of service
Predominantly beverage services
Propeller and jet aircraft

Domiciles
Number 1–6
Located in U.S. cities
Transfer opportunities

Scopes of Operation
Flight attendants aware of schedules for given time frame

Flight attendants away from home 1–3 days
Travel through minimal time zones
Multiple segments per day
Trip duration ranges from ½ hour to 3 hours

Special Features
　　Training: Room and board provided by company; 3–5
　　　　weeks in duration
　　Uniforms: Initially purchased by flight attendant; replaced
　　　　by company
　　Expenses: Meals, hotel, ground transportation all paid by
　　　　company
　　Advancement: Possible promotion to inflight manage-
　　　　ment, instructor, other departments

INTRASTATE

Airline Characteristics
　　Governed by Public Utilities Commission
　　Flies within boundaries of one state
　　Offers scheduled service to commuter passengers
　　Serves small- to medium-sized communities
　　Short-range routes

Service and Equipment
　　One class of service
　　Beverage services only
　　Propeller and jet aircraft

Domiciles
　　Number only one
　　Located in same locale as airline headquarters

Scopes of Operation
　　Flight attendants aware of flight attendant schedule for
　　　　given time frame
　　Flight attendants away from home 1–2 days
　　Travel within one time zone
　　Multiple segments per day
　　Trip duration ranges from ½ hour to 2 hours

Special Features
　　Training: Room and board provided by trainee or com-

pany; training usually 3–4 weeks' duration

Uniforms: Initially purchased by flight attendant or company; replaced by company

Expenses: Meals, hotel, ground transportation all paid by company

Advancement: Possible promotion to inflight management, instructor, other departments

CHARTER

Airline Characteristics

Flies within U.S. and between U.S. and foreign countries

Offers nonscheduled service to pleasure passenger groups; military contracts for troops and supplies

Serves variety of locales

Medium- to long-range routes

Service and Equipment

All one class of service

Variety of food/beverage services

Narrow-body and wide-body jets

Domiciles

Number one or two

Located in U.S. gateway cities

Transfer opportunities

Scopes of Operation

Flight attendants aware of schedule on trip to trip basis

Flight attendants away from home up to 2 weeks

Travel through multiple time zones

One or multiple segments per day

Trip duration—no restrictions

Special requirements: Foreign language, visas, water survival skills

Special Features

Training: Room and board provided by trainee or company; 2–5 weeks in duration

Uniforms: Initially purchased by flight attendant; replaced by company

Expenses: Meals, hotel, ground transportation all paid by company

Advancement: Possible promotion to inflight management, other departments

---

QUALIFICATIONS

Most airlines have available a fact sheet that describes the company, training, uniforms, domiciles, salary structure, and employee benefits. In addition, each airline has established minimum eligibility requirements for screening applicants. You must meet these standards to be considered for the flight attendant position.

ELIGIBILITY REQUIREMENTS

· *Age*   The average minimum age is eighteen to twenty-one. A candidate is eligible for hiring up to within one year of the stipulated retirement age.

Height   The average is 5'2"–6'0". However, there are some airlines that will hire individuals with a minimum height of 5'1", while others will hire up to a maximum of 6'2".

Weight   All airlines consider weight in proportion to an individual's height and bone structure.

Vision   Each airline specifies a minimum vision requirement ranging from 20/20 to 20/200. In most cases, an airline will allow a flight attendant to wear glasses or contact lenses.

Health   Candidate must be in excellent physical condition and able to pass an examination given by the company physician before employment.

Sex   Females or males may apply for the flight attendant position.

Marital Status   Single, married, widowed, divorced, separated may apply; you may even have a family or dependents when applying.

Citizenship   Most airlines require an applicant to be a U.S. citizen. If not a U.S. citizen, applicant must have a permanent working visa or resident alien card. Passport must not restrict entry to countries served by your airline.

Work and Education   An applicant must be a high school

graduate. Because of ever-increasing competition, an airline will look favorably on college-level experience of at least two years. Although it is not a requirement, any public contact work and/or experience will put you in a more competitive position.

Foreign Languages   The majority of airlines do not require a foreign language. However, in the hiring process for international flying, it would be considered an advantage to speak a second language such as French, German, Spanish, or Japanese.

Appearance   You are evaluated according to your overall physical appearance. Concentrate on a neat, natural look, with no extremes. In addition, emphasis will be placed on a clear complexion and straight white teeth.

General   An airline looks for mature individuals who display a pleasant personality. If an applicant has all of the qualifications required by an airline, the employer will consider him/her a "preferred" candidate or applicant.

BENEFITS AND COMPENSATIONS

Most industries offer their employees fringe benefits and salary increases. The attraction to the airlines for most people seems to center around the travel privileges, but the industry really offers much more than that. Guaranteed benefits include a structured salary scale, insurance, vacations, retirement programs, and leaves of absence. You have the opportunity to partake in these programs for the duration of your career.

SALARY

The salary scale varies among the airlines according to negotiated agreements between the flight attendant union and the company. Pay is usually determined by the number of hours flown in any given month. As a general rule, each airline has established a minimum number of hours for which flight attendants are paid a base salary. Any hours flown over this monthly guarantee, up to and not exceeding a specified maximum number of hours, are compensated for by a negotiated hourly rate of pay. Some airlines may pay their flight attendants by the mile, regardless of the number of flight hours accumulated. Some flight attendants are paid extra for flying certain equipment, e.g., jet versus propeller aircraft.

Depending on the particular airline, extra pay may be allotted for understaffing, night flying, over-water flights, reserve status, and specialized working positions. For hours spent completing required emergency and services training and for attending compulsory meetings, a flight attendant will be paid a contractual dollar amount, or an hourly flight-time rate for the accumulated number of hours.

Some airlines offer their flight attendants the opportunity to participate in publicity assignments for which extra pay is received. These nonflight assignments can include Career Day programs, commercial advertising, hosting at marketing functions, and sales campaigns in which flight attendants represent or promote the individual airline.

INSURANCE

A valuable benefit in any company is the range of insurance plans available. As a flight attendant, several programs are automatically provided you by the employer. You also have the option of extending coverage of health and medical benefits through additional purchases and payroll deduction plans. Some of the services offered include dental, hospitalization, accident and life, surgical, maternity, and optical. Most of these policies are implemented through a group insurance plan, allowing for lower rates on premiums.

VACATIONS

Vacations are determined by the individual number of days allotted per flight attendant based on seniority. You will be granted one or two weeks of vacation with pay after the first year of service. Increases of up to a maximum of four to six weeks are granted with seniority.

RETIREMENT

More and more flight attendants are staying in their profession until eligible for retirement benefits. As programs improve through negotiations, flight attendants are being given the option of flying until age sixty to seventy and collecting full benefits or electing to take an early retirement based on age and years of service with reduced benefits. You will often find that the airline will contribute to the financing of this program through profit-sharing plans.

PASS AND TRAVEL BENEFITS

The most popular attraction to the airline industry is the benefit of free and reduced air travel. The privileges vary with years of service and from airline to airline. They may include passes on a positive-space or space-available basis and opportunities to travel on other carriers that have a reciprocal agreement with your airline. Other people eligible for your travel benefits may include parents, spouse, and dependents.

Often a wide range of reductions in hotel accommodations, car rentals, and tour packages around the world are available to airline employees.

LEAVES OF ABSENCE

A leave of absence may be granted on an individual basis because the flight attendant position allows for temporary replacement by a reserve group or a surplus situation exists at a domicile. Such leaves may be used for the purpose of furthering your education or having children, or for reasons of a medical, personal, or emergency nature. General sick-leave time is also awarded with a specified number of hours and days on an annual basis.

TIME TO REAPPRAISE

If you now feel you have enough data to choose a particular airline, you have done your homework. Once the particular kind of carrier has been selected, it is time to reevaluate by balancing the pros and cons against your stated goals and objectives. Your reappraisal must include a flexible attitude toward experiences and circumstances that affect your progress. If you can now identify your expectations with those of an airline, your career campaign has helped to prepare you for the interview process. Only YOU can make the right choice.

3

INTRODUCING
THE CANDIDATE—
WRITE ON!

You have now spent many hours analyzing your potential as a candidate for the flight attendant position. The time and energy invested in developing a self-profile, establishing career goals, and investigating the airline market will prove advantageous as you proceed to the next phase of the job campaign.

You will be communicating who you are, what you have accomplished, and your career aspirations through the written word. All airlines require that you complete an employment application form before being considered for an interview. In addition, the writing of a résumé will serve as a valuable reference tool in pursuing your career.

RÉSUMÉ

A résumé is a concise, factual statement of your personal data and background experiences. It should be designed to reflect you as an individual by highlighting special skills and accomplishments. It should neither oversell nor undersell your capabilities.

Although it is not a requirement, a résumé may be the competitive edge you need to stand out from the crowd. The construction of the résumé has a twofold benefit: it leaves an interviewer with a visual reminder of a candidate and demonstrates that you are sincere in seeking the position by preparing ahead of time; and for the interviewee it serves as a quick reference for pertinent data to be supplied on an application form or to help supplement answers given during an actual interview.

The first impression of any written work is its overall appearance. A résumé should have a professional look from the quality of the paper to the layout of relevant facts. The final résumé should be typed (preferably on an electric machine) on twenty-pound weight paper with a 25 percent rag content. It should be the standard 8½-by-11-inch size, and white is preferred, although pastel-colored paper is acceptable.

To be realistic, do not expect to write the final copy of a résumé the first time around. Proper placement on the page as well as even spacing will add to a neat appearance. The finished product must be approximately one page in length with all pertinent information included in a concise, comprehensive format. You will want to avoid the appearance of overcrowding and yet make every word count. This will require continual editing and revision.

The format used reflects your individual style. There are no absolutes in résumé writing. However, there are two general approaches that are widely used: outline and essay. Decide which method would best illustrate your assets and capabilities. You want to present yourself in a professional manner, so remain consistent in your approach.

Outline A listing of information in chronological order starting from the present and continuing back through the years. Each subject area is arranged in a series of short, factual phrases. It is the preferred and most appropriate style for persons embarking on a new career.

Essay Employs composition style of writing. Suitable for individuals who feel that their vast work and educational experiences can best be summarized in paragraph form.

The material included in a résumé will vary from one person to the next. Decide which of the following subject areas to incorporate into your own résumé.

RÉSUMÉ

Name & Personal Data	Full name, complete address and telephone number (including area code), height, weight, date of birth, marital status, and condition of health.
Professional Objective	A brief, clearly stated definition of your career goal within the airline.
Educational Background	List most recent educational experience first, then work backward in time. Include secondary and college level education with locations and graduation dates. Emphasize any degrees, certifications, major fields of study, and note special awards and achievements.
Work Experience	Document your employment history in inverse chronological order. Include name and address of firm and your specific job title. Be sure to emphasize those positions and responsibilities that dealt with a direct service to the public.
Volunteer Work	Organizations and causes to which you donated time and energy. List names, places, dates, and nature of work contributed.
Military Experience	Name branch of military, years served, and rank attained. List any special skills, training, and honors received.
Special Skills	Knowledge of foreign language, first aid, sign language for the deaf, water survival techniques, and other related skills.

Hobbies/ *Interests*	Leisure-time activities, including recreational interests and participation in the creative arts. Might also note membership in professional organizations and clubs.
References	Use one of two techniques: (1) State "Will be provided upon request," or (2) Name approximately three individuals, their professions, addresses, and telephone numbers. Obtain permission from those persons you list and be certain they are in a position to attest to your job performance and character.

Before you are ready to submit the final copy of your résumé, it is imperative that you check it for overall content, writing skills, and presentation. Do you feel it is an honest, objective inventory that will leave a favorable impression in the mind of the employer? Is your résumé free of personal opinions and editorial comment? Have you checked for punctuation, spelling, and grammatical errors? Has your paper been produced so that there are no typographical mistakes, erasures, or smudges? After you have reviewed your own work, give it to someone who can read it with a discerning eye. Ask for constructive criticism and, if necessary, revise, edit, and proofread again.

Once you are sure your résumé is complete, it is best to have it duplicated professionally. Avoid the use of ditto, mimeograph, and carbon copies. Quality reproduction can best be achieved through the use of photocopy processes. The copies come close in appearance to the original work and can be obtained at a nominal cost.

There are several ways of offering your résumé to a prospective employer. One is to leave it with the interviewer at the conclusion of the meeting. Another way is to mail it directly to the airline. If the latter procedure is followed, you must also submit a covering letter as part of your presentation.

COVERING LETTER

Every résumé that is sent through the mail should be accompanied by a personalized letter of intent. This letter should be designed to state your desired position within the company, call attention to the enclosed résumé, and interest the employer in granting a personal interview. When composing the letter, keep it brief and to the point. Make every word count, as you did in your résumé. If you are sending résumés to more than one company, each letter of introduction should be individually typed and tailored to a particular airline.

It is essential to use an acceptable business letter format. To achieve a professional appearance, the letter should be properly centered on one sheet of paper, single-spaced, and include all the necessary components. The following should be included:

Return address   Give complete address, including street, apartment number, city, state, and zip code. Avoid abbreviations.

Date   Month, day, and year résumé is submitted.

Inside address   Direct the letter to the proper company representative within the Personnel Department or Employment Office. When possible, send the correspondence to a specific person whose name may be obtained by calling the airline. Remember to include his/her title, the correct name of the company, and the complete mailing address. Again, avoid abbreviations.

Salutation   If name is available, use greeting of "Dear _(name)_:" Include "Mr., Mrs., Miss, or Ms.," whichever is appropriate. When a name is not ascertained, use the proper business greeting. The salutation should be followed by a colon (:).

Body   Begin the letter by introducing yourself as a qualified candidate for the flight attendant position. Highlight your most outstanding attributes and experiences by referring to the enclosed résumé. Conclude the letter by asking for an opportunity to be interviewed. Throughout your writing, remember to be honest and concise.

Closing   Use the standard business closing, such as "Sincerely" or "Very Truly Yours."

Signature   Sign your full name (first, middle initial, and last) in ink. Type the same directly below.

Enclosure   Use notation at bottom left margin of the page to refer to your enclosed résumé and/or application, e.g., "Encl."

APPLICATION FORMS

An application form must be completed by each candidate prior to the initial interview. Although this is a requirement of all airlines, the forms are not standardized. They will vary in length and complexity, and are in fact a test in themselves. Each question has been designed for a specific purpose. Your answers to some of the questions will reflect your ability to organize your thoughts and to communicate your attitudes and ideas. The impact of *what* you say is dependent upon *how* you present the information.

When filling out an application form, there are several rules of thumb to follow. Read all pages through carefully before writing down any data. You may find the form is used for a number of job classifications and you need only complete those portions relevant to the flight attendant position. Another suggestion is to work out your answers on a sheet of scratch paper so that your final statements on the form are concise and free of errors. Fill in *all* blank spaces; if the question does not pertain to you, write in "N/A," "not applicable," or draw a line through the blank space. Also, be sure your answers are either typed or neatly printed in ink.

Depending on the airline, you may be able to request an application form through the mail or pick one up at their nearest Employment Office. Completing this form at home affords you certain advantages. First of all, you have time to review all your answers thoroughly and may want to have another person offer constructive comments. It also allows you the chance to type the final copy and make duplicates for future reference.

On the other hand, you might be required to fill out the application form at a recruiting location. Under these circumstances you will want to have all information readily available. It is helpful to have a copy of your résumé with you for reference. In addition, consider bringing a card listing facts not contained in your résumé, but sure to be asked on the application. This information can include: social security number; driver's license number; previous employment factors such as rates of pay, former supervisors, and reasons for leaving; names and addresses of references; if not a U.S. citizen, alien registration number; and medical facts concerning history, vision, hearing, and disabilities. You should anticipate having to supply information such as expected salary, date available to report for training, and willingness to relocate, and you should be ready to answer essay questions concerning why you feel qualified for the flight attendant position.

The final step in completing the application form is to sign the document. This signature verifies that all facts are honestly represented and that you understand that any false statements or omissions are grounds for rejection.

PRESENTING ...

YOU, the candidate. With résumé, letter of introduction, and application form assembled, it's now time to ask yourself some very important questions by analyzing the entire package objectively. Imagine yourself in the role of a personnel representative reviewing this material. Would you interview this person based on what is written and the manner in which the information is presented? Does the package portray a high quality and an overall professional appearance? Does this applicant meet the basic eligibility requirements? If you can consider the candidate qualified and competitive, your presentation has been effective. Should you decide to enhance the materials presented, you may include letters of reference from previous employers. When you are *totally* satisfied that your introductory package is complete, you may proceed with your job campaign.

4

MAKING THE MOST OF YOUR INTERVIEW

In an interview, each individual is there to make a decision based on information exchanged. The interviewer must choose the most qualified candidate by using established criteria that meet the company's hiring standards. You, as the interviewee, have the opportunity to evaluate the airline and decide if it can meet your expectations and satisfy your occupational goals.

INTERVIEW EXPECTATIONS

Before going into an interview you should have a realistic idea of what the airline expects of you as an applicant for the flight attendant position. The interviewer will make observations about you throughout the interview process. The way in which you portray yourself visually and verbally determines your acceptance or rejection as an employee. You will be evaluated in terms of your appearance and behavior. Let's summarize those criteria the interviewer will be using.

From the moment you walk in the door, an interviewer forms an impression of your physical appearance. Your height and weight are obvious factors, as well as your complexion, hairstyle, teeth, nail care, and makeup. Other considerations influencing your general appearance are your posture and style of dress.

You also convey a message about yourself through your attitude and behavior. In a subtle way, the interviewer can determine your degree of self-confidence, poise, type of personality, sincerity, and maturity level.

QUESTIONS FOR THE INTERVIEWEE

An interviewer will initiate topics of conversation from two sources. First of all, expect to be asked about the information you provided on the application form. Second, an interviewer will ask direct, spontaneous questions to test your knowledge of the flight attendant career, the airline with which you are interviewing, and the industry in general. If you have been doing your homework thoroughly, you should have no problem expressing yourself.

Listed below are some examples of thought-provoking questions commonly asked during a flight attendant interview. Think about what the answers may reveal to the interviewer about your personality and reasoning ability. *How* you respond, displaying common sense, quick thinking, and a sense of humor, is just as important as *what* your answers convey.

Why do you want to be a flight attendant?
What attracted you to our airline?
What do you feel is the most important quality needed to be a successful flight attendant?
Describe yourself.
Do you have any faults? What are you doing to overcome them?
What are the major responsibilities of a flight attendant?
What do you see as the disadvantages to the flight attendant profession?
How do you react in the face of unfamiliar situations?
What are your assets and how will they help you in the flight attendant profession?
What do you know about the operation of this airline?
What are your long-range career objectives?
How has the image of the flight attendant changed?
What else do you think I should know about you?

Your interviewer will be asking many more and different types of questions—all of which have their own purpose. Your answers help to illustrate certain qualities about yourself that will aid the interviewer in making a decision regarding your employment. For example, your answer to the question, "How do you react in the face of unfamiliar situations?" might indicate to an interviewer your ability to cope with new problems. Answers to other questions could be indicators of your attitude, dependability, and values. This is just one phase of the interview process.

PREPARING FOR THE INTERVIEW

Up until now your preparation has involved *thinking* about yourself, and expressing your ideas in written form. However, during an interview you will be called upon to convey these thoughts *verbally* when face to face with the interviewer. One way to know if you are ready to meet the challenge is to practice with other people.

PRACTICE INTERVIEWS

Set up a mock interview session with your friends or family. Using questions from the previous section, give your answers as if in the actual interview. At the completion of the mock session, ask yourself how you felt about your responses. Were they logical in thought? Were your answers concise and to the point? Did you respond with knowledge about the subject?

Also, analyze your behavior. Were you poised and self-confident or did you feel uneasy? Did you have good eye contact with your interviewer? Were you aware of your body language? For another point of view, ask the interviewer for feedback on your presentation.

Now reverse roles and assume that of the interviewer. It will provide a different perspective of the interviewee. Make a note of the interaction that took place. What behavior did you observe and what responses did you hear that left you with a positive impression? What came across negatively?

Analyze each session. What techniques would you like to employ in your interviewing style that would make you a more effective candidate? Which ones will you want to avoid? To make this experience work for you, keep practicing until you feel confident in what you say and how it is expressed.

QUESTIONS FOR THE INTERVIEWER

Another step in preparing for the interview is to think of questions you might want to ask a potential employer. You will have to judge whether the time and atmosphere of the interview are appropriate for your inquiries. Some typical questions are: "Where are your newly hired flight attendants stationed after training?" or "How much time is allowed between the hiring date and when I would have to report to the training center?" By developing your thoughts in advance, you demonstrate your maturity and professionalism.

APPEARANCE

Probably one of the most important phases of your preparation will be to make an objective appraisal of your appearance. First of all, decide what you are going to wear. Dress in good taste—business attire is standard. Styles change frequently, making it difficult to recommend specific apparel and accessories, so use your judgment in selecting items that will convey a conservative look. Your clothes should be neat and clean and, above all, they should compliment your figure or physique. Additionally, you'll want to be sure your hairstyle is appropriate, your nails have been manicured, and your complexion is clear. You should also keep a close watch on your weight at all times. Remember, if you look good, you feel good.

LAST-MINUTE CHECKLIST

Have on hand an extra copy of your résumé.
Take along a small note pad and a couple of pens.
Make sure you have accurate directions to the employment
office.
Allow adequate travel time to avoid a late arrival.
Take one final look in the mirror on your way out the door.

TYPES OF INTERVIEWS

All airlines utilize a combination of interview processes that differ in duration and style. You could be asked to participate in any or all of them.

SCREENING INTERVIEW

This procedure is most effectively used when an airline must reduce the large volume of applicants to a more select group. It may also be identified as a preliminary or initial interview.

The location could be in an assigned airport facility such as the airline employment office or off the premises at a hotel. In either case, you enter a room where other applicants have been assembled. While you are waiting to be interviewed, you may be asked to complete an information card, listen to a presentation by a personnel representative, or both. You will then be called one by one for your interview.

The ratio of personnel in a screening interview is one interviewer to one applicant. The session lasts approximately five minutes, during which the interviewer must evaluate the candidate and make a decision based on a few questions and a quick glance at your application. Because the time is so limited, your qualifications, appearance, and manner must make a positive first impression.

PANEL INTERVIEW

The panel interview deals with a smaller number of applicants, and the airline can go into greater detail with each candidate.

Most panel interviews are held at an airline employment office. Should you live in a city other than that in which the interview is being conducted, the airline provides free round-trip transportation.

The ratio of personnel in a panel or "board" interview is approximately three interviewers to one applicant. The interviewee sits before a panel of company representatives, all of whom are familiar with the scope of the flight attendant profession. As one member asks you a question, the others make observations. During the twenty- to thirty-minute period of the interview, you can expect to be asked questions regarding your background, the airline industry, and the flight attendant position. Another technique employed is to describe an in-flight situation and ask how you would handle it. These "for-instance" types of questions are used to test your judgment and common sense.

GROUP INTERVIEW

This type of interview looks at the individual candidate through the process of group dynamics. Special emphasis is placed on the applicant's ability to interact with others.

If you live in the vicinity of the airline employment office, most likely the interview is held at that location. However, if you live away from a major airport area, the group interview is held at a hotel or you are provided transportation to the appropriate city.

The ratio of personnel is one or two interviewers to five to twenty-five applicants. The session could last as long as one and a half or two hours. The seating arrangement for the applicants is usually in a circular fashion, allowing for open discussion. The interviewer may sit with the group, acting as its moderator; any additional interviewers assume the role of observer. By this method the interviewer is able to distinguish an applicant's personality, appearance, leadership abilities, intelligence, communication skills (listening and verbal), and competitive nature. Indirect questions posed to the group as a whole include general and situational topics in order to prompt a verbal exchange.

PERSONAL INTERVIEW

This type of interview affords an airline the opportunity to take an in-depth personalized look at its applicants. It is a summary or recap of the information you have supplied to the airline.

Personal interviews are usually conducted at major domiciles or airline headquarter facilities. If you are not within driving distance the airline will fly you to the proper location.

The ratio of personnel is one interviewer to one applicant. You can expect to spend ten minutes to approximately one hour. Sitting face to face with the interviewer, you are asked direct questions as to how your background and present-day experiences relate to the flight attendant career. At the completion of this type of interview, an interviewer will have an in-depth picture of the candidate.

INTERVIEW CLIMATE

The success of an interview is determined by the conditions affecting its environment and the effectiveness of its participants. As the one being interviewed, you play an important role in creating a favorable atmosphere through your actions and words. Keep the following points in mind. They can help you become more comfortable as an interviewee.

As a Common Courtesy:
> Be prompt. If you find you are going to be late, call the interviewer. If unable to attend, call for alternate appointment.
> Greet interviewer by name.
> Introduce yourself.
> Refrain from smoking.
> Do not chew gum.
> Thank the interviewer, then shake his or her hand.

Remember that the Interviewer:
> Is aware of your apprehensions.
> Wants the interviewee to feel comfortable.
> Prefers candidates with outgoing personalities.
> Might like to do the talking and judge your reactions.
> Might prefer that you do most of the talking.
> Looks for pattern of success through the information provided in your interviews, applications, and résumés.
> May be affected by health concerns, personal life, time of day, telephone interruptions, etc.

For those Questions and Answers:

Be honest and sincere—don't exaggerate.

Stick to the subject.

When you feel you have answered the question sufficiently, STOP; don't be intimidated by lapses in conversation.

Answer all questions. If you don't know the answer, admit it.

Change possible negative responses to the positive.

Pay attention to the tone of your voice.

Control rate of speech.

Listen with interest.

Don't talk from notes.

Avoid answering questions with just a "yes" or "no."

Express a positive attitude. Show interest, enthusiasm, and pride. Demonstrate a sense of humor when appropriate.

About Your Body Language:

Shake hands using a firm grip.

SMILE.

Be aware of your facial expressions.

Maintain good eye contact throughout the interview.

Watch your sitting position; don't slouch or fidget.

Control excess energy; don't play nervously with objects, tap fingers, etc.

Be aware of using excessive gestures; be sure the ones used are in harmony with what you are saying.

Never wear dark glasses.

Concentrate on maintaining a good walking posture when approaching or leaving an interviewer.

AFTER THE INTERVIEW

Immediately following an interview, make a practice of reconstructing the session in your mind and on paper. Be objective in your critique. Jot down your impressions of what transpired, the people involved, and the physical environment. Also make a note of the topics discussed, the specific questions that were asked, and how you responded. This evaluation can help you decide if there is room for improvement in your self-expression. Incorporate this information into your job-campaign portfolio for possible future reference.

The most effective means of critiquing the experience is, once again, to ask yourself some very important questions.

How did the interviewer make me feel comfortable?
What made me uneasy?
How did I display my enthusiasm?
Was the summary of my background and present-day experiences concise and relevant to the interviewer's questions? In what way?
Did I listen with interest?
Were my questions to the interviewer logical and timely?
Were there any distractions that influenced the interview? What were my reactions?
Which of my responses elicited from the interviewer a positive reaction? What was interpreted negatively?
Was I able to substantiate my occupational goals?
Did I remain consistent in providing information verbally that had been previously stated in my application and/or résumé?
What questions were asked that I could not answer?
Was my appearance suitable for the interview and did it reflect a style that was natural for me?
I would rate my overall impression of the interview as Excellent _____, Good _____, Fair _____, Poor _____.

It is a special courtesy to send a written "thank you" to the interviewer regardless of your appraisal of the session. This brief acknowledgment of the interviewer's time and interest can be accomplished rather quickly and has a positive effect. It may be just the reminder that the airline needs, and you will leave an impression of thoughtfulness and professionalism.

While anticipating an airline's decision about your employment, use the time constructively. Make a comparison between your career expectations and what you've learned an airline can offer. Base the comparison on your previous research and the information disclosed during the interview process so that you can be ready to answer with a definite "yes" or "no."

The flight attendant profession is a highly competitive field. In the late 1970s, approximately one out of every hundred candidates who were interviewed was hired. In essence, the airline has a plentiful market of qualified applicants from which to make a selection. How you present yourself in the interview(s), on the application form, and possibly through a résumé, i.e., as a TOTAL CANDIDATE, are the major criteria for your competitive standing.

In the past, applicants have been rejected for many reasons. Some people are turned down for poor grooming or appearance, while others are rejected because of a lack of maturity. Other reasons include a poor attitude, low confidence level, lack of enthusiasm, failure to communicate, or a low intelligence quotient. Displaying unrealistic ideas about the flight attendant profession and the airline industry as a whole also limits a candidate's chances.

If you do not hear from an airline within a couple of weeks, it is an indication that you have not been accepted. Don't become discouraged. Turn this disappointment into a positive learning experience and go on to interview with other carriers. If your interviews are not proving successful, reevaluate your occupational goals. Perhaps the flight attendant profession is not for you.

You may be one of the fortunate candidates to have made it past the interview. An airline will notify you by mail or telephone that they would like you to come back for another interview, or you have been accepted for the flight attendant position pending the results of a physical examination. Whether you accept the offer or not, you must notify the airline as soon as possible of your decision. If you have decided that this is the airline for you and have received final confirmation of your employment, you have reason to be proud. You've achieved the goal you set out to accomplish in your career campaign.

The airline informs you of the date you are to report to training and how to get there. You can also expect to receive a pretraining packet of materials to study prior to the first day of instruction. With suitcase packed and ticket in hand, you're on your way to the training academy!

SECTION II

FLIGHT ATTENDANT TRAINING: EXPECTATIONS AND REALITIES

"There is a lot of magic in the training class. Underneath the finesse of gracious hostessing is a powerful machine that can handle medical emergencies, crash landings, and punctured life rafts."
JEANNA ROBINETTE, FLIGHT ATTENDANT, TRANSAMERICA AIRLINES

"Six weeks at the TWA training center taught me more discipline than I had learned in my tender twenty-one years. Discipline that I apply to my life today."
SAM CHAUDOIN, FLIGHT ATTENDANT, TRANS WORLD AIRLINES

"Once I reached training I was happily surprised to find that excellence in this job involves infinitely more skill and knowledge than I had anticipated."
CELESTE EVANS, FLIGHT ATTENDANT, PAN AMERICAN WORLD AIRWAYS

"At last training was over, and those gold wings pinned on my chest represent my dream of a lifetime come true."
PETE RAMSEY, FLIGHT ATTENDANT, CONTINENTAL AIRLINES

"The best advice I could give to someone starting training would be 'Be flexible.' All those changes you are asked to make are positive and help fulfill your potential as an asset to your company."
KARALEE MCWHORTER, FLIGHT ATTENDANT, BRANIFF INTERNATIONAL

5

ORIENTATION TO TRAINING

Congratulations! You've made it through the searching, applying, and interviewing processes. The gratification of being accepted for training is enough to spur you on to the challenge of a new career as a flight attendant. Through the specialized airline training program you will learn that working as a flight attendant is not just a job, but a way of life.

PREPARING FOR THE TRAINING ACADEMY

In order to make the most of this new experience, look forward to your new career realistically and with a positive attitude. Expect the training period to be challenging, difficult, exciting, and rewarding. Assume it will be one of the most unique, if not the most memorable, experiences you have yet to encounter. If you perceive training to be a totally new learning experience, you will gain knowledge that will prove to be invaluable for the rest of your life.

Before leaving for the training center, you must be mentally and physically prepared. There is a new industry to observe and a new language to learn. New concepts in serving the public and saving human lives will be taught. The underlying pressures of meeting weight restrictions and rigorous training schedules will demand more energy of you than you may have had to expend in the past. Maintaining an open mind and good physical health will allow for easier management of your overall well-being once you begin training.

Your notification may come over the telephone, but most often an airline will send you a congratulatory letter accompanied by a package of instructions and pretraining materials. If you do not live in the same city as the training center and are traveling there by air, you are advised of the necessary transportation arrangements on your airline or another carrier.

Included in this letter are facts about the training program and the expectations the airline has of its trainees. The instructional period involves a very comprehensive course of study. For this reason, you might be sent a pretraining package of materials, the contents of which you are expected to assimilate before your arrival at the training academy. In this way, the airline industry and its language are familiar to you before training, and you learn more easily once in class. Study and/or memorize the enclosed material, which may include such subjects as: the twenty-four-hour clock, time zones, Greenwich time, airline route system, city and airport codes served by your airline, basic airline terminology, and a brief history of the company. You are usually advised in this letter whether or not you will be tested on this information at the beginning of training.

The airlines must schedule training classes well in advance, so pay particular attention to your assigned starting date. It may be within the week or anywhere up to six months away. Upon notification of the proposed training date, allow time to attend to personal affairs. If you are presently employed, plan on a date when you will submit your resignation. And then, if possible, give yourself a couple of weeks to get your life in order and study pretraining materials.

WHAT TO PACK

The airline that hires you will suggest the standard types of clothing, expenses, and personal effects that might be necessary during training. A word to the wise: take *only* what you will need for training. You want to make it as easy for yourself as possible. Although there are no established restrictions on the amount of luggage you may bring, consider that there is a very good chance you are going to be the only one to transport your belongings from the airport to the training center and you will be leaving the training center with more than you brought (flight attendant uniform and luggage items).

APPAREL

There are several factors to consider when deciding what clothing to bring to training. Keep in mind the geographical location of the training school and its climate for that particular time of year. Second, your curriculum dictates that business attire be worn in the classroom and on observation trips. You will also need to pack casual clothing and sportswear for recreation and the period spent in emergency training. The following are examples of the types of clothing for men and women considered appropriate for flight attendant training.

Classroom
    dresses, suits
    combination of blouse/sweater with pants/skirt
    shirt, tie, slacks
    optional jackets, vests
    dress shoes

Emergency Training
    jeans, slacks
    blouses, shirts, sweaters, T-shirts
    jumpsuits
    tennis or rubber-soled shoes

Observation Trips
    suits and ties
    dresses, suits, pantsuits
    blouses, shirts, sweaters
    inflight serving garment (if issued and required)
    dress shoes

Recreation
    bathing suit

jeans, shorts, slacks
tennis attire
casual shoes

Inappropriate Attire
"see-through" garments
low-cut dresses, blouses
extremely short skirts
items in need of repair
items not meeting appearance standards

EXPENSE MONEY

Airlines vary in their pay procedures for the training period. Many airlines do not place the trainee on the company payroll until after graduation. In this instance, your room and board are usually provided, but you will need a sufficient amount of money for your personal expenses.

There are some airlines, however, that do pay their trainees a salary or living expense. Usually when the trainee is compensated, the money issued to that person is expected to be used for accommodations at nearby hotels during the period of training (unless the academy is within commuting distance from home). Special room rates are offered through mutual agreement between the airline and the hotel. Trainees often elect to share living quarters with each other in an effort to keep expenses at a minimum.

It is advisable to plan also for expenses that are incurred after training. You will be sent directly from the training academy to your new base of operation immediately after graduation. Plan to bring sufficient funds to help "set up house" once you reach your new locale. Your expenses will range from a few nights' lodging in a hotel to deposits for an apartment and utilities. When planning to have large sums of cash on hand, be sure to bring it in the form of traveler's checks for safekeeping.

PERSONAL ITEMS

Items that you should consider packing are a camera, travel alarm clock, and personal toiletries. All valuables should be left at home since there are usually no safes provided at the training center. Again, bring only the necessities. With two to four trainees sharing each room, storage space is at a minimum. If requested to bring along a birth certificate and/or passport, allow time to retrieve these documents before packing.

POSTTRAINING PROVISIONS

In addition to deciding what to bring to the training center, it is important to give some thought to what you will need after graduation. In anticipation of settling into new living quarters, consider packing dishes, towels, appliances, and other household goods along with the rest of your wardrobe that you are not taking to training. It is advisable to prepack these items so as not to place that responsibility on a family member or friend. Most airlines will allow each trainee a specified amount of cargo to be shipped free of charge to a new domicile. Mark each shipping box with your name and a number that corresponds to a master list of contents. Eventually, they can be labeled with your new address and shipped to you after graduation.

LEAVING FOR THE TRAINING ACADEMY

Verify your packed belongings against a checklist, then take an inventory of your appearance to be sure you create a favorable impression upon your arrival.

CHECKLIST

Overall Appearance
    business attire
    weight below maximum
    no strongly scented perfume/after-shave

Hair
    clean
    neat, natural style
    well-trimmed sideburns, mustaches, and beards

Nails
> clean
> natural shape
> polished/buffed
> well manicured

Complexion
> clear
> attractive, natural makeup

To ensure a prompt arrival at the training academy, allow ample travel time. Follow the instructions sent by your airline regarding transportation and expected arrival time and date. You will be issued a one-way business pass on your airline or another carrier if you live in a different town from the one in which training is conducted. Since this may be your first experience in flying on a standby basis, you are usually advised of the possible flights that you can take in order to arrive at the training center on or before the day of your orientation. The purpose of arriving early is to allow time to get settled in your new surroundings.

The day has finally come for you to set out in your new career. Now that your suitcases are packed and your personal affairs are in order, you are ready to leave for the airport. Your flight to the training city will no doubt be an exciting one, and don't be surprised if you become acquainted with other trainees on the same plane!

Once you arrive at your destination, ask an airline representative for instructions on how to get from the airport to the training complex.

TRAINING FACILITIES

For the next three to six weeks the flight attendant training academy will be your home away from home. Instructional facilities vary with each airline, but for the most part they are modern and multifaceted. It is here that each new trainee is transformed into a professional flight attendant.

The entire flight attendant training complex is situated near a major airport and may be adjacent to the airline's corporate headquarters. The proximity to an airport provides accessibility to aircraft for "hands-on" training and observation trips.

Each complex consists of a series of buildings that includes a center of learning with classrooms for lecture as well as procedural training rooms, staff offices, recreational facilities for relaxing through many types of sports, and in many complexes, dormitory-style living facilities.

TRAINING STAFF

A flight attendant curriculum is only as effective as the professional staff of instructors and support personnel. Under the guidance of a manager or director of training, a team of specialists devotes its time and energy to promote the high standards of a professional flight attendant.

Since the majority of the teachers are former or present flight attendants, their professional expertise and personal experience contribute greatly to a trainee's education. Most instructors specialize in one subject area within the training program. Their duties and responsibilities range from teaching classes to counseling students. The instructors may be the single most important factor in the training program, as it is they who evaluate the trainees, based on performance and testing. They are also responsible for supervising academic activities, as well as the conduct of each student.

Guest speakers are invited to share their fields of expertise with the trainees. These may include pilots, union representatives, domicile staff members, and credit union representatives, all of whom bring to the classroom supplemental information that will become useful to the trainee after graduation.

LENGTH OF TRAINING AND CLASS SIZE

Most airline training programs run an average of four weeks. The length depends on the extent of inflight services and the number of aircraft to be studied. Classes usually meet five days a week, Monday through Friday, with weekends reserved for observation trips and special assignments. But, as in any other course of study, you must take the initiative to allot a number of hours outside the classroom in order to keep up with your work.

If one thing can be guaranteed in training, it is that you are never alone. There may be approximately sixty students at a time in one training class. The size of the class naturally depends on the number of flight attendants needed by an airline and the time frame in which an airline must interview, hire, and train new flight personnel. If the classes are small, you still work with other people in groups, as this will be typical of your actual job experience. If classes are as large as sixty or more, they are usually divided into smaller, more workable teams.

ORIENTATION DAY

The first day of training is an especially informative one. The excitement of starting a new career is heightened by the staff's introduction to all aspects of the flight attendant training period.

During orientation, you meet the supervisors and instructors assigned to specific groups, as well as learn more about the background and history of the airline. Rules and regulations such as classroom conduct, hours of instruction, academic standards, break periods, and appropriate attire are spelled out so that there is no possibility of misinterpretation as to what is expected of you during training.

Next on the agenda is an explanation of facilities and what transpires in every area of the academy. Then the necessary paperwork must be completed for your files. At some point during the first day you will have your picture taken and this will eventually be placed in your personnel file. This photo may also be used on your identification badge for use in secured areas. There may be payroll forms and tax-withholding statements to fill out and a dossier to complete for future publicity assignments. Everything that you document this day will be the basis for your permanent file as a flight attendant.

Every trainee is then issued a flight attendant manual, the most important reference tool you will own. You are required to have this manual on hand during all training instruction and on every flight you work thereafter. It is divided into sections that deal with different aspects of the flight attendant profession. The emergency procedures section is a requirement of the FAA. It is the responsibility of each flight attendant to keep his or her manual up to date by the inclusion of any revisions and bulletins issued by the company.

During orientation you are also assigned your permanent employee identification number and your seniority rank. Your seniority number within your own training class is determined by age, or social security number. If determined by age, the oldest person in your class becomes number one in seniority, and so on down to the youngest. This ranking in training is used to select observation trips and your first domicile by means of a bidding process. Once on the job, your seniority number is determined by your graduation date. The purpose of being assigned a seniority number is to identify your priority status among all flight attendants at your domicile and systemwide for your airline.

It is possible that a weight check and some testing may also take place on this first day of training. If you have prepared in advance, you should have no apprehensions about either. Unfortunately, if you happen to be over your maximum weight or fail to prove your comprehension of pretraining materials, your career as a flight attendant may be very short lived. You will most likely be released from training and given a one-way ticket home. However, upon successful completion of any testing and all the rigors of orientation, you are now ready to begin your classroom instruction in the hopes of becoming a full-fledged professional flight attendant.

TRAINING
CURRICULUM

The goal of each training program is to graduate individuals who will represent the airline in a professional manner, since an airline's competitive standing depends, in part, on the public image of its flight attendants. The training is demanding, challenging, and tough, but so is the job. The objectives listed below are those that define the role of the flight attendant.

OBJECTIVES

Safety

> To minimize potential hazards through precautionary measures and safe work habits.
>
> To recognize and respond to unusual situations that may jeopardize the well-being of passengers and crew.

Service

> To perform job responsibilities in a timely and efficient manner so as to properly market the services of your airline to the traveling public.
>
> To anticipate and fulfill the needs of passengers and render assistance in order to make their trip comfortable and enjoyable.

Appearance

To maintain proper uniform standards and good grooming habits.

To portray an image of self-confidence through poise and appropriate mannerisms.

Attitude

To display empathy, enthusiasm, and a sense of commitment in the performance of duties.

To exhibit maturity when complying with company and contractual obligations in an intelligent and responsible manner.

Communication

To convey expertise when responding to passengers' inquiries about your airline and the travel industry.

To relay feedback from passengers and fellow crew members to the appropiate personnel.

METHODS OF INSTRUCTION

Each airline has its own methods for teaching the flight attendant curriculum. Even the emphasis on technique varies from one program to another. Most academies employ a combination of group lectures, workshops, observation trips, hands-on training in actual planes, the use of "mock-ups," and self-study programs. You may be certain, though, that whatever approach is used will be comprehensive, well organized, and realistic. Each trainee is responsible for fulfilling the objectives of training with a predetermined standard of excellence.

AREAS OF INSTRUCTION

The principles and objectives established in flight attendant training are achieved through a variety of major learning areas. All classes and instructional materials center around these subjects: duties and responsibilities, food and beverage services, appearance and grooming, emergencies, and communication skills.

DUTIES AND RESPONSIBILITIES

This part of training takes you from checkin to checkout, explaining in full what your duties and responsibilities are as a flight attendant. A flight attendant training program could not begin without a good working knowledge of the language of the airline industry, i.e., airline terminology and airport and airline codes. Hand in hand with this instruction is the process of time conversion—learning about the twenty-four-hour clock, and time zones.

Another one of the areas of study is aircraft familiarization. For every aircraft flown by your airline, you must learn its exterior identifying features as well as its interior design. This learning is accomplished by viewing pictures, walking through available aircraft, and making use of training mock-ups. When studying the parts of a plane, trainees are also instructed on the theory of flight and contribution of weather factors.

There are certain rudiments of the flight attendant job that are taught at the training center but perhaps fully understood only after experiencing them on the job. Specifically, they are scheduling procedures, hours of service, and contract legalities. A course is usually offered for interpretation of the contract under which a trainee will someday be guided. This instruction is quite detailed and can be challenging to the newcomer in the profession. It is essential to learn the fundamentals of these contractual agreements in training since their application can be put into practice only on the job.

It is necessary that all flight attendants become knowledgeable about the travel industry in order to better serve the public. Trainees are taught to read timetables, tickets, and the OAG (Official Airline Guide). Travel assistance is also offered to passengers through a flight attendant's ability to interpret airline information. Another aspect of the travel industry that is introduced during training is the influence of the regulatory agencies: the FAA and the CAB. Much of the flight attendant's job is governed by federal regulations and restrictions, and a thorough understanding must be achieved if enforcement of these policies is going to have an impact on passengers.

On almost all domestic and international flights today there is some type of money exchange. Usually this involves the sale of alcoholic beverages, collection of money for the air fare on board, and the charging of passengers for rental of audio headsets. All trainees must learn not only how to handle these monies in a safe, secure manner, but also how to make change and convert currencies of different countries, if traveling internationally. Keeping accurate records of collection and surrendering the money to proper authorities is an important part of this instruction.

A flight attendant trainee is introduced to a wide variety of forms and paperwork. You are expected to become familiar with their purpose, and to know how to complete and distribute each item properly. Included in these classes at international training academies is special instruction on documentation procedures used when flying from one country to another.

Classes are held during initial training to learn about the company benefits extended to flight attendants. Discussed in these sessions are travel privileges, insurance and medical programs, allowable expenses, savings plans, and vacation and sick-day allotments.

FOOD AND BEVERAGE SERVICES

The emphasis in this part of training is on service and presentation. Each airline has its own variety of food to market to the passenger. You learn different techniques and procedures according to the type of aircraft and the vast differences between narrow-bodied and wide-bodied services. After viewing films or slides and watching instructors demonstrate how a service should be presented, you are given the opportunity to practice through the use of hands-on training.

Your ability to present a service based on a detailed set of procedures is developed through participating in mock sessions. Here you actually do the work in a specified time frame. To make this part of training more realistic, galley equipment and supplies are available for use in the mock-ups. Even if your airline serves only beverages, there is still a proper order of presentation to be learned. Guidelines are established to help you make use of the time and supplies on board, so that each and every passenger is offered courteous and gracious service.

APPEARANCE AND GROOMING

A polished, professional appearance certainly has merit in the flight attendant training program. The importance of a neat, attractive appearance is twofold: the image you portray to the public is representative of your airline in general; and your self-confidence, poise, and sense of professionalism is in many ways dictated by the way you look.

Areas of grooming that are highlighted at the training center include skin care, hairstyling, nail care, makeup, poise, posture, health and hygiene, and a periodic check of your weight. With relatively few exceptions, the appearance standards are designed to apply to both male and female flight attendants.

The importance of adhering to appearance and weight standards is stressed from the first day of training. Appearance counselors are on hand to offer advice on the appropriate selection of styles and coloring to enhance a trainee's features and complement the uniform.

At some point during training you will have the opportunity of wearing the uniform of your airline for the very first time. On board an airplane, the uniform you wear becomes a symbol of leadership to the traveling public. Your total appearance as a flight attendant centers around how you look in this uniform and how you enhance it by your personal grooming. In order to achieve a high standard of quality among all flight attendants wearing the same uniform, regulations are established and discussed with you in training. These policies define what is acceptable in terms of accessories and an overall professional look for each trainee.

It is your responsibility to meet scheduled uniform-fitting appointments. This is an exciting time—seeing yourself in the uniform that portrays the flight attendant you want to be. The fittings are usually held within the first week of training so that alterations and distribution of finished articles can be accomplished before graduation.

It is important that you maintain a certain weight because

your uniform articles are custom tailored to your build and they are expected to last for several years. Since the material is selected for durability (as well as design and comfort), you should follow the proper cleaning instructions to care for your uniform.

It is the trainee's responsibility to buy the initial uniform at a total cost of $400 or more—but subsequent replacements and uniform changeovers are usually free throughout the remainder of your career. The major apparel pieces include such items as jackets, pants, skirts, blouses, coats, shirts, smocks, scarves, dresses, ties, and vests. You may elect to pay the entire amount in one sum at the training center or have the amount deducted on a monthly basis once you begin to receive a salary. You can expect the company to furnish, free of charge, a suitcase, flashlight, airline insignia and/or wings, flight attendant manuals, and name pins. Accessories available for purchase may include a hat, gloves, shoes, umbrella, boots, and hand luggage.

Flight attendant trainees can develop and enhance a professional appearance during training.
Photo courtesy Delta Air Lines

Trainees practice food and beverage services at the training academy.
Photo by Mark Stevenson
Courtesy Trans World Airlines

Reading and testing are integral parts of the flight attendant's training.
Photo courtesy Delta Air Lines

Trainees must learn the types and uses of emergency equipment before working on board an aircraft.
Photo courtesy Transamerica Airlines

EMERGENCIES

The time spent in emergency training is a valuable and rewarding experience since it stresses the main reason for flight attendants being on aircraft. Although you may never be faced with an emergency situation while flying, no person is allowed to graduate from the training center without a demonstration of their competence and proof of complete comprehension of all safety aspects of the job. Approximately one week is devoted solely to emergency training.

As a trainee, you are required to operate all emergency equipment and demonstrate evacuation procedures. You are also expected to react automatically in emergencies without need for review. In order to fully comprehend emergency evacuation procedures, training sessions are held simulating critical situations. All trainees are instructed in mock-ups that are rigged to represent aircraft in adverse conditions. The simulators are equipped with tapes of people screaming, mechanisms that tilt aircraft structures to unnatural attitudes, billows of smoke, and simulation of flames inside and outside the cabin. To add further realism to this training, classmates role-play as handicapped passengers who must be briefed and given special consideration in emergency evacuations.

In addition to learning the location and use of all emergency equipment on board, trainees are given the opportunity to slide down an inflated evacuation chute. Since it is too costly to continually deploy and repack the slides on an aircraft, one is usually set up as a permanent structure outside the plane, where you must climb a ladder and enter the chute from a platform. You may also experience what it feels like to evacuate onto the airplane's wing and slide down the extended flaps to the ground. When training for over-water flights, trainees learn how to deploy and launch inflatable rafts and become familiar with the operation and use of related equipment. The purpose of teaching such proficiency in evacuating aircraft is to meet the requirements set down by the FAA. Regardless of the size of the plane, the number of usable exits, or the number of people on board, an aircraft must be evacuated within ninety seconds or less to meet with government safety standards.

Flight attendant trainees watch an emergencies instructor deploy an inflatable life raft.
Photo by Mark Stevenson
Courtesy Trans World Airlines

An instructor demonstrates the use of flotation devices to flight attendant trainees during ditching class.
Photo by Mark Stevenson
Courtesy Trans World Airlines

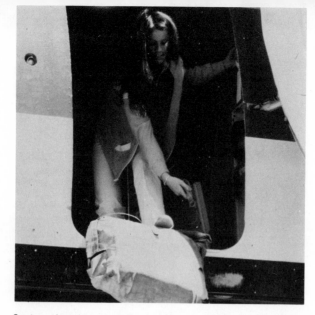

Instruction in emergency training includes knowing
how to deploy evacuation slides.
Photo by Mark Stevenson
Courtesy Trans World Airlines

Other topics and demonstrations during emergencies week
include fires, decompression, first aid, and unusual incidents.
When learning about fires that may occur inside or outside the
aircraft, you are taught the different classes of fires, fire-
fighting techniques, and the type of extinguishers found on
board the aircraft. In general, a flight attendant's immediate
response and action to a fire differ, depending on whether it
occurs on the ground or in the air.

Since most commercial aircraft today fly at very high altitudes, you are taught to recognize different forms of cabin
pressure loss. Information on the characteristics of a decompression and the use of emergency oxygen systems is given to
familiarize you with the mandatory procedures to be followed
in the event of a change in pressurization.

Since safety is the most important element of every flight,
you are taught to recognize symptoms of illness and injury,
and to administer first aid accordingly. Your responsibilities
range from bandaging small cuts to applying cardiopulmonary
resuscitation in a life-threatening situation. Your role as a
first-aider is defined through the instruction of techniques and
use of emergency equipment and supplies. During training
you become familiar with many forms of illnesses and injuries

that require you to employ good judgment, quick reaction, and a sense of genuine concern for your fellow man.

Emergency and first aid procedures are a continual learning process. Expect that upon graduating from the training academy you will have to prove your competency each year at recurrent emergency training sessions through written and/or practical examinations. During these periods of instruction, you review and are tested on current procedures and equipment, and learn new policies instituted since you last attended. If you review emergency procedures before each flight you take, recurrent training should be a positive experience.

COMMUNICATION SKILLS

A trainee must realize that acquiring all this new knowledge is inconsequential unless it can be conveyed to passengers. Courses in verbal/nonverbal skills, human relations, and transactional analysis help you develop a rapport and style of conversation necessary for effective communication on the job. Situations are suggested by instructors, and it is up to the trainees to role-play the part of flight attendant and passengers. These reenactments simulate actual situations that may be encountered on board the airplane.

As a flight attendant you will be exposed to many different nationalities and cultures. Your respect for the customs and idiosyncrasies of passengers from other countries will help you communicate with foreigners.

Classroom instruction helps trainees become familiar with on-the-job duties and responsibilities.
Photo courtesy Delta Air Lines

STANDARDS OF PERFORMANCE AND CONDUCT

Your behavior and attitude while at the training center are monitored continually. The codes of conduct established in training are meant to achieve the highest possible standards for you as a flight attendant.

PERFORMANCE-EVALUATING CRITERIA

Attitude   Your attitude must be positive and enthusiastic. You are expected to display a congeniality and a genuine interest as demonstrated in classroom participation. Instructors and staff will take note of the amount of initiative and cooperation you display, as well as your receptiveness to constructive criticism. A positive attitude is conveyed through consideration and respect for your classmates and your desire to learn new materials.

Dependability   Reliability, punctuality, trustworthiness, and attendance in class comprise your dependability record. Any trends of negative behavior are sure to be noted and discussed so as to curb a potential problem.

Judgment   A professional flight attendant learns in training to evaluate information promptly and accurately, and to make sound, logical decisions. The ability to plan ahead also displays good judgment and organization.

Stability   In training you are also evaluated on your ability to maintain composure under normal and abnormal conditions. You are expected to remain calm, in control of your emotions, and to accomplish all duties in a determined, professional manner.

Behavior   Conduct yourself with dignity and maturity. Self-assurance, tactfulness, and good manners also play a major role in your behavior while at the training center. Anticipating needs and developing conversational ability are the criteria for getting along with others.

RULES OF CONDUCT

You are responsible for your own actions during training. Failure to adhere to the codes of conduct could result in discipline or ultimate dismissal from training. Listed below are those infractions that are grounds for disciplinary action or dismissal while at the training center or throughout your career as a flight attendant.

Cheating on tests

Possession, selling, or distribution of unauthorized or illegal drugs

Drinking alcoholic beverages less than twelve hours before checking in for a flight

Behavior that reflects poorly on the company

Damage to company property

Insubordination

Abuse of travel privileges

Sleeping, or drinking alcoholic beverages, while working flights

ACADEMIC EVALUATION

You will be tested and evaluated on the comprehension of training materials. Written examinations are given in which the standard of excellence must be 85 percent or greater. In the event of failure, retakes are allowed but they are few and well monitored. Another form of testing is through oral examination. Again, the same standards of performance apply.

The practical application of materials is another method of evaluating your comprehension. Testing of this type takes place during emergency drills, workshops on food/beverage services and communication techniques, and on observation flights.

It is most encouraging to know that the failure rate during flight attendant training is minimal. Failure is attributed mostly to poor attitude, inability to meet language requirements, exceeding maximum weight, or excessive absenteeism. However, statistics show that nineteen out of every twenty trainees are motivated to achieve the highest standards of performance through a strong sense of commitment and a desire to learn.

Look upon training as a rewarding, valuable experience. Keep an open mind and make a positive attitude your outlook on learning. After meeting all of the pressures of training, you will earn your wings and a place among today's professional flight attendants. Your first reward for your achievement is the day of graduation.

Immediately upon completion of the graduation ceremonies you are sent off to your new domicile to begin a career as a flight attendant. The departure from the training center is an emotional one. You will have endured many good and challenging times with your training class, and now everyone goes his or her separate way. Make the most of your experience at the academy and use it as a valuable tool as you embark on a new way of life. . . . "WELCOME ABOARD."

President Frank Borman pins wings on flight attendants at one of Eastern's graduation ceremonies.
Photo courtesy Eastern Airlines

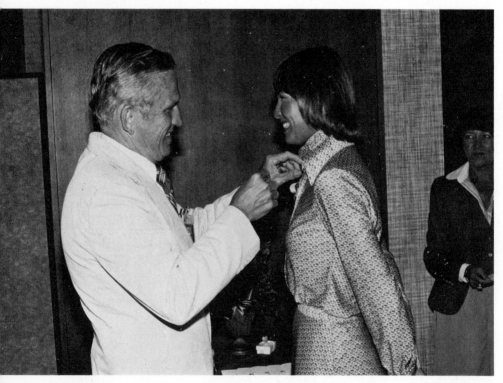

SECTION III

THE FLIGHT ATTENDANT AS A PROFESSIONAL

"I make the job as challenging as I can. I try to be extremely perceptive, to solve any problem that might arise, and to be efficient yet gracious."

DOLORES FOLEY, FLIGHT ATTENDANT, UNITED AIRLINES

"Safety is the essence of our profession. We are trained, drilled, and are constantly alert, ready for, even anticipating the emergency that, in fact, we hope never happens. It's ironic."

JEANNE CHILTON, FLIGHT ATTENDANT, TRANSAMERICA AIRLINES

"When I left to begin flight attendant training, I had no idea of the avenues that would open up to me in the airlines, as well as in other areas. The different people, countries, experiences, and benefits allow a life-style totally unlike that of any other career."

PATTI BAUM, FLIGHT ATTENDANT, TRANS WORLD AIRLINES

"I like knowing that passengers can depend on me for leadership should the need arise. Passenger confidence in my leadership abilities is gained by my 'presence.' Presence being the way that I greet them, the manner in which I work, my appearance, dedication, and sincerity—my professionalism."

KATE MCNAMARA, FLIGHT ATTENDANT, UNITED AIRLINES

"Flying lets me have a career for me and still be home with my family far more than I would be if I worked nine to five, five days a week. If you are looking for a job that is routine—this one is not for you."

KARALEE MCWHORTER, FLIGHT ATTENDANT, BRANIFF INTERNATIONAL

7

COMMUNICATION CODE SYSTEMS

A s you begin your responsibilities as a flight attendant, one of your first tasks is to learn the "language" of the airline industry. As the airlines grew in size and territory, this necessarily universal language emerged. It encompasses not only a specific terminology but also a coding system for easy identification of airports, cities, and air carriers, plus the use of the twenty-four-hour clock. It is essential to achieve an effective communication process between the airlines in general, the departments and personnel within, and the traveling public.

TIME ZONES

An integral part of a flight attendant's job is a knowledge of various time zones and their respective geographical regions. The earth's surface is divided into degrees of longitude and latitude: longitude is measured east and west of Greenwich (pronounced Gren-itch), England; latitude is measured north and south of the equator. The lines of longitude are called meridians. Greenwich has been designated as the starting point, or Prime Meridian, for the twenty-four time zones around the world. This is called Greenwich Mean Time (GMT).

There are a total of 360 degrees longitude around the circumference of the earth. If you stood in Greenwich, England, and drew an imaginary line halfway around the world at 180 degrees longitude, you would find the International Date Line. Through international agreement, this was established as the point where a new calendar day begins.

To determine what the time is in any part of the world, the 360 degrees of longitude are divided into twenty-four time zones, each comprising fifteen degrees. As the earth rotates on its axis, for each fifteen degrees, one hour of time elapses. It is easy to find the time in any zone. For each zone east of you, add one hour. For each zone west of you, subtract one hour. For example, if it were 8 P.M. in Greenwich, England, 120 degrees (or eight time zones) west of there would place you in San Francisco where the time is twelve noon.

For our purposes we will be concerned with the time zones of the United States and its territories. In 1883, the United

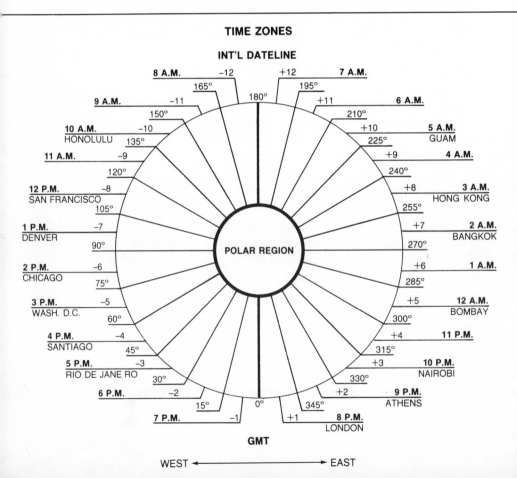

States adopted a four-zone system for the continental U.S.: Eastern, Central, Mountain, and Pacific. The boundaries of these time zones were designed to follow the 75th, 90th, 105th, and 120th degrees longitude west of Greenwich. It wasn't until 1947 that Hawaii established its standard time on the 150th degree longitude, to correspond with Alaskan standard time. It should also be noted that the U.S. territories of Puerto Rico and the Virgin Islands are in the Atlantic time zone, which is one hour later than Eastern time. The divisions follow geographical and political boundaries; therefore, they are not straight lines as are the lines of longitude.

As a flight attendant, you are expected to be able to relate proper times to passengers. Local times are expressed as standard time, i.e., Pacific standard time, Eastern standard time, etc. The only variance from standard time is during the months of April through October, when the United States (with the exception of Arizona, Hawaii, and Michigan) observes Daylight Savings time. This is when the United States adjusts its clocks one hour forward during the summer months to allow for more daylight into the evening hours.

U.S. TIME ZONE BOUNDARIES

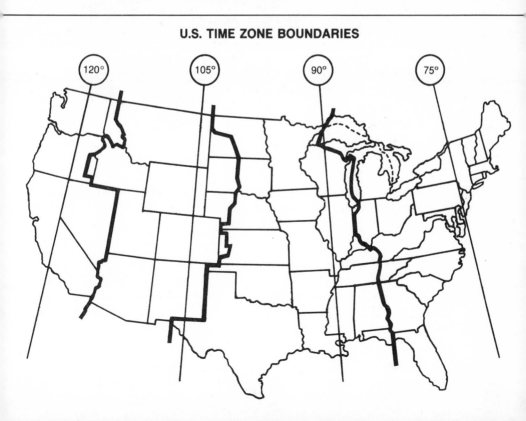

THE TWENTY-FOUR-HOUR CLOCK

If you thought 1500 was 5:00 P.M., you just missed your flight. You should have a full understanding of the various methods of time conversions utilized by the airlines. Since the airline industry is a twenty-four-hour operation, the use of the twenty-four-hour clock is the established means of determining time.

"A.M." and "P.M." are not used as they are in the conventional twelve-hour clock. The twenty-four-hour clock assigns a specific number for each hour of the day. These times are always written as four-digit figures: the first two digits represent the hour, and the last two digits designate the minutes past the hour.

The twenty-four-hour clock starts one minute after midnight, which is written as 00 (hour) 01 (minutes): 0001. The first twelve hours of the day in the twenty-four-hour clock are represented by their true numbers, i.e., 1 A.M. = 0100, 2 A.M. = 0200, etc. Note, a zero precedes the single-digit hour to complete the four-digit number (see A.M. Clock). The noon hour (1200) begins the second half of the day and the times are converted according to the following formula: twelve noon + P.M. hour = time on twenty-four-hour clock.

Examples (refer to P.M. Clock in figure):
12 noon + 3:00 P.M. = 1500
12 noon + 6:00 P.M. = 1800
12 noon + 8:00 P.M. = 2000
12 noon + 11:00 P.M. = 2300

Therefore, midnight is written as 2400, the end of one day and the beginning of the next.

Now look at some more conversions, keeping in mind that the last two digits denote the minutes:
1:25 P.M. = 1325
4:10 P.M. = 1610
7:01 P.M. = 1901
10:58 P.M. = 2258

The opposite also holds true. To convert the times of 1300 to 2400 from the twenty-four-hour clock back to the twelve-hour clock, simply subtract twelve and add P.M. Examples:

2330 - 12 = 11:30 P.M.
1955 - 12 = 7:55 P.M.
1600 - 12 = 4:00 P.M.
1415 - 12 = 2:15 P.M.

As a flight attendant, note that the twenty-four-hour clock is used in your company-issued flight schedule. Your flight times, departure, arrival, layover, and duty times are written in twenty-four-hour notations, and it is expected that you have a thorough working knowledge of this system.

A.M. HOURS

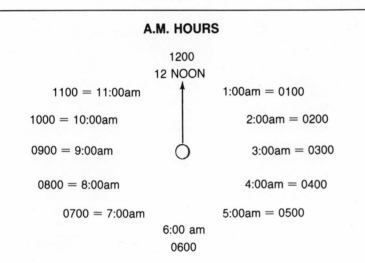

1200
12 NOON

1100 = 11:00am   1:00am = 0100

1000 = 10:00am   2:00am = 0200

0900 = 9:00am   3:00am = 0300

0800 = 8:00am   4:00am = 0400

0700 = 7:00am   5:00am = 0500

6:00 am
0600

P.M. HOURS

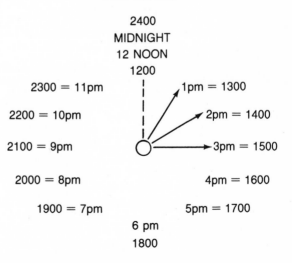

2400
MIDNIGHT
12 NOON
1200

2300 = 11pm   1pm = 1300

2200 = 10pm   2pm = 1400

2100 = 9pm   3pm = 1500

2000 = 8pm   4pm = 1600

1900 = 7pm   5pm = 1700

6 pm
1800

AIRLINE CODES

Each airline is identified by a two-letter code. These symbols help you to interpret information from airline publications and ticket coupons. Listed below are some of the U.S.-based carriers and their designated codes.

OC	Air California
TS	Aloha Airlines
AA	American Air Lines
BN	Braniff International
CO	Continental Airlines
DL	Delta Air Lines
EA	Eastern Airlines
FT	Flying Tigers
FL	Frontier Airlines
HA	Hawaiian Airlines
RW	Hughes Airwest
NW	Northwest Orient Airlines
OZ	Ozark Airlines
PS	Pacific Southwest Airlines
PA	Pan American World Airways
RC	Republic Airlines
TI	Texas International Airlines
TV	Transamerica Airlines
TW	Trans World Airlines
UA	United Airlines
AL	USAir
WA	Western Airlines
WO	World Airways

AIRPORT/CITY CODES

Each commercial airport in the world is identified by a three-letter code. The world of air travel has expanded so much since airplanes first went aloft that a coding system was developed for easy identification of cities and their airports. To eliminate any possible confusion or duplication, no two airports are assigned the same code, nor can the code look or sound similar to that of any other airport within a range of two hundred miles.

Originally, when flying was simple, airports were designated by a two-letter code. As time progressed and service grew, another letter was added to the code to provide more flexibility. If at all possible, identifiers are chosen by the FAA to be the first three letters of the airport name. However, this is not always feasible since some codes would have been the same letters as certain navigational aids and instruments.

Some codes are derived from other means, such as taking letters from the middle of airport names or, in some instances, identified for historical reasons. For example, ORD, O'Hare International Airport, is named after the original facility located in Orchard, Illinois.

In the Appendix you will find a listing of major cities and their three-letter codes for most countries. The number of codes required for memorization depends on the airline for which you work and its routing structure.

8

FACTORS
OF FLIGHT

■f a passenger asked you what makes an airplane fly, could you answer the question correctly? Would you be able to explain the noises and sensations of takeoff and landing? Could you reassure someone who might be apprehensive about flying that the rough ride during turbulence is a normal occurrence?

To satisfy passengers' natural curiosity, reassure those who have a genuine fear of flying, and for your own enlightenment, you should become familiar with the principles of flight and learn how the basic parts of an aircraft function. Then, take that one step further and understand the conditions under which a plane and its crew must operate.

FORCES AFFECTING FLIGHT

Today's modern jet is designed to use the body of air surrounding it in order to sustain flight. Much like the bird that man has longed to imitate, the airplane is specially built with movable parts to achieve this motion and control the resulting forces.

Did you ever wonder what keeps an airplane suspended in midair? What is it that enables an aircraft to ascend, cruise, and descend? To understand what makes flight possible, first think of air as having pressure or weight. This pressure is altered by the change in direction and velocity of air currents, and also by the presence of an object passing through the air. Imagine that this object is an airplane. As it travels through the atmosphere, the air flow around its surface is changed and forces are created by its movement. Sir Isaac Newton discovered that for every force there is a counterforce—for every action an equal and opposite reaction. The four forces that affect the flight of an aircraft are lift, weight, thrust, and drag. Each must be in balance with its opposite in order to maintain flight. The design of the airplane is responsible for achieving this balance.

Lift is the upward-acting force on an airplane. To overcome the natural gravitational pull toward the earth's center, the wing of an aircraft is designed to accelerate the flow of the surrounding air and create a low pressure on the wing's upper surface. The curvature of the wing contributes to the reduction of air pressure relative to the surrounding air. This imbalance of pressure allows an airplane to lift to a higher elevation. This lifting force opposes weight.

Weight is the downward-acting force on an aircraft. According to Newton's law of physics, all objects in the earth's atmosphere are drawn toward the center of the earth. Without this gravitational pull, or weight, an airplane would not have a force to counterbalance lift, and the airplane would continue to move away from the earth and be lost in space.

Thrust is the forward-acting force produced by an engine or propeller. This force is parallel to the line of flight since it is in essence pushing the aircraft along in its path. The power of the engines gives an airplane the propulsion to move forward, but it is counterbalanced by the force of drag.

Drag is the backward-acting force on a plane in flight. An airplane is designed with protruding exterior features that cause a certain amount of resistance to air currents, enabling the movement of the plane to be controlled in flight. Drag is the force that acts parallel with and opposite to the direction of flight and must be overcome by thrust if a plane is going to fly.

DIRECTIONAL MOVEMENTS

The ability of an aircraft to change direction in flight is due to its rotation around an imaginary straight line known as an axis. Picture an aircraft in flight as an object teetering on top of a pinnacle. The very point on which the object sits is its center of gravity and allows for free movement. There are three possible directional movements. It can move from side to side, up or down, or turn in a clockwise or counterclockwise motion. These three directional movements when applied to an aircraft are known as roll, pitch, and yaw, respectively.

Roll is the movement of an aircraft on a horizontal axis as when one wing is higher than the other. An imaginary line passes through the fuselage from nose to tail, and the plane rolls around it. There are hinged parts on each wing called ailerons and spoilers, which move up and down in the airstream to control the plane's rolling action.

Pitch is an aircraft's movement on its lateral axis. A plane changes altitude when the nose moves up or down. Imagine a line passing through the plane from wing tip to wing tip. A seesawlike motion is achieved when the plane uses this line as an axis. The hinged parts on the tail section called elevators that move up and down cause the pitch of the airplane.

Yaw is the movement of an airplane around its vertical axis. When the nose of the aircraft moves to the left or right, then the airplane is said to yaw. The axis around which it turns is an imaginary line that passes through the center of gravity of a plane from top to bottom. A hinged part of the tail section called the rudder moves from side to side to produce the yaw of a plane.

The orientation of a plane in relation to its position around all three axes is known as the aircraft's attitude. These resulting angles caused by roll, pitch, and yaw are evident in flight and on the ground. For example, a "nose-high attitude" means that the aircraft's nose is higher than the tail section, as in a climb.

AIRCRAFT PARTS AND DESIGN

The airplane is aerodynamically designed to withstand the forces exerted on it by air in motion. It is made up of many parts, each of which is unique in design but in harmony with the other parts, to improve the performance of the plane. The movement of an aircraft is dependent on the operation and condition of its integral components, all of which are controlled from the cockpit. There is great attention to detail when designing a plane, since its ability to perform is determined by the shape, distribution, and comparative size of all its parts.

There are minimum standards established for an aircraft's performance. A plane is subject to a thorough inspection before every flight. It is the joint responsibility of the cockpit crew and station maintenance personnel to conduct this inspection and make the necessary repairs if an airplane is to function properly and safely.

In defining location and direction on an aircraft, the following terms are used, as a general rule:

Forward:	the front part of the plane
Aft:	the back part of the plane
Left:	left-hand side facing forward (port)
Right:	right-hand side facing forward (starboard)
Inboard:	closest to the plane's center line (imaginary line from nose to tail)
Outboard:	farthest from the plane's center line

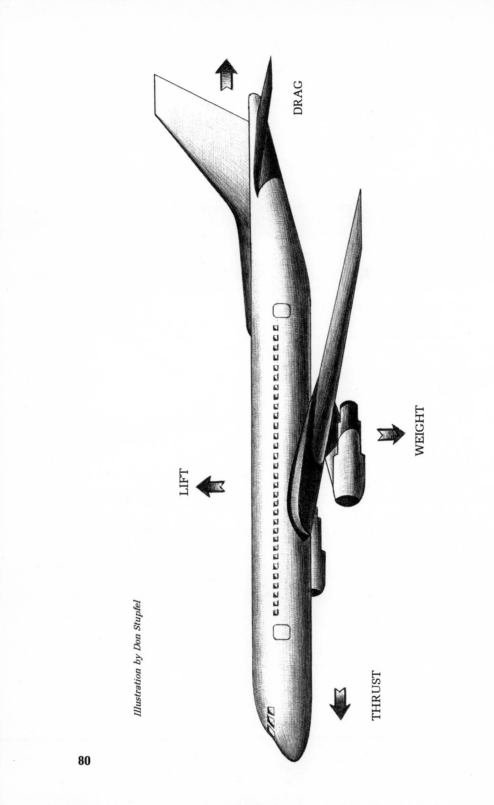

DRAG

WEIGHT

LIFT

THRUST

Illustration by Don Stupfel

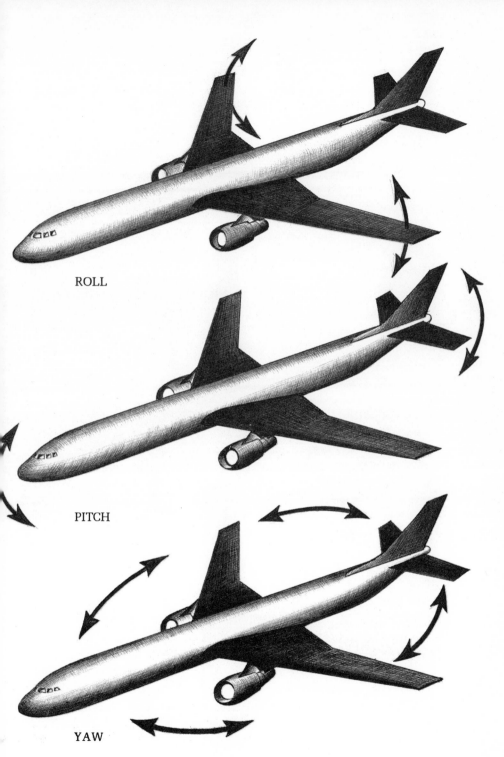

ROLL

PITCH

YAW

Illustration by Don Stupfel

It is interesting to note that aviation terminology is closely akin to nautical terminology. This is a carry-over from the early shipping days, the birthplace of the transportation industry.

Let's now look at an airplane and its components from tip to tail. Each large section of a plane includes a multitude of movable control surfaces and fixed structures that all work in concert to make that aircraft fly. The entire assemblage is designed to achieve perfect control for smooth, comfortable flying.

FUSELAGE

This is the main body of the plane, which is comprised of the cockpit, passenger cabins, and cargo area. Attached to the fuselage are wings, a tail structure, a power source, and a landing-gear system.

RADOME

The radome, the forwardmost part of the fuselage, known as the aircraft's nose, houses a radar system that is designed to detect weather conditions. In order to assure the safest and smoothest flight possible, the device warns the pilots of some forms of turbulence and storm activity in and around the plane's flight path.

WINGS

Without wings an airplane would be an unguided missile. The wings are designed to be flexible to absorb stress and are made of numerous movable parts that control changes in the aircraft's directional movements. As newer, faster, and more efficient jet aircraft are designed, the wings are becoming thinner and more multipurpose.

The design and location of the wings depend on the type of aircraft to which they are attached. Their placement on the fuselage varies according to the size, weight, and range of the aircraft. The wings also function as the storage facility for the aircraft's fuel supply.

Illustration by Don Stupfel

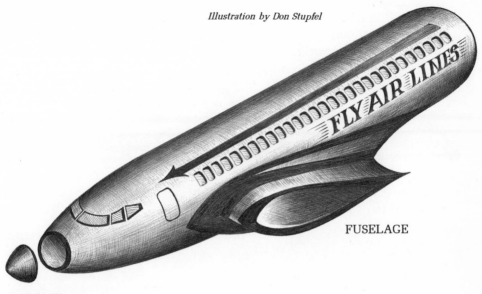

FUSELAGE

RADOME

The shape of the wing is extremely important, as it is the primary lifting air device. The leading edge and top surface are rounded and taper to the trailing edge. As previously explained, the lift of an aircraft is achieved by less pressure on the upper surface of the wing than on the lower surface. The curved wing allows the air passing over it to travel farther than it would over a flat surface. This causes the air to move faster to cover the distance and results in a loss of pressure, therefore increasing lift.

Leading Edge The front part of the wing is known as the leading edge. It is the first portion of the wing to come into contact with the air and is rounded to deflect the air up and over the surface. The leading edge is comprised of movable parts that aid in increasing lift at slower speeds.

Trailing Edge The last part of the wing to move through the air is called the trailing edge. It is narrow, tapered, and equipped with movable surfaces called flaps (discussed later) that increase the area of the wing. The change in shape and size of the trailing edge is responsible for altering the lift and drag of the aircraft.

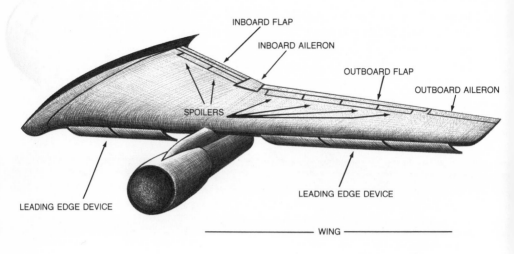

Illustration by Don Stupfel

Ailerons The ailerons are movable surfaces on each wing that act to vary the lift around the plane's horizontal axis (roll). Operation of the ailerons helps to turn or "bank" the aircraft. The pilots' steering wheel(s) control the ailerons.

When the ailerons are in a neutral position, the airflow and resulting forces across the wing surface are equal. When the ailerons are in a deflected position (up or down), a difference of pressure develops. Lowering the aileron on one wing causes that wing to go up, because of its increased lift. Raising the aileron simultaneously on the opposite wing causes that wing to go down, because of the decrease in the amount of lift. The plane then turns toward the lower wing.

Flaps and Leading Edge Devices The movable surfaces on the trailing edge of the wing are known as flaps and are the basis of the lift/drag concept. In order to provide additional lift during takeoff and landing, the flaps move on a hinge or track to provide a larger lifting surface area. Leading edge devices are found on the leading edge of the wing and move forward and down, also increasing the wing's lifting surface.

Spoilers Spoilers are hinged panels mounted in the top of the wing forward of the trailing edge flaps. When raised, they interrupt the airflow, causing loss or spoiling of lift. When used on both wings symmetrically, they function as speed brakes by reducing both lift and speed. When used one side at a time with the ailerons, they augment roll control for improved response. They are also used on the ground during landing to improve braking and reduce stopping distance.

Vortex Generators   Some planes have little raised metal tabs fixed on the upper wing surface known as vortex generators. They help direct the airflow over the wing to reduce drag and supplement lift.

EMPENNAGE

The empennage, more commonly known as the tail assembly, is located at the aft end of the fuselage. There are many variations depending on the size and type of plane, but the purpose of an empennage is to stabilize the aircraft. It is composed of a rudder, stabilizers, and elevators.

Vertical Stabilizer   The finlike fixed structure on a plane's empennage is the vertical stabilizer. It extends upright from the fuselage and helps the airplane fly in a straight path. This rigid structure is used to stabilize the aircraft around the yaw axis and has a rudder attached at its trailing edge.

Rudder   The rudder is the movable part of the vertical stabilizer. It swings on a hinge much like the rudder of a boat to help steer the airplane, i.e., it moves left and right to control yaw. If the rudder moves left, the airplane turns left, and vice versa. The pilot controls the rudder by pushing on pedals with his feet.

Horizontal Stabilizer   The fixed structures on the empennage that resemble small wings are called the horizontal stabilizers. These stabilize the aircraft and provide attachment points for the hinged elevator.

Elevators   The elevators are the movable surfaces behind the horizontal stabilizer. They move up and down to control the pitch of the aircraft. For example, when an elevator is moved downward, lift is created and the nose is forced upward, thereby resulting in a nose-high attitude of the plane. Movement of the elevator is controlled in the cockpit by pulling back (or pushing forward) on the steering wheel, more commonly called the yoke.

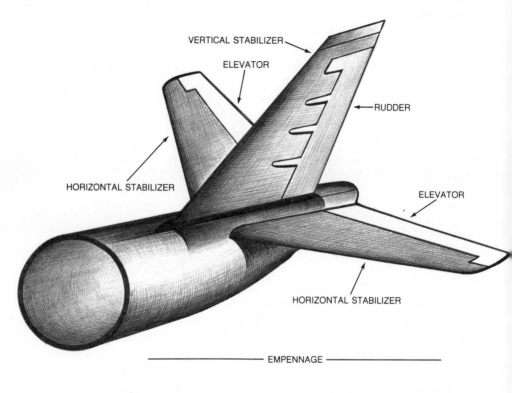

VERTICAL STABILIZER

ELEVATOR

RUDDER

HORIZONTAL STABILIZER

ELEVATOR

HORIZONTAL STABILIZER

———— EMPENNAGE ————

Illustration by Don Stupfel

LANDING GEAR SYSTEM AND WHEELS

The mechanism responsible for support of an airplane on the ground is known as the landing gear. Located on the bottom of the fuselage and wings are separate retractable units known as the nose gear and main gear respectively. These structures are raised and stored in wheel wells in the belly of the fuselage during flight to reduce drag. As a plane lifts off the runway, the gear is retracted hydraulically, and then extended in the same manner prior to landing. Both nose and main gear systems operate simultaneously. Should there be a malfunction of the landing gear, a warning device in the cockpit indicates the problem and they can be lowered by alternate or back-up methods.

Main Gear   This gear assembly is composed of struts, wheels, and brakes and is located midway between the nose and empennage. Lock mechanisms and sensors assure that the main gear is completely down and locked, or fully retracted and locked. Aircraft may have two, three, or four main landing gears.

Nose Gear   The nose gear assembly is located between the nose and the main gear. It provides support for the forward section of the fuselage and is also used for steering when the plane is on the ground. The nose gear doors are of a clamshell type and consist of two doors that are flush with the surface of the fuselage when closed.

POWER SOURCE

Recall that Newton defined a law of physics: "action and reaction are equal and opposite." When applied to the movement of an airplane, this theory implies that there must be a means of pushing air backward in order to produce a forward movement of the plane. This is done on some airplanes through the use of propellers, but more commonly on larger airplanes through the operation of jet engines.

The principle of propulsion is the same, regardless of the type of engine. Air is ingested, compressed, mixed with fuel, ignited, expanded, and expelled out the back of the engine, producing thrust in the forward direction. The number, size, and location of engines vary according to the type of aircraft. They are mounted on the wing and/or tail section. The outer covering of an engine is known as a cowling and the pylon is the mounting that attaches the engine to the wing.

EXTERIOR LIGHTS

Navigational lights are strategically located on a plane's exterior and serve to alert other aircraft as a visual indicator of the plane's position and direction. All planes have the same color coding and light positioning scheme so that a consistency is achieved for all sizes and makes of aircraft for safety purposes. A red light is on the left wing tip and a green light is on the right wing tip. White lights are used to indicate a plane's right and left outboard trailing edges of the horizontal stabilizers. Landing lights are located on the leading edge of the wing, nose landing gear, or lower flap surfaces and serve much the same purpose as headlights on your car. Also, there are red upper and lower flashing anticollision lights for identification purposes. See and be seen. A spotlight is located on the tail section of some aircraft to illuminate the airline's logo.

THE INFLUENCE OF WEATHER

The effects of weather greatly influence the progress of a plane on the ground and in the air. On the ground, it is subject to those same conditions—such as snow and ice—that impede the motion of any other form of transportation. Inflight, an aircraft is completely independent of any contact with a ground surface, so it becomes vulnerable to surrounding adverse atmospheric conditions. The responsibility rests with the flight crew and dispatchers to construct a flight plan for the aircraft that will avoid the most severe weather and promise the most comfortable and safe flight possible. Weather is the most common element in air traffic delays and cancellations. Therefore, it is your responsibility as a flight attendant to be able to explain the reasons for weather-related flight irregularities to your passengers.

A basic knowledge of our atmosphere will help you understand how weather affects the flight of an airplane. The atmosphere surrounding the earth is composed of a combination of gases. Nitrogen and oxygen make up about 99 percent, while the remaining 1 percent is a mixture of other gases. The atmosphere is divided into upper and lower layers. The layer closest to the earth's surface is known as the troposphere. It extends five to ten miles up and includes many changes in temperature. For every thousand feet of elevation, the temperature decreases approximately 3.5 degrees Fahrenheit. The upper layer, called the stratosphere, usually remains at a constant subzero temperature.

As the warmer air near the earth's surface rises, it comes in contact with the very cold air of the upper atmosphere. Since cool air is not capable of retaining as much moisture, this sometimes creates a condition known as condensation. The water is squeezed out and the liquid manifests itself in the form of droplets. These droplets unite with each other to form clouds, rain, ice, snow, and other potential weather hazards.

AIR MOVEMENT

Since an airplane is affected by the characteristics of the air around it, let's take a look at the types of air movements that are contributing factors.

Wind is the term used to describe air in motion. These currents of air vary in their intensity and velocity depending on the terrain. Mountains, valleys, and water surfaces create different wind patterns. Wind can also bring about a change affecting a pilot's control of the aircraft during takeoff, landing, ascent, and descent, as well as influence the speed and direction of flight.

Jet Streams are high-speed wind currents that travel in narrow paths high in the earth's atmosphere. They can be as strong as 100–150 miles per hour and move in streams from west to east. The jet stream is the result of troughs between large, constant air masses and is influenced by the earth's rotation.

Turbulence is an atmospheric condition characterized by sudden changes in wind direction and velocity. It may be caused by physical features of the land, or the wake from a preceding aircraft. The degree of turbulence depends on the frequency and severity of the airflow disturbance. Turbulence can be occasional, intermittent, or continuous.

The severity of turbulence ranges from light to extreme. Characteristics of mild turbulence are light choppiness, bumpiness, and slight changes in the plane's attitude. Objects remain in place inside the aircraft and seat belts may be required.

Moderate turbulence is greater in intensity, resulting in rapid bumps and jolts. There is a slight variation in indicated airspeed and the craft's altitude and attitude. The aircraft remains in control, but unsecured cabin objects may be dislodged. The use of seat belts is usually required during this disturbance.

Severe turbulence causes a series of violent thrusts and jolts. Cabin occupants and unsecured objects are tossed about and there are large variations in the plane's indicated airspeed. The aircraft also suffers large, abrupt changes in altitude and attitude, and seat belts are required.

Extreme conditions in air turbulence may cause structural damage to the aircraft and injury to passengers and crew who do not have their seat belts fastened. Every effort is made to alter the craft's flight plan to avoid these conditions.

Clear air turbulence (CAT) is a disturbance of air currents in clear air and can happen without warning. It is associated with high altitudes and needs no storm activity for its inception.

ADVERSE WEATHER CONDITIONS

Flying an airplane would certainly be easier if weather conditions were always clear and visibility good. Fortunately, flight crew members are highly trained to deal with adverse situations, and controlling systems are on hand to monitor and guide a flight's progress. Airplanes are also built to specifications to withstand a tremendous amount of structural stress and still offer safe passage to everyone on board.

Restrictions to a pilot's visibility are manifested in different forms of atmospheric conditions. They include clouds, fog, smoke, haze, and precipitation, and blowing dust, sand, and snow. It is for this reason that instrument landing systems are used to guide an aircraft to land rather than relying only on the pilot's ability to make visual sightings.

Clouds As moist air is carried upward, it combines with the colder air to form condensation known as clouds. Clouds vary in height, size, shape, and density. They are classified into types by altitude, method of formation, and composition. Where there are vertical air currents, typical cloud formations are of the cumulus type, i.e., billowy accumulations of condensation. Thunderstorms are severe forms of cumulus clouds. Stable air produces stratus clouds, which are spread out in layers or sheets. Fog is a form of low stratus clouds. It is possible to avoid isolated clouds, but precautions are still taken, since they tend to travel rapidly.

The amount of cloud cover varies from clear to scattered, broken, and overcast. The base of a large cloud cover is known as the ceiling. If the cloud coverage is too low at an airport, i.e., visibility is extremely poor, landing may be postponed until the ceiling lifts. This usually happens later in the day as the ground warms up and the air rises.

Fog A type of condensation frequently found in coastal regions is known as fog. It can linger near the earth's surface and be quite limiting to visibility. Airports are often closed to takeoff and landing traffic, and planes are grounded when the fog is too thick. However, it has been known to lift as rapidly as it appears, resulting in unpredictable flight schedules.

Thunderstorms Storms range from mild to violent and incorporate high vertical wind currents and precipitation in the forms of rain, snow, and hail. Certain atmospheric conditions are necessary for the occurrence of thunderstorms. These include unstable air, relatively high moisture content, and some amount of electrical charge.

Lightning A buildup of electrical charges in cloud formations produces lightning. The heaviest lightning activity occurs during various months of the year, depending on locale. Spring is a particularly bad time through the Midwest and south-central United States. Lightning rarely damages an aircraft seriously, because in flight it is not grounded. If lightning does strike, it enters the aircraft at one point and simply exits at another. Noticeable effects are small pit marks or holes on the plane's surface where the lightning struck, and this usually occurs when flying through rain, hail, sleet, or snow. An excessive buildup of electrical charges and lightning activity sometimes results in a phenomenon known as "St. Elmo's Fire," where a bluish corona is visible, and may occur inside or outside the plane. Electrical activity such as this can also affect the aircraft's instruments and radios.

Ice When temperatures are below freezing, water vapors are transformed into ice crystals. If encountered on the ground, ice reduces the aircraft's efficiency on runways and taxiways, and creates traction and braking problems. When ice and frost are encountered inflight, they increase drag and weight, and decrease lift and thrust. Jet planes have anti-ice systems (hot bleed air from the engines) to rid the wings' leading edges and engine inlets of ice buildup.

One of your responsibilities as a flight attendant is to understand those aircraft functions and weather conditions that affect the progress of flight. Passengers look to you for reassurance. By exuding a confidence through acquired knowledge, you can allay any existing fears and instill a sense of well-being. After all, passenger safety and comfort are your prime responsibilities.

AIRCRAFT FAMILIARIZATION

What makes a DC–9 different from a B–747? Or an Airbus from an L–1011? Is it enough to know the number and location of engines, and the length of the aircraft? There are many more characteristics that help distinguish one aircraft from another. You are expected to be familiar with all aircraft flown by your airline. Identification of aircraft exteriors ánd a working knowledge of their interiors is learned by studying distinguishing features.

There are a few aircraft manufacturers that supply the majority of passenger-carrying airplanes in the United States. Ranking among the largest are Boeing, McDonnell-Douglas, and Lockheed. Even though one airline may purchase planes from several different manufacturers, there is a basic similarity in the interiors.

AIRCRAFT IDENTIFICATION

Pictured in the first half of this chapter are basic aircraft types and a listing of individual characteristics. Discussed in the second half of the chapter are the interiors common to all aircraft types. Each airplane is constructed to meet airline specifications. The components of the interiors will vary in number, size, location, and design. This is meant as a general overview for identification purposes.

CONCORDE/SST (Supersonic Transport)

Fuselage length	61.66m
Wingspan	84'
Tail height	12.2m
Passenger capacity	128–144

Narrow-body aircraft. Four engines, two mounted on each wing. It has a rapierlike shape; small interior; beak nose, hinged; two-across seating; slender delta wing. Average range is 3,050 km. Average cruising speed is 1,450 MPH

Photo courtesy Braniff International

AIRBUS 300

Fuselage length	175'11"
Wingspan	147'1"
Tail height	54'2"
Passenger capacity	229–345

Wide-body aircraft. It has two engines, one on each wing. Average range is 1,967 nm. Average cruising speed is 560 MPH

Photo courtesy Eastern Airlines

B–707 SERIES   100   300

	100	300
Fuselage length	138'3"	145'6"
Wingspan	130'10"	145'9"
Tail height	40'11"	41'7"
Passenger capacity	125	150

Narrow-body aircraft. There are four engines, two mounted on each wing. Average range is 3,000 to 4,200 nm. Average cruising speed is 600 MPH

Photo courtesy Pan American World Airways

B–727 SERIES 100, 100QC 200

	100, 100QC	200
Fuselage length	133'2"	153'2"
Wingspan	108'	108'
Tail height	34'	34'
Passenger capacity	94	155

Narrow-body aircraft. There are three engines, all mounted on the aft section. Average range is 2,000–2,400 nm. Average cruising speed is 600 MPH

Photo courtesy Delta Air Lines

B–737 SERIES

	100	200
Fuselage length	90'7"	96'11"
Wingspan	93'	93'
Tail height	37'	37'
Passenger capacity	107	119

Narrow-body aircraft. There are two engines, one mounted on each wing. Average range is 1,000 nm. Average cruising speed is 575 MPH

Photo courtesy Frontier Airlines

B–747   **100**   **SP (Special Performance)**

Fuselage	225'1"	176'10"
Wingspan	195'7"	195'7"
Tail height	63'6"	65'10"
Passenger capacity	350–400	305

Wide-body aircraft. Four engines, two mounted on each wing. Average range is 5,000 nm. Average cruising speed is 600 MPH

Photo courtesy United Airlines

B–767 SERIES

Fuselage length	158'5"
Wingspan	155'
Tail height	50'5"
Passenger capacity	208

Wide-body aircraft. Two engines, one mounted on each wing. Average range is 2,200 nm. Average cruising speed is 640 MPH

Photo courtesy Boeing Commercial Airplane Company

DC–8 SERIES   61   62   63

	61	62	63
Fuselage length	187'4"	157'5"	187'4"
Wingspan	148'4"	148'4"	148'4"
Tail height	43'	53'5"	43'
Passenger capacity	259	189	259

Narrow-body aircraft. There are four engines, two mounted on each wing. Average range is 5,590 nm. Average cruising speed is 575 MPH

Photo courtesy United Airlines

DC–9 SERIES

	10	30	50	80
Fuselage length	104'4.8"	119'3.6"	133'7"	147'10"
Wingspan	89'4.8"	93'3.6"	93'4.2"	107'10"
Tail height	27'5"	27'6"	28'5"	29'3"
Passenger capacity	90	115	135	70–172

Narrow-body aircraft. There are two engines mounted on the aft section of the aircraft. Average range is 1,581 km. Average cruising speed is 549 MPH

Photo courtesy Hughes Airwest

DC–10 SERIES   10   30   40

	10	30	40
Fuselage length	170'6"	170'6"	170'6"
Wingspan	155'4"	165'4"	165'4"
Tail height	57'6"	57'6"	57'6"
Passenger capacity	255–380	255–380	255–380

Wide-body aircraft. There are three engines, one mounted on each wing and one on the tail assembly. Average range is 4,522 nm. Average cruising speed is 587 MPH

Photo courtesy World Airways

L–188

Fuselage length	104'8"
Wingspan	99'
Tail height	32'10½"
Passenger capacity	85–99

Narrow-body aircraft. Four turboprop engines, two mounted on each wing. Average range is 2,500 nm. Average cruising speed is 405 MPH

Photo courtesy Lockheed California Company

L–1011

Fuselage length	177'8"
Wingspan	155'4"
Tail height	55'4"
Passenger capacity	230–400

Wide-body aircraft. Three engines, one on each wing, one on tail structure where the fuselage meets. Average range is 2,000 nm. Average cruising speed is 575 MPH

Photo courtesy Eastern Airlines

AIRCRAFT INTERIORS

In order to maximize a feeling of comfort and spaciousness for the traveler, yet maintain a practical working environment for the pilots and inflight crew, aircraft manufacturers have capitalized on advanced technology in designing the interiors of today's planes. The descriptions that follow are of those aircraft cabin components that are common to all passenger-carrying commercial planes. Every aircraft, for instance, has a cockpit, passenger seats, lavatories, etc. Differences occur in size, number, location, and design scheme. As a flight attendant, you must be familiar with the location, function, and operation of your airline's cabin interiors and their integral parts in order to effectively execute your job responsibilities.

COCKPIT

The cockpit, also known as the flight deck, is an enclosed space in the forward part of an aircraft in which flight operations are conducted. It houses a team of flight personnel and an array of instruments and devices, all of which are responsible for the control, navigation, and communications of flight. The compact design of the cockpit allows for maximum pilot efficiency. The complex equipment is arranged around each crew member's seat so that all controls are easily accessible from a sitting position.

The most prominent features of the cockpit are the flight stations. These are the seats occupied by the pilots for the duration of each flight. Their number depends on the type and size of the aircraft. Basically, there are three flight stations in the cockpit. The forwardmost seat on the left side as you enter is that of the captain. Adjacent to this seat on the right-hand side is the copilot's (first officer's) station. Directly behind the copilot sits the flight engineer (second officer).

Additional space in the cockpit is utilized for other purposes. There may be one or two more seats situated directly behind the captain for authorized personnel such as flight managers, FAA officials, and pilot trainees.

In the remaining space, storage units are provided for airplane documents, flight bags and manuals, and uniform coats.

The cockpit is the center of operation for an aircraft and its flight crew.
Photo courtesy United Airlines

Emergency equipment found in every cockpit includes oxygen masks, smoke goggles, fire axe, and CO_2 extinguisher.

CABIN CONFIGURATION AND DESIGN

The passenger cabin makes use of the largest amount of interior space in any aircraft. The cabin is comprised of seats aligned in rows. Common to all narrow-bodied aircraft is a center aisle from front to back, dividing the cabin into left and right sides. On wide-bodied aircraft there are two center aisles. The seats are divided in this manner to allow for ease of service and passenger mobility. The rows are grouped into sections or zones that are divided by bulkheads and additional floor space at exit rows.

Passenger-seat rows are numbered, usually so that row one is the forwardmost row, and the numbers increase through to the last row of the cabin. Each seat is identified by an alphabetical letter. The window seat on the left (as you face the cockpit) is designated as the "A" seat and the remaining seats in the row are lettered consecutively to the right-hand window seat.

The majority of all cabins are divided by a curtain or screen into first class and coach sections. In first class, the seats are wider, fewer in number, and there is more space between each row. Featured on some aircraft is additional space for lounge tables, swivel chairs, and a stand-up bar.

In coach, there are more seats in each row and more rows per cabin. In a charter or all-coach configuration a high volume of passengers is achieved by several means: the seats are reduced in size, the space between each row is decreased, or bulkheads and extra storage spaces are eliminated.

Common to all aircraft are exits from front to back. All commercial aircraft are required by the FAA to be equipped with an adequate number of exits to facilitate an evacuation of all passengers in an emergency. These exits are of a door or window design and each is marked with illuminating signs overhead and on the exit itself.

The overall design of an aircraft interior must not only be functional for safety and service, but must also be a visual presentation of the airline. Since the airlines are involved in a competitive industry, they concentrate on designing cabin interiors that portray a unique image. Each airline specifies to the manufacturer a motif, color scheme, type of carpeting, partition designs, and incidental decoration.

PASSENGER SEATING AREA

All aircraft passenger seats are designed for comfort and built to meet specified safety requirements. The seat back and bottom cushions are padded and new designs include contouring for lower back support. These cushions can be utilized as flotation devices in the event of a water evacuation.

During flight, a seat back can be reclined to a degree so as not to interfere with the passengers seated in the row directly aft. On some aircraft, where there is three-across seating, the back of the vacant middle seat can be folded forward. This provides for a feeling of spaciousness and a flat surface area for use by the occupants of the other two seats.

Attached to each seat is a seat belt designed with a mechanism for easy connection and quick release. Should the belt be of insufficient length to accommodate an oversized passenger, extension belts are available on every aircraft.

Passenger convenience items located at every seat include ashtrays, armrests, tray tables, and seat pockets. In each row, passenger seats are divided by armrests which, in most cases, are removable or may be folded back between the seats. On the back of each seat is a pocket containing an airsickness bag and the airline's inflight publication. Route maps and inflight shopping publications are sometimes in this pocket as well.

The most important item included in this pocket is a passenger briefing card to illustrate the aircraft's safety procedures including evacuation and use of exits and oxygen. Also attached to the back of each passenger seat is a fold-down tray table. Those passengers seated directly behind a bulkhead require "plug-in" tables or find auxiliary tables contained in the armrest unit.

Every seat has a passenger service unit within reach from a sitting position. Located in the armrest or directly above the seat, panels include a switch for an overhead reading light, a flight attendant call button, and an air vent nozzle. Should the aircraft be equipped for audiovisual entertainment, a channel selector, volume control, and headset outlet are located in the armrest or in a panel over the passenger's shoulder in the seat back.

The area around a passenger is just as important as the seat itself. For safety purposes, oxygen masks are housed in a pod above or in front of a passenger's seat. Although these masks are not visible other than during an emergency situation, be aware that there is usually one more mask available than there are seats in each row. The floor space beneath each passenger seat is allotted for the storage of carry-on items. A restraining bar underneath the front of each seat prevents movement of this baggage.

FLIGHT ATTENDANT STATIONS

Flight attendants are assigned specific seats during takeoff, landing, and turbulence. These stations are called jump seats and are located at emergency exits. Their number and location on board are based on the seating configuration and safety requirements. When limited space at certain exits in the middle of the passenger cabin does not allow for a separate jump-seat facility, a passenger seat is designated for crew use.

The jump seats located directly adjacent to door exits are specially designed so that the seat bottom automatically folds upright when not in use. All jump seats are also equipped with seat belts. On some jump seats shoulder harnesses are supplied as part of the required safety features. Within reach is an emergency oxygen supply. The number of masks depends on whether the seat is designed for single or double occupancy. First aid oxygen bottles and fire extinguishers are other types of safety equipment found near flight attendant jump seats.

For communication purposes, most jump-seat facilities are equipped with phone receivers for calls from one area of the plane to another, and announcements over the public address system. This is the means by which direct contact is established between flight attendants, flight attendants and pilots, and from flight attendants to passengers. The interphone system controls are located within arm's reach of the flight attendant.

A flight attendant control panel is situated near the jump seat. Incorporated into the panel is an assortment of buttons and switches that regulate the cabin's lighting, entertainment, and call systems. The larger the aircraft, the more complex the controls. The number of controls also varies according to the location of the jump seat. Generally, the most fully equipped panel is situated near the lead flight attendant station.

CABIN CALL SYSTEM

An organized call system between the cockpit, the flight attendants, and passengers is an integral part of every aircraft. Calls can originate from flight attendant jump seats, the flight deck, galley areas, lavatories, and passenger seats. The entire system is usually color-coded so that each time a bell or chime is heard a certain color lights up on an overhead panel (in view of a flight attendant jump seat) to indicate the origin of the call. To clear the indicator light once a call has been answered, press the "reset" button located on the flight attendant control panel or at the source of the call.

CABIN LIGHTING SYSTEM

A variety of lights in a passenger cabin is used to create an effect for the specific time of day and services offered. Flight attendants have the means of controlling the brightness of the lights in the ceiling and along the sidewall of the fuselage.

Cabin lights also contribute to safe working conditions. There are entry lights at each main cabin door, and overhead lights are located in galley and flight attendant work areas. On night trips, when cabin lighting has been turned to "dim" or "off," an auxiliary light can be used to illuminate the area just outside lavatory doors.

CABIN ENTERTAINMENT SYSTEMS

Aircraft used on medium- to long-range flights may be equipped with audiovisual entertainment. Music can be transmitted over the public address system for boarding and deplaning. Once in flight, most larger aircraft use a prerecorded set of audio programs on tape that are transmitted to each passenger seat. Headsets are issued that plug into the outlet at the passenger's seat. This same system provides for the audio portion of inflight movies when shown on board. The visual portions of these programs are projected onto screens or viewed over television cassette players.

BUFFET GALLEY

A thorough description of buffet/galley design and equipment is discussed in Chapter 17, Food and Beverage Services.

STORAGE AND CLOSET FACILITIES

Storage compartments are available on all aircraft to accommodate passenger carry-on items, and include shelflike structures as well as closed overhead compartments. No heavy packages, sharp items, or newspapers should be on open overhead shelves, as there is no way to restrain their movement. There are also closets for hanging garment bags, and others for storage of bulky and odd-shaped items, such as baby strollers, fishing poles, guitars, crutches, and canes. All designated storage areas must be latched closed for takeoff and landing, and when advised that severe turbulence is imminent.

If the airline does not specify that flight attendant luggage be checked for each flight, provisions are made for crew storage inside the cabin. The specific locations are outlined in the flight attendant manual.

LAVATORIES

The number and location of lavatory facilities depend on the passenger capacity of the aircraft and the cabin configuration. On smaller planes, there may be only one lavatory. On the medium- to wide-bodied aircraft, bathrooms are situated for passenger convenience throughout the plane from front to back.

The lavatories are complete with standard features of a sink, toilet, mirror, dispensers for soap and tissues, and a waste receptacle. Even within the limited space, there are several compartments available for additional supplies. Extra soap, towels, toilet and facial tissue, sanitary napkins, paper cups, and airsick bags can be found just below and directly adjacent to the sink.

A flight attendant call button is also located in the lavatory. A passenger rings this button to call attention to the flight attendant that help is needed. Should a passenger be unable to open the door from the inside, the door can be unlocked from the cabin. When a lavatory door is locked, an OCCUPIED sign is seen from the cabin. If the lavatory is not locked, a sign reading VACANT or TOILET is visible.

PASSENGER CONVENIENCE ITEMS

Bassinets for infants are furnished on certain aircraft. While not in use they are secured in designated areas. Drinking fountains are self-contained units located throughout the cabin for passenger use. Aside from the water spigot and accompanying drain, there is a container for paper cups and a slot where they can be deposited after use. A variety of reading matter and stationery is displayed in magazine racks that are located on bulkheads or within storage facilities visible to passengers. For safety purposes, all material contained within the rack is secured by a bar, elastic strap, or partial covering.

As a flight attendant, you must recognize all the aircraft flown by your airline on sight and be able to function quickly and efficiently within the confines of the fuselage. To an inquiring passenger, can you explain: How fast are we flying? How many passengers can this plane accommodate? Where is the lavatory? How do I recline my seat? Where are the magazines? The only way to be comfortable with your work environment is to study and experience those features necessary for aircraft identification and familiarization.

10

TODAY'S AIR TRAVELER

The majority of people who comprise today's air travelers are business persons and vacationers. Their attraction to the airplane as a mode of transportation stems from the reduction in travel time, frequency of flights, and the proven safety record.

Due to the competition among airlines today, the passenger is offered many classes of service, including first class, coach, economy, night coach, and charter. On any one flight, passengers in a particular cabin may have paid varying prices for the right to occupy a seat. However, it is your responsibility as a flight attendant to see that each passenger is given the same consideration and attention regardless of the price paid for the ticket.

The business traveler usually has important time commitments and depends on the airline to operate according to schedule. Interruptions should be kept to a minimum since this traveler is either working or resting before arriving at his or her place of business. Unless these passengers want to converse with you for any period of time, respect their need for a quiet atmosphere.

Many vacationers purchase round-trip tickets for pleasure purposes, desiring to travel independently of other passengers. Some organize into groups and book passage on a charter basis. Vacation costs are reduced through the availability of tour

126

packages. Passengers can elect to partake in these arrangements, which include hotel accommodations and ground transportation, as well as lower airfares.

Commercial airlines enter into large group sales as a source of revenue for their companies. A separate plane is sometimes chartered or the group is boarded with other travelers as a portion of the entire passenger load. Most of the passengers in these groups have a common interest. For instance, groups of conventioneers plan to travel together by plane in order to make their business excursion pleasurable. Other groups, such as sports teams, ballet companies, and military troops, also travel together for a common purpose. Your flight attendant duties on board with charter groups deviate slightly from normal service. Although your safety responsibilities remain the same as on any other flight, the atmosphere in the cabin changes to a more casual service. People are up out of their seats visiting with each other throughout the flight. Although it is difficult for you to move down the aisle on some charter flights to perform your duties, realize that people are enjoying themselves and are most willing to cooperate with your requests in order to receive a more efficient service.

The passenger is the very reason you are on board as a flight attendant and you should regard the customer as an integral part of your job and the airline. Today's air traveler is more discriminating than ever before. As people travel more frequently they become seasoned, sophisticated and, at times, blasé. They demand comfort and efficient service, so you should be aware of the different types of passengers on board and know how to handle their special needs.

SPECIAL CARE PASSENGERS

Individual passengers may require special consideration in-flight. It is important to recognize how you can be of assistance to your passengers and what actions should be taken to make their flight more comfortable. Be aware of your responsibilities regarding federal laws and airline policies in dealing with certain passengers. There is no typical passenger. Every person on your airplane is unique and each should be given personalized attention.

There are several ways in which you are informed that passengers requiring special assistance are on your plane. If you are not advised during a briefing or via a manifest, the passenger may choose to tell you directly once on board. In most cases such passengers will be brought on the aircraft prior to others in order to allow extra time for settling in their seats. This gives you and the other flight attendants the opportunity to personally meet the special passengers and discuss their particular situations.

FIRST RIDERS

There is a first time for everything and for some of your passengers it may be their first experience on a plane. If they seem apprehensive about flying, explain the sounds and sensations they may experience during the course of the flight. Offer a visit to the cockpit before or after a flight to give them a better understanding of the competence of the crew and the safety of air travel. Most first riders are so excited about being in their new environment that their fears soon subside and anything you do for them is appreciated.

EMERGENCY TRAVELERS

For some passengers the need to travel may be due to sudden news about an accident, serious illness, or death of a loved one. They may be confused and distraught, and may not want to be disturbed at all. Sometimes a passenger is accompanying a casket on the same plane and may be permitted to witness its boarding from the ramp. In general, offer assistance to emergency travelers and be sympathetic to their emotions.

VIP'S

"Very Important Passengers" include celebrities, political and sports figures, high-ranking executives, and people whose faces and names are in the news. They may want special treatment inflight, or they may prefer to go unnoticed and to not be disturbed. It is up to you and the other flight attendants to offer any assistance possible and to assure their privacy, if desired.

UNACCOMPANIED CHILDREN

Most airlines allow children to travel by themselves if they meet certain age requirements. They are escorted to the plane and introduced to the flight attendant in whose charge they remain until met at their destination. A paper is included with their ticket that informs the flight attendant of the person who will be meeting the child, along with the name, address, and telephone number of the parent or guardian. If the child is connecting to another flight, you must see that he or she is not left unattended.

Offer comfort and reassurance to these children if they are upset and give them whatever toys and games are available on the plane. Once other passengers board, introduce the children to their seat partners and keep an eye on them throughout the flight. They may be especially interested in visiting the cockpit before or after the trip. Making these children feel like very important travelers will certainly add to their enjoyment.

FAMILIES WITH SMALL CHILDREN

Parents are very appreciative of any help you can extend to them when traveling with their children. You can assist them in settling into their seats by storing belongings and offering to be on hand when needed. If one of the children is an infant, offer a bassinet, if possible, after takeoff. During the flight, try to serve children's meals first so parents can enjoy their meal at their convenience. Advise parents that you have provisions for heating baby bottles and, if available, you can offer additional infant-care items from the flight attendant kit.

ELDERLY PASSENGERS

A helping hand can be offered to elderly passengers who may not be able to fend for themselves. Take special care to note any physical impairments or loss of agility for which you

A young child traveling alone makes a new friend—his flight attendant—
on board.
Photo courtesy Delta Air Lines

may have to compensate. (For example, if they are hard of hearing, stand directly in front of them to speak.) Do not rush them through their meal or hurry them while they are walking through the aisle. Offer to do things for them to avoid any unnecessary exertion on their part.

IRATE PASSENGERS

There are many reasons why some of your passengers may be visibly irritated or upset. Sometimes the problem is private, brought on by personal or business-related causes. At other times, problems have arisen through some mishandling by the airline. Perhaps the passenger's baggage was lost, the food choice was not available, a delayed flight caused a missed connection, or an unpleasant encounter with a company representative occurred. For whatever reason a passenger is irate, the passenger's individual need will dictate how you should handle the situation. Some passengers want proof that something is going to be done to correct the problem and visible results, and others simply ask for understanding and listen to your explanations and suggestions. Try not to take sides over the issue and reassure the passenger that there are valid reasons for whatever upset them.

INTOXICATED PASSENGERS

The problem of dealing with passengers who are obviously intoxicated is compounded by their inability to reason. Your main concern is for their safety, that of the other passengers, and to prevent any disturbance. If a person has had too much to drink, cut off the supply of alcohol and notify the lead flight attendant and captain of the circumstances. Be tactful and discreet when dealing with these passengers.

FOREIGN-LANGUAGE-SPEAKING PASSENGERS

If, on a domestic flight, a foreign-language-speaking passenger boards, ask escorting friends or family necessary questions about the language spoken, the passenger's destination, and meal and beverage choices. Determine if anyone on board speaks the same language as the foreign passenger, to facilitate communication. Remember that these passengers are at a disadvantage, so pay them special attention and make an effort to communicate through the use of hand motions.

HANDICAPPED PASSENGERS

Handicapped and disabled persons have special needs and requests. Be understanding, compassionate, and use common sense in assisting these passengers. Respect their feelings and dignity by speaking directly with the handicapped persons as opposed to their companions. The Federal Aviation Administration requires that handicapped persons be briefed individually about safety and emergency procedures.

Disabled passengers are categorized into two groups: ambulatory and nonambulatory. Those who can walk about, such as the blind and deaf, may prefer to do so unassisted. Nonambulatory passengers, such as paraplegics, are usually accompanied by a friend or relative since their capabilities in moving about are limited. Passengers' handicaps are also classified by physical and mental disabilities.

Types of handicapped passengers you may encounter on a flight and your responsibilities toward them are listed below:

Oxygenated Passengers   These persons use a supply of oxygen provided by the airline throughout the flight. There is an additional cost for this service and the container of oxygen is installed prior to flight under the passenger's seat. Continually check on the passenger's well-being and enforce no-smoking regulations.

Blind Passengers   Give blind passengers the opportunity to dictate how you can best be of assistance. Some do not regard their condition as a handicap since they have learned to become self-sufficient. Respect their dignity and be tactful in your approach. When boarding, offer to guide blind passengers to their seats. If they require your help, extend your arm or elbow for them to hold. Stay approximately a half step ahead of these passengers and be specific when giving directions. If the passenger uses a cane, store it during takeoff and landing, unless it is the collapsible type, in which case it may be stored in the seat pocket.

Some blind passengers may be accompanied by a Seeing-Eye dog. This guide dog is allowed to remain in the cabin at the feet of the blind passenger and is usually accommodated at the bulkhead row. Avoid petting or feeding the dog and advise other passengers to do the same.

During your preflight safety briefing, be explicit in your verbal description of emergency features. Let the blind passenger touch the objects you are discussing and describe the exact location of emergency exits. Reassure the passenger that the dog's safety has also been considered in the emergency procedures devised by the airline.

Other means of assistance include a description of passenger comfort items, lavatory location, and audio operation. During a meal service, describe the food and tray items, and their location on the tray. Offer to read a menu to the passenger and advise verbally when cabin signs are lit.

Deaf Passengers The same principles of assistance concerning blind passengers also apply to the deaf and hard-of-hearing. Your communication techniques when briefing these passengers or describing service features should center around sign language, hand gestures, and written notes. If the passenger can lip-read, be explicit in forming words when you speak.

Since deaf passengers cannot hear announcements, use briefing cards and pictures to personally describe what is being said. Inform them of the illumination of all signs and make a point of checking on them throughout the flight.

Nonambulatory Passengers Air travel is now available to passengers for whom it was previously unfeasible. Special provisions and procedures have been implemented by the airlines to transport those persons who cannot walk. Such handicapped passengers include paraplegics, stroke victims, and those who have suffered leg amputations. Aisle chairs allow the passenger to be taken directly to the airplane seat. A travel companion assists with visits to the lavatory if the passenger is not catheterized.

Aero-Stretcher Passengers Passengers confined to stretchers are permitted to travel on commercial airlines provided certain requirements are met. The disabled passenger must be accompanied by at least one other person, and additional seats must be purchased to allow for the size of the stretcher.

133

Only after obtaining clearance from a medical doctor and advising the airline in advance can an aero-stretcher passenger be accommodated. The maintenance department is responsible for preparing the seats in the cabin where the stretcher is to be installed. The passenger is transported to and from the airplane by ambulance personnel. It is for this reason that an airline may consent to carry an aero-stretcher only on a direct flight—there are usually no provisions to transport a stretcher passenger from one airplane to another.

Your responsibilities to aero-stretcher passengers involve fastening their seat belts, ensuring that the shoulder harnesses are attached for takeoff and landing, and briefing them on emergency evacuation procedures. If pull curtains are included with the stretcher apparatus, ascertain whether the passenger prefers to have them opened or closed during the flight.

Mentally Handicapped Passengers The airlines and in-flight crews have a right to know of any persons on board who have confirmed mental disabilities. Your actions and attitudes toward these passengers are determined by the severity of their handicaps, which may range from slight retardation to full committal as mental patients. The person escorting a severely disturbed passenger must advise the airline twenty-four hours before a flight of the passenger's name and destination, and offer assurance that medical authorities have sanctioned air travel.

ARMED PASSENGERS

Passengers authorized to carry weapons must have special permission to board a commercial aircraft. Advance notice is given to the airline when reservations are booked for a flight. These persons are escorted through the security screening area. Such persons include federal, state, local, and foreign law enforcement officers. Armed persons must introduce themselves to the captain, and all other crew members are advised. If more than one armed person is on board, they should be made aware of each other's presence. Do not call public attention to these passengers, and refrain from serving them alcoholic beverages.

PRISONERS

You may have passengers on board who are being extradited or transported to prison facilities. They will be in the custody of one or two armed guards and may be handcuffed. The captain and the airline decide whether or not a prisoner is to wear handcuffs on the flight. There is advance notification to airlines and flight crews, and prisoners are boarded first and deplaned last.

Prisoners and their escorts are seated in the last row of the aircraft. The prisoner sits in the center or window seat (but never at a window exit), and the guard sits on the aisle. No alcoholic beverages may be served to either party, and flight attendants should check to see that all items are returned on meal trays.

TRANSIT ALIEN

A transit alien is a person who is traveling without a valid visa and is the responsibility of the cabin crew while on board. The flight attendant receives the passenger's ticket and immigration forms and does not allow the transit alien to deplane on stopovers. Upon arrival at a final destination, the transit alien is released to the proper authorities.

DEATH IN FLIGHT

If you have reason to believe that a person has died on your flight, be discreet so as not to draw attention to the matter. Advise the captain and crew. Only qualified medical authorities can pronounce a person dead. Have the captain notify officials on the ground to meet the plane upon arrival. Make note of all events that led up to the incident, for legal purposes, and respond to all directions from the captain and ground personnel. Make a full written report, including name and address, time and date, description of incident, witnesses, flight number and crew, and any other pertinent facts.

135

PETS IN CABIN

Some airlines allow passengers to bring pets on board. Such pets allowed in the cabin include dogs, cats, and birds, and the passengers are required to produce valid health certificates for the animals.

The airline must be informed of the pet when the passenger makes a reservation, since only one per cabin is allowed on most carriers and passage may have to be denied. There is a supplemental charge and the pet cannot be accepted on board unless in a kennel that fits underneath a seat. A passenger should consider bringing a pet on board only if the animal is small enough to fit comfortably in its container, as the pet must remain under the seat for the duration of the flight.

PASS TRAVELERS

One of the benefits of working for an airline is to enjoy free and reduced air travel. As a flight attendant, some of your passengers may be airline employees who are taking advantage of their privileges. Although revenue passengers are given priority in seat selection and first choice of meals on board, the pass traveler should be treated with the same respect and courtesy afforded to all other passengers. Remember, you may be one yourself some day!

CREW SCHEDULING

A smooth inflight operation depends on skilled scheduling of the crews. Each airline has an organized system to schedule its flight attendants for work duty. Scheduling is achieved through the joint efforts of the company and flight attendant scheduling committee, who design feasible work patterns based on the available number of crew and the trips that must be staffed.

CREW DESK

The crew desk is the center of operation and activities for flight attendant scheduling. Schedulers are responsible not only for monitoring the crew complement for each flight from its domicile, but also for keeping a tally of each flight attendant's total monthly flight time. The job of the personnel working on the crew desk is a tedious one that requires a great deal of concentration and knowledge of contract scheduling provisions. Flight attendants must check in to the crew desk when reporting for flight duty. If there are scheduling problems, the schedulers can clarify them. The size of their work load depends on the number of flight attendants at their domicile. They rotate shifts on a twenty-four-hour basis to monitor all flights for one day and prepare for the next. You may not be happy with their decisions at times, particularly when your schedule is changed at the last minute. But keep in mind that decisions are not always in their control. When you consider the amount of work that a crew scheduler must accomplish, the number of flight attendants requiring assistance, and the occurrence of irregular flight operations, you realize the great responsibility placed on them for keeping a domicile's operations running as smoothly as possible.

SENIORITY RULES!

If there is one thing you learn immediately as a flight attendant, it is that seniority rules in almost any work-related situation. Upon graduation from the training center, you will be assigned a seniority number that gives you a rank among all other flight attendants flying for your airline on a systemwide basis. You accrue flight attendant seniority as long as you remain on active flying status. Most companies allow their flight attendants to continue to accrue seniority during leaves of absence and while on special assignment with the company or union. A decision to quit flying permanently means forfeiture of all your rights as a flight attendant, including your seniority status. If you transfer to another department but remain with the airline, then your seniority among all employees is based on your length of service with the company.

SENIORITY SYSTEMS

Company (Airline) Seniority
Determined by: Length of service with airline.
Affects: Vacation bids, pass and reduced travel.

Flight Attendant Seniority During Training
Determined by: Birthdate or social security number among
    training class
Affects: Observation trips, selection of domicile

Systemwide Flight Attendant Seniority
Determined by: Graduation date from flight attendant train-
    ing
Affects: Rank among all flight attendants in airline, transfers
    to other domiciles, filling temporary assignments, pay
    scale

Domicile Seniority
Determined by: Length of service among all flight atten-
    dants at your domicile
Affects: Rank among all flight attendants at domicile, work
    schedules, work positions, filling of temporary positions
    offered at domicile

HOURS OF SERVICE

Many people in the general public see one of the greatest
advantages to being a flight attendant as the small number of
hours that you spend on board a plane. What most people don't
realize is that you also spend many hours on duty in places
other than on an airplane. All rules governing flight schedules
and other hours of service are called legalities. They are limitations negotiated by your union and defined in the contract
for easy reference. The company must abide by these rules, but
that's not to say there won't be any exceptions. Any deviation
from stated contract items is called waiving legalities. This is
not condoned as a common practice, but occasionally legalities
are waived in order to avoid serious scheduling problems.

An explanation of the hours that govern flight attendant
work schedules can be given only on a general basis. There are
differences in the types of operations, e.g., domestic, international, charter, and many variations in individual contract
stipulations. For the purpose of understanding the different
types of legalities, you will find averages and brief definitions
discussed rather than rules for each airline. All of the following are used as guidelines by the company and union when
creating monthly work schedules for flight attendants.

FLIGHT HOURS

The hours spent on an airplane inflight are considered

flight-time hours. For most airlines, this time is determined from "block to block," i.e., when blocks are removed from the wheels of the nose gear as the airplane leaves the gate until blocks are put in place at the arrival gate. All time away from the gate is actual flight time, even though the airplane may never have become airborne.

There are maximum and minimum numbers of hours that a flight attendant may work in a specified period of time. In the following figures, you will notice that domestic times are usually on a monthly basis, and international and long-range schedules may be governed by quarterly restrictions. The reason for this is that long-haul flights may constitute a number of hours far exceeding domestic rules. However, after a period of approximately three months, the total of international flight hours are on a par with other flight attendant schedules.

Maximum Monthly Flight Hours
Domestic: 75–85
International: 85–100; not to exceed 240–255 hours per quarter

Minimum Monthly Flight Hours
Domestic: 55–72
International: 67–74
Determines base pay

Maximum Weekly Flight Hours
Domestic: No more than 30 hours in 7 days; must have a 24-hour rest break for every 7 days
International: Does not apply

Maximum Daily Flight Hours
Domestic: 8 in 24-hour period
International: 12–14 in 24-hour period

DUTY HOURS

The time from check-in with the crew desk until release by the company after the completion of a daily flight schedule is known as duty time. For instance, if you checked in at 1400 and were released from duty at 2310, your duty time for that day would be nine hours and ten minutes.

There is a formula pay scale devised by each airline union agreement under which you are paid for a prorated "credited" time. This is a combination of duty and flight time, and there are guaranteed credited times established for each day of duty. A flight attendant is paid for actual flight time or for credited time, whichever is greater.

Maximum Daily Duty Times

Domestic:	10–14 hours scheduled
	14–16 hours irregular operations
International:	13–16 hours scheduled
	16–20 hours irregular operations

LEGAL REST

Each flight attendant must be granted a minimum number of hours free from duty. This time is known as a legal rest. The length of a rest break is determined by a negotiated number of hours off between duty periods.

When a legal rest is spent away from your home domicile, it is known as a RON (remain overnight) or a layover. At the termination of your last flight for the day, your duty time extends approximately thirty more minutes before you are actually released to your legal rest. The length of your layover is determined by your next scheduled outbound trip.

There are many factors which determine the length of a legal rest. Suffice it to say that the number of hours needed for a rest is governed by:

number of hours flown
time of day in which duty period began
distance between hotel and airport
next scheduled outbound trip

Another type of rest provision is utilized on long-range operations. When nonstop flights exceed approximately eight to ten hours, the inflight crew must be granted rest breaks on board the aircraft. Two or three contiguous passenger seats are designated and placarded as crew rest seats. They are to be occupied only by flight attendants on a rotational basis for the purpose of a rest period during the course of a flight.

BIDDING PROCESS

Work schedules devised by the airline and union are made available to all flight attendants at regular intervals. Most major carriers publish work schedules once a month for the purpose of allowing flight attendants to "bid" for flight schedules and regular days off. This selection process is accomplished according to domicile seniority. Other airlines, such as some supplemental carriers, do not allow their flight attendants to bid for schedules because of the irregular nature of their operation.

There are a great many variations to bidding and they are spelled out in the individual contractual agreements of each airline. All examples cited and illustrated are a composite of the forms and procedures used by most of the major carriers.

To begin the bidding process, schedules are printed, duplicated, and posted around the second or third week of the month. From the posting date to a predetermined closing date and time, the flight attendants may peruse the choices and record their preference of schedules.

BID PACKAGE

The means of conveying monthly flight attendant schedules and bid information is through a bid package. There are several components to this package, each of which works in conjunction with the others, and the completion of which relays your bid preferences to the company. Depending on domicile procedure, the package will be either placed in your mailbox, sent to your home, or available near the crew desk area.

Information Sheet: A cover letter is included with the bid package to convey important bid information. It gives the exact closing date and time for the submission of bids, and the date on which bids will be awarded. If changes in trips or schedules occur after the package is printed, notification is given in this letter.

Trip Sequences: A trip sequence is a unit of duty designated by the company. It can consist of two or more flights and is identified by a special number known as the "ID." As an example (see right), 1 ID #100 consists of flights #2 and #1,

ID #	# of F/A	A/C	FLT #	DPTR CITY	ARVL CITY	RPT TIME	DPTR TIME	ARVL TIME	FLT TIME	DUTY TIME	L/O	CREDIT TIME	ACTUAL TIME	RON	MEAN EXP.
100	12	747	2	SFO	BOS	1145	1300	2105	505	635				Boston Park Hotel	
		747	1	BOS	SFO	0805	0905	1210	605	735	1200	1110	1110		$30.00
101	4	DC8	12	SFO	SEA	0700	0800	0948	148		142				
		DC8	23	SEA	SFO		1130	1315	145	645		430	333		$ 6.00
102	4	DC8	58	SFO	SEA	0900	1000	1148	148		242				
		DC8	167	SEA	LAX		1430	1642	212		48				
		DC8	112	LAX	SFO		1730	1836	106	951		506	506		$ 8.00
103	3	737	444	SFO	SMF	0400	0500	0534	31		26				
		737	379	SMF	SFO		0600	0635	35		145				
		727	76	SFO	OMA		0820	1320	300	920	2355			Omaha Plaza	
		727	663	OMA	LAX		1315	1420	305		110				
		737	542	LAX	SFO		1530	1606	106	636		1031	820		$35.00
104	3	727	39	SFO	SAN	1100	1200	1323	123		47				
		727	740	SAN	SFO		1410	1528	118		123				
		737	643	SFO	FAT		1651	1735	44		30				
		737	525	FAT	LAX		1805	1855	50		135				
		737	600	LAX	SFO		2030	2136	106	1036		533	521		$10.00

and together these two flights make up one trip sequence. Below are the definitions for the abbreviations used in the trip sequence form. You will note, from the upper left of the diagram, that San Francisco is the domicile responsible for covering this trip, from October 1 through October 31.

ID #:   numerical identifier for entire trip sequence
# of F/A: number of flight attendants required to cover the trip based on type of aircraft
A/C: type and model of aircraft to be flown
Flt. #:   flight number of each segment
DPTR city: departure city; point of origin
ARVL city: arrival city; point of termination
RPT time: report time for check-in; time duty period begins
DPTR time: departure time
ARVL time: arrival time
FLT time: flight time from block to block; written in local time per segment
Duty time: total time on duty for each day
L/O: amount of layover time between trip segments

143

Credit time: combination of flight time and duty time; number of hours that determines pay

Actual time: total flight time for entire trip sequence

RON: remain overnight; prearranged hotel accommodations

Meal Exp.: total meal expense allowance per trip sequence

Lines of Flying: The flight attendant actually chooses a schedule by referring to a second form called Lines of Flying (see below). On this chart, the days of the month are written across the top. A line of flying is simply a work schedule showing how the trip sequences fall within the month. For example, if the flight attendant gets the line of flying identified by #1 at the left-hand side of the page, she/he would be flying trip sequences ID #100 on the 8th, 10th, 15th, 17th, 22nd, 24th, and 29th for a total of 78 hours and 10 minutes. Note that the use of the arrow shows the trip covers two days. She/he would be free from duty from the 1st through the 7th, as well as on the other empty slots. If, for instance, the flight attendant wished to work at the start of the month, line of flying #3, incorporating flight sequences ID #103 and 104, might be a preferred choice.

FLIGHT ATTENDANT WORK SCHEDULES
LINES OF FLYING

Month _____ Equipment _____ Domicile _____

Line #	# F/A	1	2	3	4	5	6 S	7 S	8	9	10	11	12	13 S	14 S	15	16	17	18	19	20 S	21 S	22	23	24	25	26	27 S	28 S	29	30	Total Time
1	12								100→		100→			100→		100→					100→		100→		100→					100→		78:10
2	4			101	101	101	101	101				101	101	101				101	101	101	101				102	102	102	102				73:40
3	3	103→		104					103→		104			103→		104			103→		104			103→		104						79:06

BIDDING AND AWARDING PROCEDURES

When the lines of flying for the following month are posted, it is each flight attendant's responsibility to submit her/his line preferences, commonly known as "bidding." Obviously, flight attendants with top seniority will get their first choices, as seniority within the domicile is the basis for awarding bids.

In addition to bidding for line preferences, some airlines allow you to bid for specific work positions; first class, coach, etc. On other carriers, work positions are assigned by a purser or a lead flight attendant prior to each trip. Before certain lines can be bid, you must ensure that proper qualifications are maintained, such as over-water training and language requirements.

Bid choices may be submitted either in written form or over the telephone, depending on your airline's policy. They are usually due approximately one week after posting, and it is each flight attendant's responsibility to see that they are turned in on or before the due date.

RESERVE

There is a greater number of flight attendants at each domicile than needed for regular schedules, creating a pool or reserve of extra staff. This group has the responsibility of being on call or available for trip coverage and is usually comprised of the most junior flight attendants at the domicile. Reserve lines are posted in the same manner as the lines of flying posted for regular line-holders and the process of bidding is similar except that reserves bid for days off rather than trip sequences.

Reserve schedules are governed by contractual agreement for the purpose of protecting the number of work hours and pay provisions. As a reserve, you are guaranteed payment for a specified number of credited hours, whether you fly that number or a lesser amount. This payment is called a base salary. Should you exceed your monthly flight-time guarantee, you will be compensated at a negotiated hourly rate of pay.

Junior flight attendants alternate reserve months or stand straight reserve until senior enough to hold a line every month. However, there are some airlines that require all flight attendants to be on reserve on a credit basis. What this means is that the responsibility of standing reserve is shared equally by every flight attendant at the domicile, regardless of seniority.

RESERVE TRIPS

There is a systematic order to assigning reserve trips. At the completion of a trip you are usually responsible for checking in at the crew desk, reporting your name, arrival time, total flight time, and other pertinent information. Your name is recorded according to your arrival time and date, placing you in a rotation order among all other reserves. As reserves are called out on trips, your name moves to the top of the list until you are eligible for your next trip after you have had a legal rest or your scheduled days off.

It is to your advantage when "standing reserve" or "holding pool" to be prepared at all times. Plan ahead to determine when you will need your uniform and make sure it is at home and not at the cleaners when the crew desk calls. Keep your trip schedules within easy reach of your telephone for handy reference. Make good use of your legal rest, allowing sufficient time to sleep and eat.

SCHEDULING EXCEPTIONS

At times it seems as though scheduling exceptions *are* the rule. There are many variables to scheduling procedures that affect not only differences in flight time and trip coverage but also your monthly pay.

DEADHEADING

At times, flight attendants must be flown to or from a particular city to cover an assignment. Then they travel as passengers—this is known as "deadheading." For deadheading you are compensated with flight pay and hours according to your contract. If you are being transported by air, the company provides you with a positive space ticket on your airline or "off line" on another carrier if necessary. When ground transportation is required, e.g., deadheading between San Francisco and Oakland, it is arranged and paid by the company. When you deadhead on a flight, you should conduct yourself in a businesslike manner. You are seated with the other passengers and, whether in uniform or street clothes, your actions have a direct bearing on the image of the airline. Observe common courtesies such as allowing passengers to board and deplane ahead of you, and when using passenger items such as pillows and magazines.

DRAFTING

When a critical coverage situation exists, crew schedulers find it necessary to "draft" flight attendants or "junior" crew them into vacant positions. As a rule, it can happen only when all scheduled line-holders and reserves are unavailable to take open trips. Flight attendants are contacted in reverse seniority order whereby the most junior "legal" flight attendant available by telephone contact or on the company premises is informed of the coverage problem and assigned the open position. There are only a few instances that would prevent a flight attendant from being drafted: illegal because of preceding or future trips; alcohol consumption within twelve hours of report time; and current sick list or leave of absence status.

Drafting is avoided whenever possible. Inevitably, it creates a domino effect, since another flight attendant is needed to cover the trip from which you were removed. However, it is the responsibility of the crew schedulers to settle coverage problems as they occur in the most expedient manner.

UNDERSTAFFING

When a coverage problem cannot be resolved, a flight may depart "understaffed" based on company guidelines, but still in accordance with FAA limitations. This insufficient crew complement is due to a number of factors, some of which include: equipment change, increase in passenger loads, length of trip, and type of service. Airlines try to ensure that planes are properly staffed, but it is not always possible.

TRIP TRADING

Flight attendants have the opportunity to swap trips with each other as long as the trade abides by all legalities and meets with the approval of the scheduling office. Requests must be submitted in writing and signed. A trip trade can take place only between two consenting flight attendants at the same domicile. Line-holders can trade individual trips or sequences, and reserves can trade days off. However, each person must be qualified for the traded position. There is also a restriction barring the trip trade of a flight attendant on vacation and the number of trades allowed per month for each flight attendant.

HOLDING TIME

Extra compensation is granted when flight attendants are required to remain with passengers on the plane at the gate. This may occur beyond a scheduled departure time or while waiting for a replacement crew on a through trip. Pay is figured on a prorated basis according to the contract.

VACATION BIDDING

Each year flight attendants have the opportunity to bid for vacation periods. As with trip scheduling, vacation days are allotted so as to maintain a sufficient number of flight attendants on active work status throughout the year. Schedule planners post the available vacation days for your domicile well in advance of the commencement of the new year. You then have adequate time to review the choices and submit your bid. Following all the correct procedures, and completing your vacation bids on or before the due date is necessary if you are to have a choice.

Your seniority with the company determines the number of

vacation days you may bid. These days can be divided into one to three vacation periods, providing they contain a specified minimum number of consecutive days in each period. Bids are submitted for primary vacations and the days are awarded according to seniority. Secondary and tertiary vacations may be bid from the remaining days available after the primary vacations are awarded. Once bids are awarded, you may have the option throughout the year to change your vacation days through a trade with another flight attendant or an interim bidding process with the company. This is done by mutual agreement between the union and company, and all requests must meet established procedures.

Compensation for vacation periods varies from airline to airline, but the usual procedure is to be paid for the trips missed or credited with flight hours on a daily basis. Regardless of the form of payment, vacation opportunities and flexible schedules are some of the greatest work advantages of being a flight attendant.

Scheduling procedures are probably the largest influence in dictating your life-style as a flight attendant. You may choose not only the number of hours you wish to fly, but also to what cities, how often, and on what type of plane you wish to work. It is up to you to abide by all regulations as set forth by the contractual agreement. All flight attendants and scheduling departments must work together to achieve a smooth, efficient inflight operation.

12

PREFLIGHT DUTIES

$\blacksquare$ he preflight duties and responsibilities of the flight attendant are crucial to a successful flight. Each trip requires a concerted team effort employing organization and flexibility in a specified time frame. Your professional attitude contributes to the achievement of the preflight demands placed on the entire inflight crew. The thoroughness with which preflight obligations are performed has a bearing on the overall effectiveness of service provided to the passengers.

CHECK-IN

It is imperative that you be prompt when checking in for your flight. Your responsibilities for flight duty actually begin by having clean and proper uniform items, an up-to-date flight manual, a working flashlight, and an appropriately packed suitcase ready for immediate use. Allow plenty of time to get to the airport, taking into account traffic delays, weather problems, or car trouble. If it seems as though you will be late, make every attempt to contact the crew desk.

Upon arrival at the inflight office, report to the crew schedulers at or before your check-in time. Do this by speaking directly with the person at the desk, making a notation by your name on a sign-in sheet, or affixing your signature to a roster. After verifying flight number and departure time, obtain any pertinent scheduling information and determine your work position if possible.

Immediately after check-in, you have a few minutes to take care of company business. Proceed to your mailbox to check for correspondence such as manual revisions, memos from your supervisor, mail from other employees, information on training or services, trip-trade requests, and complimentary passenger letters. If there is anything you need to discuss with your supervisor, now would be a good opportunity to do so. In addition, personal accounting, such as turning in expense reports for uniform cleaning, transportation, training, and publicity assignments, can be done at this time. Don't forget to pick up your paycheck and/or work schedule if they are available.

While in the inflight office, read all posted information concerning company policy, training, current service and marketing promotions, FAA bulletins, and scheduling restrictions or changes. These announcements can be found on company and union bulletin boards, in briefing books, and in newsletters.

Some airlines require that flight attendants report for an appearance and weight check prior to each flight. However, if this is not mandatory for your airline, it is still advisable to take a last-minute glance at your overall appearance.

BRIEFING

All flight attendants meet prior to passenger boarding to discuss flight information and job responsibilities. This session, known as a briefing, gives each flight attendant the opportunity to meet co-workers and be assigned individual roles.

There is one person responsible for obtaining information pertinent to your flight. This individual may be referred to as the senior, lead, first flight attendant, or, as on international flights, a purser. For simplification, this person in charge will be referred to as the lead flight attendant throughout the remainder of the book.

The lead flight attendant procures a passenger manifest, or

trip advisory, which indicates the passenger load, the meal count and choices, and special-care passengers. This person should also check that crew coverage is sufficient. The Federal Aviation Administration and individual airlines establish guidelines for the number of working crew members in relation to the passenger load. If more inflight crew are needed, the lead flight attendant should make this known to the proper personnel as soon as possible.

During a briefing there is a review of safety precautions and emergency and service procedures. Each flight attendant is delegated specific duties, as well as being assigned a jump seat, work position, and safety demonstration area. The lead flight attendant relays information from the flight data sheet and its content is discussed at length.

At the conclusion of a briefing, you are ready to proceed to the aircraft. Verify the departure time and the gate from which the flight will be leaving. On your way to the airplane, you may have to pass through a security area. As a flight attendant you are permitted to bypass this search when displaying an I.D. badge on the outside of your uniform. If you fail to present this identification, you will be subject to the same security screening as passengers.

BOARDING THE AIRCRAFT

Once you are ready to board the aircraft, do so at the proper time. An airline stipulates the exact period of time before departure when you are obligated to be on board. In most cases the larger the aircraft, the more involved the predeparture duties. Therefore, a flight attendant is scheduled to be on board from half an hour up to one hour prior to takeoff. The only time there is a deviation from normal procedure is when the inbound aircraft operates outbound as the same flight number; in other words, a *through* trip. Some passengers may decide to stay on the airplane at the layover point. For each cabin occupied by through passengers, there must be a flight attendant present. The inbound crew remains with the passengers until relieved by the next crew.

Stow your personal belongings immediately upon boarding the plane. If your airline does not designate certain stowage areas, put your crew luggage in a place that is safe and equipped with restraints, and does not take up space that is normally allotted for passengers' carry-on items. Any purses or valuable items should be stored in a closed unit, out of passengers' view, since you have little opportunity to keep an eye on them during the flight.

While each flight attendant initiates preflight duties, the lead flight attendant assumes the additional responsibility of meeting the captain and exchanging names of inflight personnel. While in the cockpit, the lead flight attendant should ascertain information regarding weather, flight time, or special conditions that might influence the planning of cabin services. If the flight crew asks for a beverage, comply with the request at this time. Once boarding procedures begin, full attention should be given to the passengers and their needs.

SAFETY INSPECTION

The most important responsibility before passengers board is to complete a preflight safety inspection. The purpose of making this check is twofold: to verify that all emergency equipment and exits are ready for use; and to ensure that each flight attendant is mentally prepared to deal with abnormal incidents inflight and the possibility of a land or water evacuation. Accidents happen without warning—be prepared in advance. The realm of your responsibility in this area varies according to airline policy and type of aircraft. Airlines that involve their flight attendants in this inspection benefit to the fullest extent. After all, who should be more qualified to state the condition of emergency equipment and exits than those who initiate their use?

A preflight safety inspection is based on knowing what to check, how to check it, and what to do if it doesn't check out.

Most airlines requiring flight attendants to do a safety check usually provide each crew member with a checklist or guide. This checklist is either incorporated in your flight manual or

153

printed on a safety card or inspection chart. Most often, your individual responsibility includes that area near and around your assigned jump seat. A thorough check is made of the jump seat itself, the exit(s) nearest your seat, and any equipment in the same location, including supplies for your safety demonstration.

An inspection should be made by visual and manual means. For example, on some emergency equipment, such as fire extinguishers, look for a seal denoting that it is fully pressurized. In other cases, gauges and lights are present to facilitate the inspection. In addition to making a visual check, sit in your jump seat to test its operation and adjust the seat belt to your size. While in a sitting position, reach out to where the nearest equipment and exit(s) are located so that in the event of an emergency your reactions are automatic.

Should you notice that any equipment is substandard, inoperative, or missing, report it immediately to the lead flight attendant. From there the information will be passed on to the captain, maintenance department, or other persons who can remedy the situation. Do not regard any discrepancy as insignificant. Some malfunctions, such as a loose jump seat, are actually serious enough to be considered "no-go" items, i.e., the aircraft's departure is delayed until they are repaired. Make your report and let the proper personnel determine the need for repair. On narrow-bodied aircraft, discrepancies may already have been noted by a flight officer who is responsible for the preliminary inspection. On wide-bodied aircraft, the lead flight attendant advises the cockpit that the safety inspection has been completed.

CABIN PREPARATION

Up to this point, each flight attendant on board has been performing the same types of duties. Now it becomes necessary to divide the responsibilities of preparing the cabin before passengers board. While some flight attendants are checking galleys, others are making routine inspections of the cabin interior and its supplies. This teamwork allows all predeparture duties to be performed simultaneously in a relatively short period of time. The lead flight attendant oversees the performance of duties in preparation for flight.

BUFFET SETUP

One flight attendant is assigned to a galley for the purpose of preparing the inflight food/beverage service(s). Upon entering the buffet, make a safety inspection of the electrical and safety equipment. This involves verifying that all lights, coffee makers, hot plates, and ovens are operable and any emergency equipment located in the buffet meets safety standards. In addition, check that all restraining devices are present and properly fitted. On aircraft with buffets below the main cabin deck, a safety inspection is also made of the personnel and cart lifts, escape hatches, and jump-seat areas.

Next, verify that food and beverage supplies are adequate for the planned passenger load. If a shortage is discovered, notify the lead flight attendant as soon as possible to allow time to obtain additional items. Prepare as much as you can in the galley before passenger boarding to allow for a more timely commencement of services inflight. Before leaving the galley, close and latch all buffet carrier doors in preparation for take-off.

CABIN INVENTORY

Observation of the cabin condition and a brief inventory of supplies is the joint responsibility of all flight attendants. The cabin interior should be tidy, clean, and well stocked. Passenger amenity items such as magazines, pillows, blankets, and timetables should be in adequate supply. In addition, ensure that you have the appropriate number of bassinets, plug-in tray tables, garment tags, "occupied" stickers or cards, smoking/no-smoking signs, and headsets, if necessary. Also, check that all reading lights, call buttons, air vents, and window shades are operable, and notice if headrest covers, armrests, or ashtrays are missing from any passenger seats. Look up, down, and to both sides as you pass through the cabin for a general check of ceiling fixtures, carpeting, sidewalls, windows, and overhead bins. Abnormalities should be reported for immediate repair.

While walking through the cabin preparing for passenger boarding, inspect lavatories and open closet curtains/doors to make sure that space is available for passengers' belongings. Confirm that there is an adequate supply of hangers near first-class storage facilities.

During the final walk-through before passengers board, familiarize yourself with the number, location, and content of any kits that may be on board. These kits, called "flight attendant," "cabin," or "traffic" kits, contain supplemental passenger service items. Materials in these kits vary from airline to airline and on particular types of flights, e.g., domestic, international, and may include any combination of the following:

HANDY ITEMS
Baggage tags
Pens, pencils
Stationery, scratch pads
Aspirin
Band-Aids
Ammonia inhalants
Deodorizing sprays
Artificial sweeteners
Decaffeinated coffee
  packets
Playing cards
Children's toys/"wings"
Matches
Baby diapers/food
Liquor seals (a locking
  device)
Decongestant sprays
Merthiolate capsules
Toothpicks

FORMS
Accident/illness forms
Damage report
Lost and found articles
Cabin discrepancy sheet
Passenger reaction forms
Headset sales accounting
Customs forms
Crew declaration
Liquor
  accounting/envelopes
Witness statements
Air-travel club
  membership
Flight-time reports
Flight attendant/flight
  verification forms
Cocktail order sheets
Passenger seating chart
Change-in-cabin fare
  status
Duty-free order forms
Supply order sheet
Flight attendant inflight
  report
Needs repair forms

FINAL STAGES OF PREPARATION

Under normal circumstances, cabin preparation is usually completed in approximately ten to twenty minutes. After selecting the appropriate cabin lighting, temperature, and boarding music to enhance the environment, a last-minute check of your personal appearance is in order. As soon as the lead flight attendant is advised that passenger boarding is going to begin, all crew members are notified to assume boarding stations. Your goal is to make a favorable first impression on your passengers.

PASSENGER BOARDING

As a special courtesy, passengers requiring assistance are boarded early. Children traveling alone, handicapped persons, elderly people, and families with small children are granted extra time to settle in their seats. This allows flight attendants an opportunity to familiarize these passengers with their seating area and the operation of their seat belts. It is also a federal requirement that all physically handicapped passengers be briefed individually on procedures to be followed in the event of an emergency evacuation. Make a note of the seat numbers of all special-care passengers.

As the remaining passengers start to enter the aircraft, all flight attendants are stationed strategically throughout the cabin(s) to facilitate boarding proceedings. Some airlines require that one flight attendant be positioned at the bottom of the entry stairs (weather permitting) or in the jetway leading to the door. In most cases, a flight attendant is standing at the entry door to collect tickets and greet passengers. A passenger's impression of the flight can be favorably enhanced by the welcome extended at the front door. The greeting should be friendly, warm, and genuine and, by all means, accompanied by a smile.

While passengers are being welcomed on board, the flight attendant at the entry door makes sure that each passenger is properly ticketed for that particular trip. Procedures vary, but each passenger must present either a validated ticket coupon or a boarding pass to gain entrance to the plane. It takes a great deal of concentration on the flight attendant's part to welcome the passenger while checking the flight number, destination, class of service, seat assignment, and date on the ticket, as well as advising the passenger of smoking/no-smoking sections. On smaller aircraft, the flight attendant taking tickets might also be the only one on hand to monitor the storage of carry-on items in closets near the entry door. As one passenger is greeted, another follows close behind and the process is repeated again ... and again ... and again.

Throughout the cabin, flight attendants monitor passenger seating. They are busy directing passengers to their seat locations and correcting problems such as duplicate seat assignments. To comply with Federal Air Regulations, carry-on items must be stowed under a passenger seat, with the exception of the bulkhead row, where bags must be surrendered for stowage in a closet. Coats or garment bags that are hung should be properly tagged with the passenger's seat number and destination. Clothing articles that are to be placed in the overhead bin should be folded neatly and placed directly above the passenger's seat.

Just when you think your predeparture duties are almost complete, you may be faced with other responsibilities, which include: repositioning family members who may have been separated in their seating assignments, delivering a predeparture beverage service in first class, relocating passengers who are seated in the wrong cabin, providing seat-belt extensions to those persons who are too large for the regular-sized belt, and offering passenger comfort items. Above all, each flight attendant should be available as much as possible in every cabin where passengers are present. Now would be an excellent opportunity to make a mental note of able-bodied persons whose assistance you'd enlist in an emergency situation.

As soon as all passengers have boarded, the next phase of predeparture duties begins. The lead flight attendant receives the final paperwork from the gate agent, which might list: the final passenger count, number of meals, special passenger information (special meal or wheelchair requests, emergency travel, VIP's), smoking/no-smoking sections, first-class passenger names, passenger status (revenue, space-available, business pass), and seat numbers of through passengers. Any other exchange of information and documentation before the door closes consists of giving the ticket coupons to the gate agent and if handed a weight manifest, delivering it immediately to the cockpit.

Announcements are made at this time regarding the flight number and destination, safety regulations about carry-on baggage and, if applicable, the title of and charge for the movie being shown on board the flight that day. When all passengers have been seated, verify first-class passenger names and other pertinent information against the passenger manifest. If menus are boarded for a meal service, they may be handed out at this time. Also, if audio entertainment or a movie is scheduled, distribute/rent headsets.

As the door closes, a final head count is made and reported to the captain. This tally should include the number of passengers, lap infants, and working crew members on board. While in communication with the cockpit, determine if the flight's altitude will warrant a demonstration of the emergency oxygen system. After all information has been related to the captain, be sure to close and lock the cockpit door as you leave.

As the stairs or jetway are pulled away from the aircraft, flight attendants attach the slide bars or arm the doors, denoting that they are "PREPARED FOR DEPARTURE."

13

INFLIGHT DUTIES

From the time you leave the gate until arrival at the destination, you have certain prescribed duties and responsibilities. Airline procedures are written for normal conditions. However, with people, places, and services changing from flight to flight on a daily basis, do not expect events to happen as a matter of course. Rely on your intelligence and common sense to adapt to unique circumstances. Your professionalism and resourcefulness have to be the final guides in managing situations on board an aircraft from takeoff to landing.

Teamwork is essential when attending to large volumes of the traveling public. Specific inflight assignments are coordinated through the lead flight attendant (or purser if international) so that every crew member contributes to the total effort. One of the best examples of an inflight crew working together is the welcoming announcement.

TAXI OUT

"Good morning, ladies and gentlemen. Welcome aboard." As the airplane begins to taxi out to the runway, the lead flight attendant officially greets the passengers over the public address system. Flight attendants stand at assigned rows, usually in the forward part of each cabin or zone, where they are visible to passengers in that area. While the announcement is being given, flight attendants are simultaneously demonstrating the safety features being described.

The content of inflight announcements is standardized throughout the industry, but the presentation varies from one airline to another. The exact wording need not be memorized, since announcement booklets or similar guidelines are provided for reference. These are written in layman's terms so that the announcements are understood by all passengers. On international flights, announcements are given in other languages so that foreign-language-speaking passengers can be addressed in their native tongues.

The way an announcement is delivered and presented is just as important as what is said. When the speaker uses a well-modulated voice, a moderately paced presentation, and a friendly, businesslike tone, a positive attitude is conveyed to the passengers. The flight attendant demonstrating the safety features of the aircraft provides the passengers with a visual interpretation of the announcement. The importance of the message being conveyed can be emphasized through body language. The flight attendant should maintain direct eye contact with passengers, stand erect, work at the same pace as the speaker, and avoid creating distractions. The goal is to ensure an effective presentation and command the attention of the passengers—after all, their lives may depend on it!

The "welcome aboard" is a cheerful greeting that includes the airline name, flight number, and destination, followed by an introduction of the person in charge of cabin service, and the captain's name for that flight. Passengers are then informed that a safety briefing card is located in the seat pockets in front of them. As the flight attendants hold up the card for all to see, the passengers are instructed to follow along while the many safety features of that particular aircraft are described. The purpose of this demonstration is to familiarize the passengers with: the location of door and window exits, operation of seat belts, use of the emergency oxygen system, the location of flotation devices and, if flying over water, the operation of life vests. To illustrate what is being said, flight attendants point to exits and their signs, and don demonstrator oxygen masks and life vests.

Time permitting, the announcer may elaborate on the type of food/beverage services to be offered inflight. If a movie or audio entertainment is scheduled, passengers are also advised as to the operation of the volume control and channel selector, and the location of the headset outlet.

At the conclusion of the announcement, passengers are told to bring seat backs and tray tables to their upright and locked positions, check that seat belts are fastened low and tight across their laps, ensure that all carry-on baggage is placed beneath the seat in front of them, and observe the no-smoking sign until it is turned off inflight.

In preparation for takeoff, conduct a final check of the cabin and galley areas. *Look* at each passenger seat area to be sure that they have complied with the safety announcement. *Advise* parents holding infants on their laps that the seat belt must be secured around only the adult. *Check* lavatories to

The effectiveness of inflight announcements depends on the flight attendant's delivery.
Photo courtesy Air California

ensure they are unoccupied and lock door if required. *Pull* on buffet carrier doors to be sure they are locked in place. *Open* and *secure* all cabin dividers, curtains, and galley doors. *Close* and *latch* all storage compartments.

Upon notification via a chime or an announcement from the cockpit that takeoff is imminent, proceed to your assigned jump seat. Assume the proper protective position designated by your airline. For example, fasten the seat belt low and tight across your lap and hook the shoulder harness, if available; place your feet flat on the floor in front of your seat, and fold your arms across your chest. Review your individual responsibilities for evacuation procedures in preparation for any accident that may occur during takeoff.

TAKEOFF AND ASCENT

You're on your way. After taxiing to the runway, the plane is cleared for takeoff. Once the plane becomes airborne, flight attendants as well as passengers must remain seated during the initial climb out.

When the no-smoking sign has been turned off a few minutes into the flight, the lead flight attendant makes an announcement to passengers regarding the designated smoking/no-smoking sections in each cabin and reminds them that there is no smoking permitted at any time in the lavatories or while walking about in the cabin.

The extinguishing of this sign is usually the indicator to flight attendants that it is safe for them to be out of their jump seats, unless otherwise advised by the captain. If lavatory doors were locked prior to takeoff, unlock them upon leaving your jump seat. Although you are permitted to walk around the cabin at this time, passengers are to remain seated with their belts fastened until the seat-belt sign has been turned off. Avoid communicating with the cockpit unless absolutely necessary for approximately the first ten minutes of flight. The period directly after takeoff is extremely crucial and the concentration of the cockpit crew should not be interrupted unless a safety matter is involved.

AIRBORNE

The scope of responsibilities performed by flight attendants while airborne involves: interacting with passengers and crew, implementing food/beverage services, monitoring the cabin environment, enforcing federal safety regulations and company policies, and maintaining a personal standard of conduct. Flight attendants attempt to achieve the above objectives on every flight through the performance of specific tasks. The extent of duties prescribed for each flight is determined by the trip duration, size and model of aircraft, and type of flying, e.g., domestic, charter, international.

The following inflight duties are categorized in very general terms. Keep in mind that any or all of them may be performed and their occurrences are quite often simultaneous.

CABIN-RELATED DUTIES

These responsibilities center around maintaining a comfortable cabin atmosphere. You must have knowledge of mechanical devices for regulating cabin temperature, and lighting and audio systems on all types of aircraft flown by your airline.

Tidiness Keep cabin as neat and clean as possible. Put unused pillows away, fold blankets before storing, and return magazines to their racks. At all times during the flight, return items to their proper storage compartments. If refuse falls to the floor, pick it up and throw it away. Empty overflowing ashtrays, keep baggage out of aisles, and ensure that personal belongings are put away. Performing these duties is to your benefit as well as that of the passengers. A clean cabin interior contributes to safe working conditions and easier management of inflight tasks.

Temperature Respond to passenger comments about the temperature. If the cabin is too cold, offer blankets. If passengers complain of being too warm, turn on their fresh air vents. Advise the lead flight attendant or flight officer of needed temperature adjustments if the controls are not located in the cabin.

Lighting Monitor cabin lights to suit the time of day. During a night flight, keep a light on at the entrance to each galley and lavatory for safety purposes. Before entering the cockpit turn the light off near the entrance so as not to disturb the pilot's vision. Offer to turn on a passenger's reading light when main cabin lights are extinguished (conversely, if a passenger falls asleep, turn the reading light out). Whether on a day or night trip, watch for call lights and their location and respond immediately.

Lavatories   Check lavatories regularly. They are a potential fire hazard if passengers disregard the no-smoking policy in these facilities. Tidy the unit and restock supplies. If odor is extremely offensive, use a deodorizing spray supplied for this purpose.

Water   Check water-supply gauges in galley areas from time to time throughout the flight. If pressure decreases or water ceases to flow, report the situation to the cockpit.

Movies/Audio   If visual entertainment is offered, make an announcement just before it begins. Instruct passengers to lower their window shades if necessary to darken the cabin. Remind them where to plug in headsets, and inform them of the correct channel for the corresponding audio program. Make screens available for viewing and begin the movie. Push the appropriate button on the flight attendant control panel, or if the switch is located in the cockpit ask a flight officer to start the projector. Monitor the film quality and sound synchronization, and advise the cockpit if any malfunction occurs.

Discrepancy Report   The need for any repair of permanent equipment or fixtures in the cabin interior is reported to the cockpit or entered in a discrepancy log book by the lead flight attendant. Such items may include the use of an oxygen bottle or fire extinguisher, and problems with cabin equipment.

PASSENGER-RELATED DUTIES

Passengers rely on flight attendants for a safe and comfortable flight. A constant vigil in the cabin(s) can contribute to anticipation of passenger needs and the prevention of accidents. Employ good judgment, quick reaction, and common sense in performing aisle checks and fulfilling passenger requests. Communication and positive interaction have a large influence on a passenger's impression of the flight and the airline in general.

Aisle Checks   A cabin should never be left unattended. One flight attendant should always be present in each cabin or zone. Make an aisle check every fifteen to thirty minutes to remind passengers of your presence. Maintain direct eye contact to aid in identifying passenger needs and requests. Be alert for signs of discomfort, illness, and any unusual incidents as you pass through the cabin. For passengers' safety, verify that seat belts are fastened every time the sign is lit.

Requests   Fill all passenger requests if time and duties permit. If you cannot fulfill the request, tactfully explain the reason.

Amenities   Offer passengers service items such as magazines, stationery, children's toys, playing cards, pillows, and blankets. Adjust air vents, reading lights, seats, and tray tables. Reoffer if the need is demonstrated after monitoring the cabin. Present all items by handing them directly to the passenger.

Work Direction   Whenever possible, start from the front of your zone and work aft. This allows for a better viewing of the passengers and demonstrates to those seated aft that you are nearing them. This procedure should be followed during cabin checks, food/beverage services, and while distributing service items and checking seat belts.

Interaction   Converse with passengers in a friendly non-argumentative manner. Answer all questions and monitor passenger comments about cabin conditions and travel concerns. If possible, refer to passengers by name, especially in first class.

Night Flights   For safety purposes, always have your flashlight available for use in the darkened cabin. Be extra respectful of passenger comfort, especially when the majority of passengers are sleeping. If empty seats are available on which a passenger can lie down, offer to remove armrests. Advise these passengers to keep their seat belts fastened throughout the entire trip, preferably on the outside of the blanket. This allows you to check their seat belts without disturbing them. For passengers who remain awake, continue to offer beverages and reading material. Voices of crew members and nonsleeping passengers should remain low to ensure a quiet atmosphere.

Food/Beverage Services   These will be discussed in Chapter 17.

Government Formalities   Distribute documentation forms such as customs declarations, landing cards, and other official papers to passengers individually. Allow ample time for passengers to supply written information and collect only those forms that passengers are not required to submit to immigration officials. Know all disembarkation procedures so that you can answer passenger questions.

FLIGHT-ATTENDANT-RELATED DUTIES

As a flight attendant, you have obligations to yourself, the inflight and cockpit crew, and the airline you represent. You are expected to maintain standards befitting a professional flight attendant. These include performing job responsibilities as an effective team member, and utilizing proper communication systems to link your efforts with company operation.

Rest Periods   Interim breaks are scheduled so that all crew members have a chance to rest. When breaks are taken, at least one flight attendant should remain in each cabin or zone at all times. If a break is spent in view of passengers, do not read, write, or involve yourself in handiwork or games. Taking a break does not mean you are off duty—maintain a dignified image at all times.

Personal Appearance   To communicate a professional image to passengers, check your personal appearance on a regular basis. Make a point of keeping your hands clean before, during, and after food/beverage services. Wear your name pin on the appropriate uniform article. Serving garments are to be worn only inflight.

Accounting Procedures   Flight attendants are responsible for the accounting of monies produced from the inflight sale of liquor, tickets, and duty-free items, and the rental of headsets. Make every effort to return change to passengers as soon as possible. If foreign currency is collected on an international flight, try to return change in the same currency received.

Administrative Tasks   A variety of forms is used to communicate to other departments what transpired during a flight. Whether accounting for monies collected inflight, furnishing information of unusual incidents, or relating passenger reaction to services, all forms should be complete and accurate. State facts only and supply a detailed description, if necessary.

Federal Air Regulations and Airline Policies   Enforcement of regulations and policies inflight depends on your knowledge of the rules and reasons supporting them. A flight attendant is expected to employ tact and diplomacy if asked to justify their purpose. Noncompliance with these regulations could subject your airline to fines and penalties. There are innumerable federal air regulations that pertain to the flight attendant position. Each deals directly with the safety of the aircraft, the passengers, or its crew. The following examples are cited to give you a general idea of those regulations you may be called upon to enforce.

"Prohibition against interference with crew members." No person(s) shall interfere with, assault, or threaten a crew member or in any way impede the progress of duties performed inflight.

"Smoking/No-smoking sections." The airlines are required to designate specific areas on board each aircraft where smoking is either permitted or forbidden.

"Admission to Flight Deck." Entering the cockpit inflight is restricted to crew members and those officials whose job responsibilities directly relate to the safety of the flight or the operation of the aircraft.

"Portable Electronic Devices." To avoid interference with flight communications and radio frequencies, passengers are not permitted to operate portable electronic devices such as televisions or AM/FM radios on board an aircraft.

DESCENT AND LANDING

When the aircraft begins a gradual descent, prepare the cabin and passengers for landing. As you proceed through the cabin, pick up food and beverage items from the passenger seats as well as magazines, pillows, blankets, and headsets no longer being used. Secure all galley equipment, latch cabin dividers open, and store auxiliary tables in their proper compartments. When the seat-belt sign comes on in preparation for landing, check to see that passengers have their belts fastened and all sleeping passengers have been awakened. Bassinets must be stored at this time and passengers must be reminded that all carry-on baggage is to be stored once again. During the last ten minutes of flight, curtail any communication with the cockpit unless it pertains to a safety matter.

As the no-smoking sign is lit, the lead flight attendant makes a preparation for landing announcement. Passengers are reminded to place seat backs and tray tables in their full upright and locked positions, to clear the area directly in front of their seats of carry-on baggage, and to refrain from smoking until well inside the terminal building. Other flight attendants make a final visual check that all passengers have complied with the safety announcement, and that all lavatories are unoccupied (and locked, if required). All flight attendants proceed to their assigned jump seats for landing and assume the proper protective position. As the airplane approaches the runway, once again review your evacuation responsibilities and procedures.

TAXI IN

As soon as the airplane touches the runway, a marked deceleration is noted until a prescribed rate of speed is achieved for a safe taxi to the gate. The lead flight attendant makes an arrival announcement after the engine noise has subsided. Passengers are told the local time and proper name of the airport and city served. A safety reminder is given to remain seated until the aircraft is parked at the gate and the captain has turned off the seat-belt sign. If the flight is continuing to another destination, passengers are advised of the next departure time and the reboarding procedures. On international flights, arrival announcements include disembarkation instructions. A sincere "thank you" for the opportunity to serve the passengers and an invitation to fly your airline again conclude the arrival announcement.

While taxiing to the gate, flight attendants continually ensure that passengers remain in their seats with seat belts fastened and that no one smokes. Ask special-care passengers to wait until other passengers have deplaned so that extra assistance can be extended. If appropriate, adjust cabin lighting and turn on ground music. Time allowing and conditions permitting, return passenger belongings within the vicinity of your jump seat.

When the airplane has arrived at the gate, the engines are shut down, the seat-belt sign is extinguished, and blocks are put into place indicating the arrival of the flight.

14

POSTFLIGHT DUTIES

As the jetway or stairs are pulled up to the entry door, all flight attendants prepare for arrival by detaching slide bars or disarming doors. On narrow-bodied aircraft it is a practice to "crack" or partially open the main cabin and buffet entry doors as an indication to persons outside the aircraft that the doors are ready to be opened. On most wide-bodied aircraft, the flight attendant is responsible only for placing the arming device in the manual position (disarmed).

PASSENGER DEPLANING

It is important that flight attendants be available in the cabin while passengers disembark. Your assistance is needed to aid in emptying closets of carry-on baggage and helping passengers to remove items from overhead bins.

As soon as the entry door is opened, the flight attendant stationed in this location has several responsibilities. Inform the gate agent of any passengers on board who need special assistance in deplaning. Check on the availability of wheelchairs that had been previously requested. Some airlines require that any money collected inflight be handed over to the agent or supervisor meeting the trip. Before surrendering any

171

forms or monies, verify that all required signatures are affixed.

In the event you are working an international flight and have arrived at a customs/immigration point, you are responsible for knowing all disembarkation procedures and regulations. The aircraft must be cleared before any passenger or crew deplane.

By this time most passengers have noticed that the "fasten seat belt" sign has been turned off and they begin to vacate their seats. If passengers crowd the entry door before it is completely open, warn them to stand back a distance to avoid possible injury. As passengers leave the aircraft, send them off with a genuine good-bye. Since people deplane at a quicker pace than they board, your farewells should be varied to avoid sounding like a recording. Intersperse your "good-byes" with "so long," "come back again," and "have a nice day." Saying good-bye to foreign-language-speaking passengers in their native tongue leaves a favorable impression.

Your responsibilities may extend outside of the airplane when releasing special passengers to proper authorities. Unaccompanied children are escorted to the authorized family member or friend. The escorting flight attendant asks to see identification of the person meeting the child to ensure that the name matches the child's flight information papers. If there is a runaway, illegal alien, or person of a suspicious nature on board, it is your responsibility to identify these passengers to security officers meeting the flight.

As passengers continue to file out the door, invite those who express an interest in seeing the cockpit to do so at this time if the courtesy is offered by the captain. Offer to help elderly passengers and families with small children retrieve their belongings and assist them into the terminal building. Your thoughtfulness is appreciated. You may also have to deal with passengers who have become inebriated or ill during the flight. If you are unable to arouse them after landing, enlist the aid of ground personnel in helping them off the aircraft.

As the last passengers deplane, advise any cabin service personnel waiting outside that they may enter the cabin at this time. Also retrieve signed documents that are returned to you by the gate agent and, if required by your airline, obtain flight times and block times from the cockpit for your records.

CABIN CHECK

Every flight attendant remains on the aircraft until the last passenger has deplaned and a final check of the cabin has been made. Whether you and your flying partners will be the outbound crew on this aircraft or a new group of flight attendants is taking over, there are certain housekeeping tasks to be completed prior to the next flight.

Inspect the entire cabin for any carry-on baggage that may be left on board by passengers. Examine overhead bins, closets, under passenger seats, and seat pockets. If valuable items such as jewelry, wallets, or important documents are found, turn them over to the proper authority and write a report of your findings. Clean out compartments that were used to store supplemental supplies so that they are ready for use on the next flight. Return all items, such as unused passenger amenities, to their proper place and throw away any obsolete flight papers that were used during flight.

If kits were used and are to be removed from the aircraft, return them to their proper location and lock if appropriate. Advise cabin service personnel of any soiled areas that need special attention before passenger boarding. If emergency equipment needs servicing, or discrepancies were noted in the cabin log book, inform a mechanic if it was not already done by the flight officer. Above all else, make a final safety check of the cabin and galley areas. Ensure that ovens, coffee makers, and hot plates are turned off.

If the flight is a "through" trip, one flight attendant per cabin occupied by passengers is obligated to remain on board until relieved by the outbound crew. If the flight has been relatively short and no cleaners are provided on arrival, tidy the cabin by returning pillows and magazines to their proper places. Fold blankets before putting them away, replace armrests, and fold seat belts over seat cushions for a neater appearance.

As a courtesy to the next crew, reorder necessary galley and cabin supplies you think they might need. Inform the outbound flight attendants when they board the aircraft of the number of passengers going through and any special conditions worthy of their attention.

As you prepare to leave the aircraft, take a few minutes to

173

check your personal appearance. All uniform items should be worn and carried in the appropriate manner when you are in public. Before proceeding into the terminal building, collect your crew luggage and personal belongings. You are now ready to begin all over again on another airplane or check in after the final destination of your trip.

LAYOVER

In the middle of a trip sequence, you may be scheduled for a layover. The lead flight attendant is expected to sign in all crew members as being present for the next flight on your schedule, as well as obtain any necessary limousine, cab, or hotel vouchers. Once you are off duty, accommodations are provided for your legal rest at a hotel near the airport or at a downtown location. If you are staying with the crew at the hotel, transportation from the airport is furnished by the airline. However, if your layover plans include staying somewhere other than the hotel, leave a contact telephone number with the operations office or crew desk in that city.

As you check out, it is your responsibility to pay all room service and telephone charges billed to your room. At the end of the layover, meet with your crew at a prearranged time for transportation, or report to the airport at the proper check-in time. Upon arrival at the airport, begin exactly as you do for every other flight.

CHECK-IN

At the termination of a total trip sequence, you are once again at your home domicile. Postflight responsibilities take approximately fifteen minutes. A formal debriefing session may be held to discuss specifics of the trip. Your attendance at a debriefing is mandatory, since job performance may be discussed. Flight attendants are advised individually of any need for further training and service procedure reviews.

When returning to your home domicile, report once again to the inflight office. Flight attendants on a reserve or unscheduled status are required to check in at the crew desk for their next assignments or to advise the crew desk that they are now available for a flight, following a legal rest. It is the responsibility of each flight attendant to ascertain correct duty and flight times and to verify that names are affixed properly to pay sheets. Forms or reports that were completed from your trip should now be distributed to the proper departments. It is especially important to submit reports of unusual incidents inflight, records of irregular operations that occurred on your trip, and constructive feedback on any aspect of the service provided to your passengers. All reports should be timely and accurate to provide an effective means of communication between the departments involved.

Before leaving the office, repeat your check of bulletin boards and mailbox for any pertinent information that may have been posted or delivered while you were out of town.

15

EMERGENCIES

An emergency situation exists on board an aircraft any time the safety of the passengers and crew is jeopardized. A flight attendant is trained to recognize hazardous conditions and deal with the dangers at hand in a determined, professional manner. Although inflight service-related duties are often the only ones viewed by the traveling public, they all rank as secondary when compared to the responsibility shouldered by the flight attendants in a potentially life-threatening situation.

LEADERSHIP ROLE

As a flight attendant, the primary purpose for your presence on board an aircraft is to assume the leadership role in providing for the safety of passengers and to increase passenger survival in the event of an emergency. The type and degree of authority you will have to exercise over your passengers depends on the severity of the situation. No problem is insignificant.

Each incident is unique. It is up to you to attempt to limit the hazards of unexpected and unforeseeable accidents, whether big or small. Consider the nature of the problem and the actions that must be taken to ward off further danger. It is necessary for someone to take control and direct the passengers' actions. This person is you, the flight attendant, and, although you may never have to exercise this authority, you are always prepared to do so.

You are dealing with groups of people who are not only unfamiliar with their surroundings, but may be apprehensive about being trapped in a confined space. It is only natural to expect a variety of human responses. The passengers' fears in the face of an emergency may manifest themselves in two types of panic: positive and negative. In extreme emergencies, some passengers may display positive panic by screaming and yelling. Other indications of positive panic may include an irrational desire to "take over" the entire situation and direct the other passengers. Since you are the one trained in the emergency systems for that particular aircraft and informed of the special conditions that exist, it is your responsibility to assume this leadership role with quick, decisive actions in order to attract everyone's attention to your commands.

The opposite of passengers' assertive actions is known as negative panic. In this case, you deal with passengers who are dazed, immobile, unthinking, and docile—almost to the point of being blasé. They are not aware of the dangers of the situation and will perhaps not move from their seats of their own volition. You must see to it that these passengers respond to your orders, increasing their chances for survival. You must recognize these different forms of behavior and react accordingly with a great sense of authority.

Your knowledge as a safety expert must be communicated to passengers in the form of commands that are short, positive, and authoritative. When shouting instructions or giving directions, use simple words and concise phrases. Avoid the use of negatives—people react more positively and with less confusion when you tell them specifically what you want them to do. Be sure to make yourself heard by using a loud, but not shrill, voice. Demand instant action of your passengers when required, and above all—BE DIRECT!

The first indication to passengers of your leadership role is through the preflight safety demonstration. It is this forethought and preliminary instruction that serves to increase passenger survival in an emergency. You cannot predict when a crisis is going to arise, so it is of the utmost importance that your safety demonstration be thorough and correct. You are preparing every passenger on board to act appropriately in the face of an emergency situation.

UNUSUAL INCIDENTS

There are some emergency situations on board that are caused by people, as opposed to those caused by mechanical means. These circumstances are particularly challenging in that you are usually dealing with someone in an unstable mental condition whose actions might be totally unpredictable. The following situations command every ounce of your patience, common sense, and good judgment.

ABNORMAL BEHAVIOR

There are no guarantees that each passenger who boards an airplane is of sound mind. As a flight attendant, it is your responsibility to be aware of any unusual behavior exhibited by your passengers and to report anyone who acts suspiciously. People will say and do strange things in the confined environment of an airplane, but it is up to you to distinguish between harmless antics and potentially dangerous behavior.

Every situation and every passenger is unique. If you feel someone's actions or statements indicate that they may interfere with the normal course of events inflight or may threaten passenger safety, immediately notify the captain. Be precise in what you report. Deciding what actions to take with the passenger becomes the ultimate responsibility of the captain.

SABOTAGE, BOMB THREATS, HIJACKINGS

International threats of violence on board an aircraft are serious offenses. Passengers who interfere with the routine duties of a crew member with malicious intent face punishment by federal law. Such interference may range from physical abuse to actual interruptions in the course of a flight. If informed that there is a bomb on board or the plane is being hijacked, you would naturally consider the situation serious and dangerous. Remain calm. Use good judgment and intelligence in following your airline's prescribed procedures to the letter.

It may be your sole responsibility to communicate a hijacker's demands. Keep the situation under control by acting promptly and positively. The safety of everyone on board may depend on your actions, so think before you act.

As in any unusual incident, regardless of the severity, file a complete report to the company upon return to your home domicile.

LOSS OF PRESSURIZATION

Commercial aircraft today fly at altitudes of 10,000–40,000 feet above sea level. To make breathing easier and to allow for a comfortable atmosphere in the cabin, the planes are "pressurized" to simulate an altitude of 5,000–7,000 feet. Most people find this altitude range allows for normal breathing.

To understand why the cabin must be pressurized for high-altitude flying you may want to review this science lesson from your school days: Air is composed of molecules of gases such as nitrogen and oxygen. At sea level, the concentration of these molecules is dense. There are more molecules packed closer together at sea level than at a higher elevation. At 35,000 feet elevation, the same amount of air has fewer molecules, and there is more space between each one (concentration is less dense). This is known as "thin air" and is incapable of sustaining human life without artificial means. It is for this reason that the air inside an airplane is compressed to the density of an elevation comfortable for normal breathing, i.e., it is "pressurized." The pressure on the inside of the aircraft now becomes greater than pressure from the air outside.

As long as there are no holes on the outside wall of the aircraft that would result in the loss of this pressurization, everyone travels along without any complication or distress. However, there is potential danger to passengers and crew when air from inside begins to escape. The size of the opening in the cabin's fuselage, the rate of pressure loss, and the amount of mechanical failure determine the severity of the problem, which is termed either a pressure leak, or, more seriously, a decompression.

PRESSURE LEAK

The pressure may "leak" out of a cabin due to a crack around the frame of a door or window. A slow, gradual escape of air in these areas is usually due to an improper fitting or worn-out portion of the rubber seal around the frame of a window or door. A pressure leak can be identified by a high-pitched whistling sound coming from the frame.

Your immediate reaction to a pressure leak should be to move people away from the door or window where the leak is suspected. There is a chance that because of the greater pressurization on the inside of the cabin, the amount of air leaking out may force a wider opening in the fuselage. Keep the area immediately adjacent to the leak clear by moving passengers to other seats if possible as a precautionary measure. Notify the captain immediately and ensure that all passengers have their seat belts securely fastened.

DECOMPRESSION

A rapid loss of cabin pressurization is called a decompression. Fortunately, a decompression seldom happens, but when it does, it is a very serious problem. A decompression is caused by a sizable opening in the fuselage, such as a rip in the cabin wall or a blown-out window, or mechanical failure of the automatic pressurization system. Examples of situations that are likely to cause a decompression are improper locking devices on some cargo doors, which cause the door to open in-flight, or the explosion of a pressurized oxygen bottle or bomb forceful enough to blow a hole in the fuselage.

In any event, once the decompression begins, it takes approximately five seconds for the greater pressure on the inside of the aircraft to become equalized with the lesser outside pressure. The severity of the decompression depends on the size of the opening and the difference between cabin pressure and flight altitude at the time of the loss.

The different types of pressure loss can best be illustrated by the use of a balloon. An uninflated balloon has the same amount of pressure on the inside as on the outside. By blowing up the balloon, you are increasing the amount of air molecules and therefore the pressure on the inside. The interior pressure is now greater, or denser, than the air pressure on the outside. A pressure "leak" is demonstrated by letting a very small amount of air escape slowly from the mouth of the balloon. On the other hand, a pinprick to a fully inflated balloon illustrates the effects of a rapid, or explosive, decompression, where there is an instant equalization of interior and exterior pressure.

The following are the characteristics and resulting cabin conditions of a rapid decompression:

a loud, sudden, explosive noise (corresponding to the "pop" of a pinpricked balloon)

sudden rush of a large volume of air (high pressure gases being sucked outside)

loose objects, dust, and debris flying through the cabin in the direction of the hole

extremely cold temperature (owing to rapid equalization of heated cabin air to outside subzero temperatures)

dense fog (contact of warm, moist cabin air with outside cold air

The immediate effects felt by passengers and crew in a decompression and subsequent descent are confusion; difficulty in breathing; impaired vision; generalized feeling of pressure against the body; distress in ears, sinuses, and abdomen; and possible rupture of eardrums. If supplemental oxygen is not obtained within the first fifteen to thirty seconds of a decompression, you become unconscious.

NOTE: In a decompression, oxygen masks will automatically drop from their compartments at passenger seats and crew stations. Additional masks are located in lavatories, galleys, and service centers. All passengers and crew should grab the nearest available mask, pull it firmly to the face to release the oxygen, and place the cup over nose and mouth with the elastic strap around the head. Adjust the strap for a comfortable fit. Stay calm, securely fastened in your seat, and try to breathe normally. Be sure to extinguish all cigarettes. Passengers with small children should place the mask on themselves first and then assist their children. Keep in mind that all of this must be accomplished posthaste.

Once flight attendants have been advised by the captain that it is safe to walk around, you can use the extra available oxygen masks at passenger rows to move through the cabin. Make your way to an available crew portable oxygen bottle so you can breathe supplemental oxygen while attending to passengers and crew who may need your help.

Make a check of the entire cabin, including lavatories and cockpit. Until the emergency oxygen system shuts itself off automatically, make certain that everyone is receiving a sufficient supply. Switch passengers requiring additional oxygen to portable bottles. Stay on your own oxygen supply until advised by the captain that it is safe to be without it. Enforce the "No Smoking" rule in the cabin while oxygen is being used. Monitor the passengers' physical conditions and treat any injuries or those persons suffering from a condition known as hypoxia.

Hypoxia is a deficiency or partial lack of oxygen in the body, and it is most prevalent during a decompression. It usually goes unnoticed in the early stages—there is no built-in alarm system in the body to warn of its presence. Individuals can be more or less susceptible to its effects. Smoking, alcohol, and drugs reduce the body's tolerance to withstand sudden changes in altitude. For instance, heavy cigarette smokers may experience earlier symptoms of oxygen decrease than nonsmokers.

The symptoms of hypoxia become more pronounced the longer the body is deprived of sufficient amounts of oxygen. In its early stages, fatigue, sleepiness, and headaches are noted by hypoxia victims. As the condition becomes more severe, the symptoms progress from breathlessness to a state of unconsciousness, if not treated with supplemental oxygen. From the moment that oxygen is denied, a victim begins to experience euphoria, an abnormal feeling of well-being. Further lack of oxygen begins to affect vision, mental processes, and body functions until, finally, mental and motor coordination deteriorates to the point of collapse. Ironically, the hypoxia victim feels no pain or discomfort.

The only treatment that can be rendered a person who develops hypoxia is supplemental oxygen as soon as possible. Recovery usually takes only fifteen seconds, but it is absolutely imperative that oxygen be administered at the earliest stages of hypoxia before a person's condition becomes critical or life-threatening.

FIRES

Fires are perhaps the most hazardous of all inflight emergencies. It is the responsibility of every flight attendant to be constantly alert to any fire danger and to correct conditions that may cause one to start. Remember that fires are just as dangerous on the ground as they are when the plane is in the air.

There is a definite difference between "fighting" a fire and "extinguishing" a fire. Depending on where and when the fire occurs, your responsibilities range from keeping a fire under control to ensuring its total extinction.

FIRE HAZARDS

Conditions that contribute to the inception of a fire exist in many forms. Any time an aircraft is being fueled there is great potential for fire. It is for this reason that no smoking is permitted during boarding, deplaning, when sitting on an aircraft that is parked at the gate, or during takeoff and landing. Smoking is probably the greatest threat to safety where fires are concerned. It is your responsibility to ensure that there is no smoking permitted when oxygen is in use, in the lavatories, while standing or walking in the aisles, and at any time the "no smoking" sign is lit in the cabin. Monitor all cigarette smokers, especially those passengers who appear to be intoxicated or have fallen asleep. Be on the lookout for lighted cigarettes that may have been left on meal trays or fallen between seat cushions. Prohibit the type of lighters in which the fuel is visible through the case—these types ignite into small torches.

Other causes of fire of which you should be aware involve poor work habits and mechanical failure. Take care not to place any paper or plastic objects near electrical hot plates and coffee makers in the galley areas. Be sure to safely stow all electrical cords and turn off the ovens when not in use. A fire can also start somewhere in a plane's air conditioning, heating, or general electrical system. Keep your senses sharp for any unusual smell or smoke in the cabin and investigate its source thoroughly.

TYPES OF FIRES

Fires are classified into three categories:

Class A fires are those that involve common combustibles such as paper, plastic, and fabric. On the plane these materials are found in seat cushions, curtains, luggage, packages, and paper supplies.

Class B fires are mostly petroleum based. They are usually caused by flammable liquids such as lighter fluid, cooking fats, and jet fuel.

Class C fires start from an electrical source. The complexity of wiring systems poses a fire danger in the cockpit, galleys, lavatories, passenger service units, and in the lighting system throughout the plane.

FIRE EXTINGUISHERS AND EQUIPMENT

In the event of a fire, each aircraft is equipped with different types of extinguishers and fire-fighting equipment. All extinguishers are cylinders that house a compressed liquid, powder, or gas. The amount and pressure of the propellant may be indicated by a gauge or seal denoting that it is ready for use. The extinguisher is designed with a nozzle for aiming the contents and a trigger to activate the flow. They are all portable pieces of equipment and are secured by a bracket to a fixed structure of the cabin.

The following types of extinguishers are common to commercial aircraft.

Water (H₂O) This extinguisher is used *only* on Class A fires—paper, cloth, wood, and flammable solids. Never use a water extinguisher on a grease or electrical fire. Soak the burning material thoroughly so that it will not smolder and reignite.

Carbon Dioxide (CO₂) This extinguisher can be used on any type of fire. Since the contents are a compressed gas, it leaves no residue. For this reason, this extinguisher is usually located in the cockpit. When using a CO_2 extinguisher, be aware of people who may be nearby. The gases could cause suffocation if emitted in a confined space, and frostbite may occur if the spray hits bare skin.

Dry Chemical These extinguishers are used on Class B fires. They are filled with a dry powder that is ejected in a spray. They are usually found in or near galley areas, where most grease fires originate.

Other fire-fighting devices include a variety of equipment. A full-face smoke mask is attached to some oxygen bottles located in confined areas such as lower deck galleys. This allows the person using it to fight a fire in the midst of dense smoke while breathing a supply of pure oxygen.

FIRE LOCATIONS

It is up to each flight attendant to be alert for the occurrence of fire and act accordingly. Following is a list of possible fire locations and appropriate responses:

1. Aircraft exterior—on the ground: notify the captain, other flight attendants, and ground personnel. Evacuation may be necessary.

2. Aircraft interior—on the ground: notify the captain and other flight attendants; if passengers are on board, have them deplane at once; remove nearby oxygen supply; and fight fire.

3. Aircraft exterior—inflight: notify captain and other flight attendants.

4. Aircraft interior—inflight: fight the fire; notify the captain and other flight attendants; extinguish the fire.

FIRE-FIGHTING TECHNIQUES

Maintaining a constant vigilance in the cabin is the key element of fire prevention. Unfortunately fires still occur, and it is your responsibility to extinguish them in the most expedient manner. The first flight attendant to arrive on the scene retrieves the nearest appropriate extinguisher and fights the fire. If an extinguisher is not in the vicinity, stay with the fire and attempt to use alternate equipment, or direct another flight attendant or passenger to obtain one for you. Also, instruct another flight attendant to notify the cockpit while you fight the fire and keep passengers away.

If the fire is electrical, notify the cockpit to cut the power source. When you have an extinguisher ready, aim the nozzle at the base of the flames. Hold the container upright and slowly progress forward with a sweeping motion from side to side. If oxygen bottles are in the area, remove them immediately to prevent an explosion.

While the fire is being contained, another flight attendant may consider making an announcement to assure passengers that everything possible is being done. Above all else—stay calm. Passengers will look to you for reassurance—panic could be your worst enemy at this point.

Additional tools include a crash axe for use on hard-to-reach fires. When fighting a fire in the cabin, handy items such as blankets, coats, and pillows may be sufficient to smother a small fire while an extinguisher is being retrieved.

ABNORMAL TAKEOFFS AND LANDINGS

Any time the normal progress of an aircraft's approach to or departure from a runway is interrupted, there is a danger of fire, a possibility of structural damage, and a general threat to everyone's safety. It is extremely important to be alert to unusual sounds, forces, and attitudes of the aircraft in determining whether an emergency situation actually exists.

The captain may have to abort the flight's takeoff or landing at the last minute for a variety of reasons. For example, there might be a malfunction of mechanical systems, interference by another aircraft or ground equipment, crowded airways, or ingestion of foreign matter into an engine. There would be no forewarning from the cockpit to the passenger cabin, so it is your responsibility to assess the situation and respond accordingly.

Always be prepared for the unexpected. There is a possibility that the plane may swerve off the runway or make abnormal contact with the ground surface during takeoff or landing. Common causes of aircraft accidents involve pilot error, failure of the landing gear system, or blown tires. Since many airports are located near large bodies of water, it is possible that an aircraft may have to "ditch," i.e., land on the water.

EMERGENCY ESCAPE SYSTEMS

Emergency evacuation from an aircraft becomes necessary when remaining on board poses a threat to human life. Before you can consider getting people out of an aircraft during an evacuation, you must be totally familiar with the equipment at your disposal and the location and operation of emergency escape systems. Your specialized training on each aircraft flown by your airline is meant to serve as a guideline and to be enhanced by constant reviews and safety checks of those systems. Knowing where to obtain and how to use all the gear on board may make saving lives a reality in case of an emergency evacuation.

PORTABLE EQUIPMENT

Each aircraft is equipped with portable apparatus that can be used to hasten the process of evacuation. They are usually secured to the aircraft structure by means of a bracketing device. This equipment can be hand carried by crew members and passengers, and could be instrumental in increasing passenger survival.

Megaphone This battery-operated device is a back-up to the plane's public address system. It is used to shout directions to passengers during an evacuation and to assemble them outside the aircraft. It is conical in shape and operates by pressing an amplifier button and speaking into the mouthpiece. Megaphones are always placed in an area immediately adjacent to emergency exits, where their use is most beneficial.

Flashlights   Federal Air Regulations require that flashlights be immediately available to each flight attendant. Some airlines require that the flashlight be worn on the person during takeoff and landing, while others affix the device to a part of the aircraft near emergency exits. As with all emergency equipment, they can only be of use to you if they are readily accessible and in operating condition.

Flotation Devices   Each aircraft has removable flotation devices in the form of seat bottom or back cushions that can be carried off the airplane in the event of a water landing. They are designed with a quick-release snap or tape and have handles sewn on the back side that allow for a secure grip.

Life Vests   All aircraft designed for over-water flights are equipped with passenger and crew life vests. They are located at each passenger seat and crew jump seat so that during a water evacuation they are readily accessible to everyone on board. (Some airlines also provide a smaller "child's" life vest whose operation is similar to the adults'.) Instructions for their use are printed on the back flap of each vest. They are equipped with inflatable chambers that can be distended by pull tabs or inflated orally via a tube. A water-activated light and adjustable waist straps are also incorporated as a part of the vest. Different colors are used for identification purposes. For the most part, passenger life vests are yellow, while crew members wear a bright red vest, making them easily recognizable as the leaders in an emergency evacuation.

Life Rafts   Standard equipment on all over-water aircraft are inflatable life rafts. They are folded into small compact units and usually stored in ceiling compartments or exit doors (as on the DC-10). In the event of a water landing, they are retrieved, carried to the closest exit, and launched outside the aircraft. Each of these rafts is designed to carry a specified number of passengers and crew and they are in adequate supply for the capacity of the aircraft.

The following is a list of all of the components and emergency equipment that may be found on board these life rafts:

Boarding ramp	Inflation pump
Hand-held life line	Repair kit
Heaving line	Bailing bucket
Sea anchor	Water bags
Knife	Desalting kits
Transceivers/beacons	Dye markers
Sponges	Whistle
Removable canopy and supports	Flares
	Flashlights
Survival instruction booklets	Compass
	Pliers
First aid kit	Mirror

FIXED EMERGENCY SYSTEMS

Essential to every aircraft structure is an emergency lighting system. These additional lights are located inside and outside the plane. Their operation is automatic on some planes, but there is always a back-up device installed in the cockpit and near flight attendant jump seats to activate the system manually. The purpose of exterior lights is to illuminate emergency escape routes and the area adjacent to the outside of the aircraft. Interior emergency lights are used to brighten the cabin atmosphere and illuminate all exit signs at doors and windows. These phosphorescent exit signs are located at every exit and in ceiling compartments throughout the cabin.

Another permanent emergency system is found on wide-bodied aircraft in the form of evacuation alarms. When doors are opened in an emergency, this sounding device is activated automatically at each exit. There is usually a button located at each door where the horn may be deactivated if not needed.

EMERGENCY EXITS

Flight attendants trained and authorized as working crew

members must have full knowledge of the location, function, and operation of all emergency exits on board aircraft operated by their airline. As you depart on each flight, and again before you land, familiarize yourself with the specific exits and their components on board that aircraft. Lives may depend on your knowledge and quick action when conditions warrant leaving a plane as fast as possible.

DOOR EXITS

Commercial passenger-carrying aircraft are built to specifications that include a sufficient number of emergency exits for the total capacity of people on board. Doors and slides of varying types and sizes provide a means of immediate and simultaneous egress for all passengers and crew during an emergency evacuation. Not only do they differ from one aircraft to another, but there may be several varieties on the same airplane.

Each door is identified by number and location. For example, the forwardmost door on the left-hand side is designated as 1L and the numbering continues aft. The same holds true for the right-hand side where door 1R is the forwardmost door on the right.

Cabin doors are those used for boarding and deplaning passengers, buffet units, and servicing personnel. They open either outward by means of hinges or upward into the fuselage. On the cabin side of the door is a movable handle and directions for its use. In addition, a porthole-type window is located on the top half of each door for easy viewing of outside conditions.

An essential component of all aircraft doors is a slide pack unit. Housed within this unit is an inflatable slide that is folded and stored on the cabin side of the door or inside the door structure itself. When deployed, it acts as a chute that provides a means of rapid escape from the aircraft to the ground for all passengers and crew.

To ensure that the slide remains attached to the fixed aircraft structure for use in an evacuation, it is equipped with a connecting device. Located at the bottom of the folded slide pack is a girt bar. This is a long bar of steel that fastens to metal brackets on the floor near the doorsill. Securing the bar to the slide pack is a lanyard device that encircles the middle of the bar.

When the girt bar is attached to the aircraft, this is known as arming the door; it is done on every flight as the aircraft pushes back from the gate. The procedure is then reversed upon arrival at the aircraft's destination. This is known as disarming the door, or disengaging the girt bar so the door is ready for normal use.

A signal is given to all flight attendants to prepare their doors for departure. On narrow-bodied aircraft, this must be done manually. However, on wide-bodied equipment, the girt bar falls into place when the arming lever is placed in the automatic position. With the girt bar now locked in place and attached to the aircraft structure, opening the door would cause the slide pack to be pulled away from its container.

Now imagine that a door is opened with the slide ready for use. As the pack falls away, inflation of the slide takes place automatically or must be accomplished manually.

When a slide is inflated, its length runs from the door of the aircraft to the ground. On narrow-bodied equipment the width is designed to accommodate one person at a time. On wide-bodied aircraft the doors and slides may be double width to allow for two lanes of exiting passengers and crew. Some slides are even equipped with antiskid material toward the bottom edge. This is meant to slow the speed of a person's descent from a great height. Most slides have strap handles along the sides, which are used by crew members who might need to reenter the aircraft.

On certain aircraft, the inflatable slides also function as rafts. Should an airplane that is not over-water-equipped make an emergency water landing, certain slides can be inverted before inflating, then deployed for use as rafts.

One exception to typical aircraft door exits is the rear door on all 727 aircraft. It opens inward at the aft end of the cabin. Just outside the door area is a lever that activates a set of movable airstairs as a means of escape.

Another type of door exit is known as a jet escape door. These doors are always armed and used only for emergency purposes. They are designed so that pulling on a handle causes the door to fall outward and down from the fuselage. Since the girt bar is always attached, the slide deploys automatically when the door is opened. There is also a viewing window on this door and placards with written instructions for its operation.

An exit door is virtually impossible to open when the aircraft is inflight. Each door is designed so that it "plugs" a hole in the fuselage from the inside of the cabin. Because of the greater pressure on the inside of the aircraft during flight, the door cannot be opened against this force. However, on the ground and without this pressurization, opening of these doors is feasible. Provided the doors are armed, slide bars attached, and there is no structural damage or mechanical failure, the door is ready for evacuation purposes.

WINDOW EXITS

On narrow-bodied aircraft the exits over the wing area are of a window design. They are smaller than doors, raised off the floor, and located adjacent to passenger seating rows. Small aircraft have one window on a side over the wing. Larger aircraft have a total of four window exits, two over each wing. A handle is located near the top of the window with instructions for its use. There is also a hand-hold near the bottom of the window to aid in its maneuverability. When the handle is pulled, the window falls in toward the cabin. With two hands, it is possible to place the entire structure on the adjacent seats.

There are no slides at a window exit. The wing and its extended flaps become the means for reaching the ground in an evacuation. There are directional arrows on the wing surface just outside the window exit that point toward the trailing edge of the wing. When followed, they lead to the flaps, which provide the additional surface needed to reach the ground from the cabin elevation.

COCKPIT EXITS

There is also a means of escape for the flight crew should their access to the passenger cabin be blocked during an evacuation. Some cockpits have windows that slide and are large enough for one person to fit through at a time. Because of the distance to the ground from these windows, an escape rope is provided. On 747's, the cockpit is located above the main cabin level. Therefore, a separate emergency door exit and slide is provided from the cockpit directly to the outside.

GALLEY EXITS

On wide-bodied aircraft with galley units beneath the main cabin deck, there are several means of escape. Normal access to this area is through the use of a personnel lift. When there is a need to evacuate a lower deck galley in an emergency situation, there is a built-in ladder along the side walls of the cart lifts. The galley attendant can climb up this ladder using the foot and hand-holds and unlatch the cabin level doors from the inside in order to climb out.

At the opposite end of the galley is an alternate escape route in the form of a hatch. The top side of this hatch is actually a piece of the main cabin floor. As the cover is pushed open from the lower deck galley, you can climb out directly into the aisle of the main cabin to escape.

EVACUATIONS

To evacuate an aircraft means to remove all passengers and crew in an expeditious manner through all usable emergency exits. The FAA requires that an evacuation be accomplished in ninety seconds or less, regardless of the size of the aircraft or number of people on board. It is your responsibility as a flight attendant to know the exact procedures as dictated by your airline for initiating and completing the entire evacuation within this specified time frame. Other people's lives, as well as your own, will depend on your efficiency and expertise. Knowing how to communicate this information is also the key to a successful evacuation.

The types of emergencies that warrant an evacuation include bomb threats, fires, and abnormal takeoffs and landings. Most airlines authorize their flight attendants to initiate an evacuation based on the recognition of conditions that are a threat to everyone's safety. Some airlines require that their flight attendants obtain permission from the captain before evacuating an aircraft. In either case, a plane must be on the ground and be at a complete stop before an evacuation can take place.

Emergency evacuations fall into two main categories: planned and unplanned. Your most effective means of preparation for these emergencies is the preflight safety announcement and demonstration given before every flight. Your only recourse once the accident occurs is to begin shouting instructions to passengers and to initiate emergency procedures.

After an emergency landing, all occupants should be evacuated in ninety seconds or less. In a planned evacuation, your chances of attaining this goal are very high, based on an organized plan and communication with your passengers. The captain advises the lead flight attendant that an emergency situation has developed. The captain relates the nature of the emergency and how much time is available for preparing the cabin. It is then the lead flight attendant's duty to ascertain where the landing is to be made, expected attitude of the aircraft, special instructions, protective position, and signals to be used. Then it is up to the lead flight attendant to communicate all of this information to all crew members on board and to delegate evacuation duties.

The passengers are apprised of the situation through announcements and briefings. All instructions are to be communicated clearly and with a calm, commanding voice. You should encourage passengers to be a part of your team—by everyone sharing in the responsibilities, the evacuation will run much more efficiently. It is up to you and your flying partners to generate a calm atmosphere by reassuring the passengers. Panic can be kept to a minimum through positive, direct crew leadership.

The first instruction to the passengers in preparation for an evacuation is to take the safety information card out of the seat pocket. Ask them to review the location and operation of all the exits, especially the ones closest to their seats. Also have them practice the protective position described on the card. Passengers should remove and stow their shoes and loosen restrictive clothing. Have everyone check to be sure seat belts are securely fastened, seat backs and tray tables are in their upright and locked position, and all smoking materials have been extinguished. If a water landing is expected, instruct passengers to don their life vests at this time. Ask them to follow your instructions and listen to all commands and announcements. Assure them that with their cooperation and positive attitudes, everyone will have the best chance of getting out of the airplane as fast as possible.

Preparation of the cabin involves reseating passengers and making sure everything is stowed and secure. Move able-bodied passengers to seats adjacent to emergency exits so their help may be enlisted during the evacuation. Secure items such as loose luggage, sharp objects and supplies, and closet doors and module covers. Lock lavatory doors so they are not inadvertently used as an exit. Adjust cabin lighting for time of day. Provide pillows and blankets for impact protection. Once all of these duties have been accomplished, the captain is advised and all flight attendants must take their assigned seats for landing.

On a signal from the captain, assume protective positions. For those passengers sitting in forward-facing seats, possible protective positions for impact are grabbing ankles or placing crossed arms on the seat back in front of the passenger. If sitting in an aft-facing seat, the brace position is to sit up straight with arms folded cross the chest and head back against a seat or wall. The purpose of assuming a brace position is to prevent the head, neck, and body from sharp thrusts forward, backward, and from side to side.

Once the airplane has landed, DO NOT MOVE until it has come to a complete stop. Everything from this moment on is going to happen very quickly, so LOOK and THINK before you act. This is no time for mistakes—muster all the courage and energy you have to achieve the most expeditious egress possible from the plane.

Begin shouting to the passengers to release their seat belts. As you leave your jump seat, assess the conditions outside the exit before opening it. If there is fire or structural damage on the other side of the door or window, redirect passengers to another usable exit. If you have just landed on water, instruct passengers to grab flotation gear and have helpers assist in launching the rafts. Once your door is opened, make sure the slide is inflated. There are usually assist handles located near the frame of each door. Use them to aid in opening the exit, then hold on to avoid being pushed out by people behind you. Send the first two people down the slide and instruct them to stand at the bottom and pull people off the slide and direct them away from the aircraft. Shout for people to come to your exit. Make verbal and physical contact with the passengers as they approach. Give them a shove if they are reluctant to jump into the slide or raft.

Many factors could affect the speed of an evacuation. It could be slow due to poor visibility, human error, or structural damage to exits and slides. Factors such as age, gender, physical health, and mental attitudes have a large influence on the progress of an evacuation. Keep shouting and pushing people out the exits until it appears that everyone has left. Time and conditions permitting, grab first aid kits, blankets, and a megaphone. Make one last check of the cabin. When you have done everything that is humanly possible without jeopardizing your own life, leave the aircraft. There is a saying among flight attendants that should be your code: "When the smoke is too thick, water too deep, or fire too hot, get out!"

POSTEVACUATION

Once outside the aircraft, people will continue to depend on your leadership capabilities. You may have a very chaotic situation on your hands. Your prime responsibility is to ensure the highest rate of survival by keeping people safe from further danger while waiting for the arrival of rescue units.

To compound the severity of the situation, certain unfavorable environmental conditions may exist. The time of day, weather conditions, and terrain have a definite influence on the chance of survival. Consider the fact that it may be night, cold, a mountainous area, with jagged loose pieces of fuselage strewn about. If the plane landed on water, make sure that people stay inside the life rafts. Exposure to the action of the waves and wind, cold temperature of the water, and the possibility of sharks is extremely dangerous.

The ranking crew member from the aircraft is in charge of postevacuation activities. Your responsibilities center around moving people away from the aircraft and keeping them in groups. It certainly is not expected of you to act beyond your means. Do your best to guard yourself and your passengers from further danger.

Expect pushing and shoving, hysterical behavior, and demonstrations of positive and negative panic. Be realistic about rescue. A positive attitude and a strong will to live should be encouraged among all survivors. Engage people in activities to occupy their time and minds. If you are involved in a ditching, tie life rafts together and cut them loose from the aircraft. Signal for assistance by using flares and beacon equipment.

Do not attempt to alter the wreckage and by no means allow passengers to smoke or reenter the aircraft. Your concerns should focus on applying first aid treatment to survivors. Common injuries after an evacuation include sprains, breaks, contusions, and first-degree burns of the hands and face.

Continue to reassure passengers that everything possible is being done in their behalf. Your professionalism as demonstrated through the entire emergency will command the respect of every passenger. These people now more fully realize that your primary responsibility on board was for their safety and welfare.

16

FIRST AID

The principles of administering first aid are the same whether on the ground or in an aircraft at 39,000 feet. The role of the first-aider is to render initial treatment of a sudden illness or injury based on the recognition of symptoms. Immediate temporary care is given to a person until professional medical help can be obtained. In this chapter we will deal only with considerations especially significant for the flight attendant. It is strongly recommended that a certified course in first aid techniques be taken.

A UNIQUE ENVIRONMENT

The administration of first aid to a passenger on an airplane can be accomplished effectively in spite of possible limitations. The primary asset to this unique environment at 39,000 feet is the constant presence of emergency-qualified personnel. All flight attendants and flight crew members have been trained in life-saving techniques and, most importantly, to work as a team when applying first aid procedures. While one flight attendant is treating the victim, other flight attendants assume the responsibilities of procuring supplies, keeping the captain informed, and, if needed, enlisting the help of qualified medical personnel on board.

In the event a passenger's illness or injury becomes severe enough to warrant medical assistance on the ground, the captain can coordinate the necessary arrangements. A radio is on hand in the cockpit at all times for direct communication between the inflight crew and ground personnel. For example, should a passenger become seriously ill on a domestic flight, a hospital or other emergency facility on the ground might not be more than fifteen to thirty minutes away through means of an unscheduled emergency landing.

Certain physical limitations on an airplane present a challenge to the flight attendant when administering first aid. The interior of an airplane is a self-contained unit of space where the ability to administer immediate care to a passenger may be restricted by the design of the seats and the seating configuration. Your access to a victim may be hindered due to the width and height of the seats and the minimal space between each row. It is possible that your ability to reach a passenger at a window seat may be complicated by one or two other passengers seated between you and the victim, or your access to the passenger may be obstructed by a serving cart in a narrow aisle.

Regardless of the confinement of space, effective first aid measures can be accomplished. The interior of an aircraft becomes a second home to a flight attendant. This familiarity with surroundings, combined with specialized training received on the operation of equipment, increases your ability to render professional first aid care.

PREFLIGHT FIRST AID PROCEDURES

Prior to departure, flight attendants make routine preparations for any illness or injury that could happen inflight. During a briefing session, you might be informed of passengers who have medical problems and may require assistance. Once on board, it is also your responsibility to make a visual check of the cabin for any possible safety hazards that could cause injury. If any defects are noted (such as a loose piece of carpeting or an unlatched overhead lighting cover), alert the proper personnel to remedy the situation immediately.

FIRST AID KIT

First aid kits are on board, placed in designated areas for easy accessibility. Their number and location depend on the size of the aircraft. The contents of these kits could include any or all of the following supplies: ammonia inhalants, merthiolate swabs, adhesive bandages and tape, scissors, burn ointment, compresses, splints, and triangular and roller bandages. An important part of the preflight safety check is to verify that all first aid kits are in place and properly sealed.

FIRST AID OXYGEN

At your disposal is a supplemental oxygen system designed for first aid purposes. Since passengers in an airplane do not have immediate access to medical facilities, it is mandatory to have equipment on board that is capable of adding comfort or sustaining life. This provision is in the form of portable bottles or masks that plug into a fixed airflow system. There are enough bottles and masks situated throughout a passenger cabin to make first aid oxygen readily accessible to every person on board. It is imperative that you know where all equipment is located and the proper operating procedures. Instructions for their use are usually written on the bottle as well as listed in your flight manual.

PASSENGER PORTABLE OXYGEN BOTTLE

A passenger first aid oxygen bottle is designed to be portable and easy to operate. It is in the shape of a cylinder that contains pure compressed oxygen. Each bottle is equipped with a gauge to indicate the amount of pressurized oxygen inside, measured in PSI's (pounds per square inch). A passenger first aid oxygen bottle usually contains enough oxygen to last for approximately one hour of continuous use. There are valves for high and low oxygen flow and an outlet in which to insert the tubing connected to a disposable mask. This mask and tubing are usually found packaged in a plastic bag and taped to the side of the bottle. The cylinder is made of metal and when full can be awkward and heavy to carry. Therefore, each bottle has a canvas strap attached that makes it easy to carry sling fashion or wear from the shoulder.

During your preflight safety check you should have verified that these bottles are all present and secured in their proper locations. Whether located in overhead bins or in separate storage compartments, each bottle must be fastened to a permanent structure in the cabin by means of a bracket that can be unlatched when the bottle is needed. When checking the pressure gauge, verify that the indicator needle falls within the prescribed range for full pressurization. You want to be sure that all bottles are ready for use before passengers board the aircraft.

FLIGHT ATTENDANT PORTABLE OXYGEN BOTTLE

A smaller version of the passenger first aid oxygen bottle is found throughout the passenger cabin. This crew bottle is almost identical to the passenger version, except that its supply of oxygen lasts only approximately ten minutes. It is used primarily as a walk-around supply for flight attendants after a decompression when they are moving through the cabin to check on passengers. However, it can be used for a passenger in lieu of a larger portable bottle, provided enough flight attendant bottles are available for crew use in the event of a decompression.

FIXED FIRST AID SYSTEM

On some aircraft, such as DC-8's, first aid passenger oxygen is available through the same source as the fixed emergency system. In this case, a supply of masks and tubing must be retrieved from specified storage compartments throughout the passenger cabin. To use this supply, the mask unit is brought to the passenger and plugged into the high-flow valve located in the service panel above the passenger's head. Still another system involves opening the oxygen pod near the passenger's seat and selecting the proper mask to be used for first aid purposes. In either case, the flow of oxygen is regulated by a toggle switch on the controlling apparatus responsible for feeding the supply throughout the plane.

ADMINISTERING FIRST AID OXYGEN

Whenever supplemental oxygen is going to be used, the first step is to ensure that no one is smoking within several rows of the bottle. Pure oxygen is highly volatile, so be sure to instruct passengers near the victim to extinguish cigarettes or move to another seat elsewhere in the cabin. While one flight attendant is retrieving a bottle, another should notify the captain that oxygen will be in use. This bottle can become a weapon if dropped, so carry it to the passenger's seat using the canvas strap and holding the bottle firmly. When you arrive at the victim's seat, lay the bottle down, securing the canvas strap to a fixed portion of the seating area.

Now you are ready to administer oxygen to a passenger. Wipe off any lipstick or protective lip covering from the victim's mouth, since these products can be flammable. Plug the metal fitting of the mask tubing into the high-flow outlet and turn the valve its full rotation to start the oxygen flow. Before placing the mask on the passenger, ALWAYS check to be sure the bottle is working properly and that oxygen is indeed being emitted. This can be done by pinching the tubing or tapping the end of the tube with your finger. If you hear or feel air being discharged, you know the apparatus is in working order.

Place the mask over the passenger's nose and mouth. The mask is similar to a cone-shaped plastic bag to which the tubing is connected. There is a thin strip of metal across the top edge of the mask that should be pinched around the bridge of the nose to allow for a proper fit on the passenger's face. To further hold the mask in place, a small elastic strap attached to the mask should be placed around the passenger's head. Verify that the passenger feels the oxygen flow and check the pressure gauge on the bottle periodically for the amount of remaining oxygen. Keep abreast of the time factor so another oxygen bottle can be prepared if necessary.

If the person requiring oxygen is an infant, there are different procedures to be followed. The plastic mask provided is too large for an infant's face and therefore would be ineffective.

Instead, cut a hole in the bottom of a small paper drinking cup and insert the tubing. Close the hole around the tubing with masking tape or an adhesive bandage. Use the low-flow outlet and, when assured that oxygen is flowing, place the cup over the infant's nose and mouth.

In administering oxygen to yourself from the crew portable bottle, follow the same procedures as those applied to adult passengers. The only difference is that the bottle is worn sling fashion, enabling you to walk around the cabin while using the supply. After you have started the flow, place the mask over your face and adjust the elastic strap for a proper fit. Breathe normally and before landing notify the cockpit of the number of bottles that were used and their location.

ADDITIONAL OVERALL RESPONSIBILITIES FOR PASSENGER SAFETY

From the time passengers board an airplane, all flight attendants are responsible for their well-being. Monitor every activity inflight with safety in mind. You should do everything possible to guard against illness or injury to passengers, your flying partners, and yourself by employing safe working habits. For example: do not fly with a cold; ensure safe storage of items in closets and overhead compartments; when serving from a cart in the aisle, avoid overstacking loose items and ensure that hot beverage containers are covered; before using glass and china, check for chips and cracks; carry only a few food and beverage items at a time; and warn passengers not to hold lighted cigarettes out in the aisle.

Above all else, maintain a constant vigil on the airplane. At least one flight attendant should be present at all times in each cabin occupied by passengers. It is your responsibility to know what is going on around you—look and listen for occurrences that are out of the ordinary.

LISTEN TO YOUR PASSENGERS

You may be personally advised of a passenger's needs. For instance, at the beginning of a flight a passenger may advise you of a heart condition. Ascertain whether a problem is antic-ipated and if the passenger is carrying medication. Another example is when a passenger requests that you store medicine in a refrigerated unit. As a rule, you should not accept such medicine for storage; instead offer a container, e.g., motion sickness bag, filled with ice so that the passenger may keep the medicine at his seat. Sometimes a passenger will ask if a meal could be served right away. It might be wise to consider if there are medical reasons for the request rather than assuming that this person is being overly demanding.

LOOK AT YOUR PASSENGERS

Another way to become aware of a person's needs is through your own observation. You should be able to recognize a vis-ual plea for help. There might be a passenger walking around the plane who appears to be in a daze, or a group of passengers is seen gathering in one area seemingly concerned about some-thing. These examples are visible signs that YOUR ASSISTANCE IS NEEDED!

YOUR ATTITUDE COUNTS

Precautionary measures do not always ensure that someone is going to avoid an illness or injury. Should your first aid training and knowledge be needed, use good judgment, profes-sionalism, and confidence when providing emergency care. Remember to treat the symptoms—you are not trained to make a diagnosis.

Your attitude is of great importance when treating an ill or injured person. People are looking to you for help and reassur-ance. As long as you are with the passengers, remain calm. Control your emotions until your responsibility has termi-nated. You should be confident that your training and com-mon sense will help you see it through.

While applying first aid, be aware of a passenger's emotional as well as his physical state. Display empathy and a positive attitude to help create a relaxed atmosphere. By using a low, well-modulated tone of voice, and controlled, purposeful movements, you help to maintain an air of calmness. Also, keep an ill or injured person comfortable by loosening restrictive clothing such as collars and belts. If appropriate, offer water, additional air, pillows, blankets, ice packs, or warm compresses.

RECOGNIZING WARNING SIGNALS

When an emergency health situation arises, it warrants your immediate attention. Aside from the obvious infirmities, you will have to evaluate the passenger's condition by heeding certain warning signals:

Skin color   Passenger's overall skin tone appears abnormally flushed, blue, or pale.

Skin temperature   Body temperature seems too warm or cold to the touch when placing the backs of your fingers against the passenger's skin.

Pupils   Pupils are dilated (large) or constricted (small) or one pupil appears noticeably larger than the other.

Numbness, paralysis   Passenger has loss of sensation or is unable to voluntarily move extremities.

Expression of pain   Holding one's body at source of pain, contorted facial expression, or sounds of anguish may be evident.

State of consciousness   Passenger seems confused, incoherent, semiconscious, or unconscious.

INITIATING FIRST AID PROCEDURES

Once you have determined that someone is in fact ill or injured, there are certain action procedures that must be followed:

Gather necessary information   Talk to passenger (if conscious), family member, seat partner, bystander; ascertain medical history and present condition; check for "medic alert" tag or other medical identifiers.

Administer appropriate first aid treatment

Notify captain Advise as to the nature and severity of illness or injury; inform of any oxygen use; inform of treatment being rendered; make intermittent reports of passenger's progress.

Seek help of qualified medical persons Medical doctor, nurse, or paramedic.

Your approach to the problem depends upon whether the passenger is conscious or unconscious. First aid treatment is easier when dealing with the conscious passenger. You are able to obtain information directly regarding: discomfort being experienced, location of pain, history of problem, medication prescribed and presently being taken, and whether passenger is currently under a doctor's care.

You are confronted with an entirely different situation when the passenger is unconscious. Your immediate responsibility is to determine if the passenger is breathing and has a pulse. If either one or both are not evident, apply the appropriate life-saving measures. Possible causes of the passenger's unconscious state can be detected by observing warning signals and questioning nearby passengers. Check the victim's entire body for any visible signs of injury.

LIFE-SUSTAINING MEASURES

The objective of life-support methods is to restore breathing and circulation. This is done by means of applying artificial respiration and cardiopulmonary resuscitation (CPR). These techniques must be applied with speed and efficiency. If delayed or performed incorrectly, irreversible damage to the victim may be the result. Therefore, it is essential that you know the proper step-by-step techniques for administering artificial respiration and cardiopulmonary resuscitation. Courses are established in schools and community programs throughout the country where certified instructors can teach you these techniques.

Respiratory arrest occurs when a victim's breathing has stopped, but a pulse is evident. Other symptoms displayed are unconsciousness, dilated pupils, and a blue tinge to the victim's skin. By applying artificial respiration, the first-aider attempts to open the airway and restore breathing.

Cardiac arrest is the cessation of the heart action, preventing the circulation of blood throughout the body. This is evidenced by unconsciousness, no respiration, lack of pulse on palpation of carotid artery, dilated pupils, and an ashen-gray tone to the skin. The responsibility of the first-aider in administering CPR is to activate the victim's heart and restore circulation.

ILLNESS AND INJURY

It is impossible to list every type of illness or injury that you may have to face on board an aircraft. Most often, these situations occur suddenly and require your immediate attention. Your airline usually provides, as an integral part of the flight attendant manual, a guide to first aid procedures to be used inflight. Possible occurrences that you may have to confront include: heart attack, burns, bleeding, sprains, stroke, airsickness, choking, respiratory failure, lacerations, ear blockage, fractures, miscarriage, shock, seizures, food poisoning, drug overdose, and appendicitis.

In treating an illness or injury, consider the overall situation and respond accordingly. Do not attempt to memorize a list of symptoms and treatments; rather, deal with the matter at hand only after a thorough evaluation.

POSTFLIGHT FIRST AID PROCEDURES

Your responsibility to a stricken passenger does not end when the plane lands. If the severity of the illness or injury warrants medical assistance on the ground, you are obligated to be on hand to relay pertinent information as to what transpired during the flight. In the event a seriously ill passenger prefers not to be met by professional medical help after the plane is parked at the gate, remain with the passenger until family members or friends arrive, or you may relinquish the custody of the passenger to your airline ground representative.

17

FOOD AND BEVERAGE SERVICES

One of the most visible and promotable features of airline travel is the food and beverage services offered inflight. An airline's competitive standing in the industry and a passenger's choice of carrier are greatly influenced by the type and quality of services offered. While safety remains the prime consideration of every airline, it is the flight attendants who assume the additional responsibility, during normal operations, of providing a gracious and efficient service to their passengers. Passengers should be treated as though they were guests in your home, so make every effort to create a comfortable and enjoyable atmosphere.

PLANNING AND PREPARATION

Much planning and preparation go into any food and beverage service on an airplane. Services don't just happen—they are the combined efforts of the personnel who develop menus and serving procedures, the kitchen staff who prepare and assemble the buffet contents, and the flight attendants who make the actual presentation to the passengers. Little do the passengers realize what goes on behind the scenes in order to quench their thirsts and please their palates. Let's look behind the scenes to see what goes into the planning of a service and how you can bring it all to the passenger's tray table with a personalized touch.

IN THE BEGINNING ...

An airline conducts an extensive amount of research before deciding what type of service is to be offered on which flights. Their main concern is to see that the service is unique, portions are adequate, and the presentation is creative. Today, when so many commercial airlines are flying identical routes, competition plays a large role in the type of service offered. Time is spent to select the finest quality of food and drink, in the knowledge that passengers have discriminating tastes and may come back to fly with your airline simply because of finer food service. Brand-name liquors and wines are chosen for inflight services because of their distinctive qualities. Particular travel markets are considered when designing menus to suit the passengers' life-styles and tastes. A great deal of testing and experimentation goes into maximizing the use of modern catering equipment without minimizing the quality of the product—all the while operating in a specified cost structure.

After many others see to it that the service is designed, prepared, and delivered to the airplane, it is the responsibility of the flight attendants to ensure a professional presentation. You are expected to follow prescribed serving procedures and keep safety in mind at all times when putting into practice what your airline hopes will please its passengers.

Teamwork is essential. Only when the entire crew works together in an organized plan can efficiency be optimized. A service should be paced to a passenger's convenience, considering the length of the flight. Use good judgment in unique situations. Just because procedures are established and provisions seem adequate, don't discount the possibility of problems arising. Remain flexible and remember that alternatives are always available. That's what you were hired for—to think on your feet.

GET READY, GET SET . . .

Your first responsibility regarding food and beverage services is to know what is being offered before you board the aircraft. Most crew schedules have some indication of the type of inflight service for each segment. If descriptions of services are not included in your flight attendant manual, they are usually available in the inflight office for easy reference after you check in. Find out what you are going to be serving and at what station the provisions will be boarded. Then consult a trip advisory for any special meal requests or changes in procedures. If a briefing is held, you are usually informed of meal choices and percentages of selection, as well as what your assignments are in the implementation of the service.

As soon as the provisions for your flight are brought on board, the attendant working in each galley must determine that all is in order for the flight. The first task is to verify that the correct number of meals and other items correlate with the planned passenger load and the caterer's checklist. If any discrepancies are noted, report them immediately so additional supplies can be obtained.

Make the galley area ready for use (commonly known as setting up) by turning on lights, hot plates, coffee makers, and other electrical appliances. Assemble and unwrap necessary supply packages such as paper cups, plastic glasses, ice buckets, and napkins. Verify the amount of liquor against the accounting sheets and make a notation of any discrepancies. The object in all predeparture duties, as discussed earlier, is to be able to begin serving your passengers as soon as the plane is airborne. Offer a predeparture beverage service if one is scheduled and brew a pot of coffee if time permits. Before leaving the galley, clear countertops and make certain that all modules and storage compartments are closed and latched for takeoff.

GALLEY FACILITIES

An airplane's kitchen is known as a galley, buffet, or service center. The galley is a relatively confined area of space considering the amount of equipment and supplies boarded for the number of passengers to be served. Rest assured, though, that the area is sufficient for your purposes and designed to make everything readily available within a few feet.

Buffets are made up of removable containerized units. This makes it possible for catering trucks to remove used supplies and deliver new units to the aircraft in a very brief, efficient operation. Depending on the size and type of aircraft, this unit may be one specialized section with several compartments or a series of individual modules. Once boarded, these units are locked in place so as not to shift during flight.

Buffet units and modules vary in size and design. Their purpose is to make the galley area concise and its contents portable. There are also means for refrigeration, freezing, and heating of food items. Since there is a basic difference between narrow-bodied and wide-bodied galley areas, they will be described separately.

On narrow-bodied aircraft, the buffets are located on one side of the cabin near an exit door through which the units are boarded. The cold-storage units are kept cool with dry ice or other refrigerants. When the ovens are boarded and in place in the buffet, they are connected to the electrical power system of the aircraft. There are on/off switches, heat controls, and timers for keeping food hot. A waste receptacle is part of the unit, as well as additional supply drawers and compartments.

To accommodate the increased number of passengers on wide-bodied aircraft, the galley designs are quite different. Service centers on the main deck are comprised of storage facilities and countertop work surfaces. On planes in which supplies and food are boarded elsewhere, this service center area is empty during takeoff and landing. During the flight it is stocked with supplies and carts and used as a distribution point for all aspects of the service.

Some wide-bodied planes have all galley areas on the main passenger level. However, on others there are buffet facilities located one floor below, known as a lower-lobe galley. These galleys require special procedures because of the physical layout. Elevators, or "lifts," are used as access routes and it is from here that all food and beverage services originate. Large modules are boarded from a cargo door and rolled into place.

The components of these modules include an array of portable carts and supplies that are sent "upstairs" to the main cabin for the service. The carts are preset and well stocked, each designed for a different purpose. Tray carts contain rows of stacked meal trays that are minus a hot entrée. Entrée carts are heated electrically for the purpose of storing hot food for the meal service.

Some carts are a combination of trays and entrées with heated units incorporated. Liquor carts contain everything from miniature bottles, beer, wine, and champagne, to napkins, glasses, garnishes, and soft drinks. Waste carts are large plastic-lined receptacles into which trash is deposited during a flight.

The service on a wide-bodied aircraft becomes essentially a mini-buffet on wheels. Carts are positioned throughout the cabin for use during the service. Flight attendants wheel the carts down the aisle, delivering food and beverages directly to the passenger from the cart. As one cart is depleted, it is parked on special "tie-downs" and is exchanged for a full cart.

Food items are boarded in smaller refrigerated units. Entrées are often frozen and boarded on long racks in freezer compartments. Having been partially cooked and frozen, they must finish cooking. A permanent part of the galley is a series of reconstituting ovens into which the frozen meals are placed in their racks. Once heated thoroughly, the racks of meals are removed and placed into the preheated entrée carts.

The liquor supply units on every plane are locked with a wire seal or similar device. Accounting forms, which must be completed prior to landing, are included. Liquor compartments are once again locked before they are removed from the aircraft.

Typical of all galleys are a multitude of supplies and serving items. The more elaborate the service and the larger the plane, the more extensive the array of buffet items. Below is a sample list common to inflight food and beverage services:

BEVERAGE SERVICES

Paper cups
Serving trays
Sugar packets

MEAL SERVICES

Preset meal trays
Menus
Pot holders

213

Coffee creamers
Coffee
Coffee pots
Tea bags
Ice buckets
Bags of ice
Ice tongs, scoop
Water pitchers
Can opener
Plastic glasses
Stir sticks
Cocktail napkins
Cocktail mixes
Garnishes
Soft drinks
Fruit juices
Milk
Bouillon cubes
Lemonade

Plate lifters
Roll baskets
Punch ladle
Silver platters, utensils
Cocktail glasses
Wineglasses
Liqueur glasses
Glass carafes
Champagne buckets
Wine bottle holders
Salt and pepper shakers
Salad bowl
Peppermills
China plates/bowls
China cups and saucers
Silver coffee service
Teapots
Carving board and
    utensils
Linen tablecloths
Refresher towels
Linen bags
Flowers

BEVERAGE SERVICES

Every airline has its own set of procedures and guidelines for food and beverage services. They vary in purpose, complexity, and style, but your manner of presentation should remain consistently professional. Organization is the key to any successful service, whether beverage or food.

SOFT BEVERAGE SERVICES

If a flight segment is very short in length (approximately thirty minutes), and there is any service offered, it is only a beverage. It is imperative to have all items and supplies accounted for and organized before takeoff to minimize delivery time inflight. Keep needed supplies within easy reach, and know your work assignment. Beverages include nonalcoholic drinks such as coffee, tea, milk, carbonated soda, fruit juice, water, lemonade, punch, and bouillon.

When serving hot beverages, make sure they are just that— HOT. No one is more disappointed than a person who asks for a hot cup of coffee and receives a lukewarm one instead. Carry a serving tray stocked with plenty of creams, sugars, and artificial sweeteners. As a safety precaution, avoid pouring hot coffee at an awkward reach. If possible, ask the passenger to put the coffee cup on your serving tray, bring the tray close to you to pour, and return the full cup. For health reasons, serve milk and similar items in their original containers accompanied by a glass. Offer beverage refills frequently, time permitting.

LIQUOR SERVICE

The airlines offer alcoholic beverages to persons twenty-one years of age or older. It is the flight attendant's responsibility to monitor the consumption on board. It is a Federal Air Regulation that you do not serve a mixed drink, beer, or wine to a passenger who appears intoxicated, an armed passenger, or prisoners and their escorts. Also, according to federal regulations, passengers may not drink alcoholic beverages from their own supply. Any drinks purchased on board must be consumed inflight and not taken off the airplane.

Offered for sale during a cocktail service is a wide selection of premium liquors, beer, wine, champagne, and liqueurs. In coach, the whiskey, vodka, gin, bourbon, and other spirits are sold in miniature bottles and offered on the rocks or straight up. In first class, miniatures may be used, but sometimes fifths are boarded.

Wine is a popular beverage among air travelers. Airlines have increased their selection of wines and champagnes to suit the passengers' discriminating tastes. Allow the passenger to choose a wine according to individual preference rather than implying that certain wines go with certain foods. Wines are included as part of a cocktail service and are available during most meal services. Always serve champagne and white wine chilled, and red wine at room temperature. If small bottles or "splits" are sold in coach, they are handed to the passenger along with a glass. First-class wines and champagnes are usually boarded in fifths and poured into a wineglass at the passenger's seat. Place the glass on the table, turn the bottle so the label faces the passenger, and fill the glass two-thirds full. As you lift the bottle away, turn it slowly and wipe the top with a linen napkin to catch any drops left on the rim.

On some flights, liqueurs are offered after a meal service. Again, the selection is premium and they are served with or without ice. Although they are usually in miniature bottles, they may be boarded by the pint or quart in first class.

Cocktail services must be performed with speed and accuracy. Carts and buffets should be well organized before you proceed down the aisle to the passengers. Have on hand plenty of ice, mixes, glasses, and other nonalcoholic beverages for those not desiring a cocktail. Charge the correct amount of money for each alcoholic beverage, and be sure to return the correct change as soon as possible (and in the same currency). Accounting must be accurate and totals of the amount of liquor sold and returned should be clearly noted on the liquor forms.

MEAL SERVICES

The meals served on board a commercial airline are as varied as every other aspect of the industry. They range from the simple accompaniment of peanuts or some sort of tidbit with a cocktail service, to a full-course dinner with all the trimmings. Beverages are served with all food items, and a separate cocktail service usually precedes afternoon and evening meals.

TYPES OF FOOD SERVICE

Most carriers have an established schedule for meals. For instance, breakfast may be offered from 0700 to 0900, lunch from 1100 to 1300, and dinner from 1700 to 1900. Services offered other than during these hours consist of beverages and light snacks. A passenger simply needs to consult a flight schedule or a reservations agent to determine what, if any, meal(s) will be served on board a flight.

Snack   One type of meal service is a light snack. It usually consists of some type of sandwich that is boarded one per passenger tray; or the sandwiches are bulk packed and taken to the passengers en masse. This type of service is most popular on all-night trips, late morning, and late afternoon flights. In other words, snacks are served on trips not falling within scheduled meal hours.

Breakfast   On early morning trips of a short duration, a continental breakfast is offered consisting of pastry, coffee, and juice. On longer trips during breakfast hours, a full meal is served to each passenger. It consists of fruit and/or juice, a pastry, and hot entrée.

Lunch   Great variety can be found among airline lunches. It may be a light lunch consisting of soup and sandwich, or a hot entrée with salad and dessert. First-class lunches may include an assortment of fruit and cheeses to enhance the meal service.

Dinner   In the evening a hot dinner is served to passengers. The most common dinner consists of a salad, hot entrée, roll and butter, and dessert. More elaborate services, such as a first-class, full-course dinner, begins with an appetizer to accompany a pre-dinner cocktail, then proceeds to a salad with a selection of rolls and butter. Next on the menu is a choice of exquisite entrées. Accompanying the entrée service is a fine selection of wines and champagnes. The dinner is followed by lavish desserts and liqueurs.

Charter   Passengers traveling on charter flights may prearrange the type of meal service they would like to enjoy inflight. There is usually no choice available once on board—all passengers receive the same meal.

TYPE OF PRESENTATION

There are two basic differences in passenger meal services. The first involves the use of a preset meal tray and is most commonly found in coach cabins. The other is a more elaborate first-class service where meal items are arranged in individual place settings on the passenger's table.

217

For convenience and efficient operation, most coach passengers are served their meals on preset trays. They are boarded in the cold-storage units and contain a sterilized package of eating utensils, a napkin, coffee cup, and salt and pepper packets. Cold food items such as salad, dessert, roll and butter are also on the tray, depending on the meal being served. The flight attendant just adds the hot entrée and a beverage and distributes the trays to the passengers.

When there is more than one course offered, as in first class, the delivery of food items becomes a succession of presentations. The meal service is brought to the passenger seat on beautifully decorated carts. China plates, sterling silver service, and floral arrangements may embellish the gourmet food selections. Items are placed directly onto the passenger's linen-lined table and cleared away before the next course. A variety of services performed on a cart at the passenger's seat may include tossing a salad, carving a rib roast, and making ice cream sundaes.

SPECIAL MEAL REQUESTS

Commercial airlines offer a variety of special meal services. To allow adequate preparation time, passengers must notify the airline at least twenty-four hours prior to departure. Meals can be ordered because of special preference, or for religious, dietary, or medical reasons. You are usually advised before a flight of any special requests via the trip advisory or during a briefing session.

Special meals should be labeled for identification. During your predeparture buffet setup, locate these meals to verify that they have, in fact, been boarded. Contact the passengers to identify their seat numbers.

Types of special meals include: low-calorie, diabetic, kosher, low carbohydrate, low sodium, vegetarian, high protein, low cholesterol, bland, and children's meals, e.g., hot dog, hamburger, spaghetti, sandwich. When a kosher meal is requested, procedures differ slightly. A special meal of this type is prepared by a kosher caterer under the supervision of a rabbi.

When boarded, the tray and entrée are encased in a plastic or foil wrap which is only to be removed by the passenger.

Respect a passenger's preference for a special meal. If the meal was ordered for dietary or medical reasons (such as diabetes), ask the passenger if the meal should be consumed at any particular time. If the passenger must eat immediately, be sure to serve that meal first.

CREW MEALS

Many cabin attendants and cockpit crews have provisions in their union contracts for meals to be boarded for the flight they are working. A crew meal may not be boarded as a matter of policy if monetary compensation for meal expenses is made on a trip-by-trip or monthly basis.

Confer with the captain at the beginning of the flight to discuss the best time to serve the cockpit crew their meals. If crew meals were inadvertently not boarded, inform the captain so alternate arrangements can be made.

If the flight attendant contract includes a clause for crew meals, or if a meal is available from the passengers' allotment, they are to be eaten only after all passengers have finished their meals. One flight attendant must remain in each passenger cabin while meal breaks are taken. You should confine your break to the galley area, or jump seat if out of view of the passengers.

GENERAL SERVING PROCEDURES

The method of serving passengers changes from flight to flight depending on the scheduled service. However, the manner of presentation should remain the same. Procedures are written as general guidelines that make your job easier and the passengers' trip more enjoyable. Throughout your career, you will receive additional training on new service procedures in the form of classroom instruction, handout sheets, or updated manual revisions.

DURING A SERVICE

After organizing the food and beverage supplies, it is time to present the service. All food and beverage services originate from a buffet or service center. The way the items are transferred from the galley to the passenger differs as much as the serving direction on each plane. If meals are run out from the buffet individually, one flight attendant is usually assigned to stay in the buffet to prepare the orders, while another flight attendant delivers them to the passengers. A service may also be done totally from carts, as on wide-bodied aircraft. Regardless of the method of delivery, it is the passengers' convenience and comfort plus the allowable time frame that should be the determining factor for how a service is to be accomplished.

Above all, a service should be well timed. Work quickly, but don't appear rushed. If it is inconvenient for you to get something when asked, explain that you will do it at your first opportunity—and then don't forget to carry through with your promise.

When serving meals, know what the entrée choices are and what is included with the meal. Use the correct name of the dish and know how the entrée is prepared so you are able to answer any passenger questions as they arise. Coordinate the offering of beverages so they are delivered to the passengers with or shortly after the meal arrives. Offer second beverages such as coffee and wines, time permitting. Keep everything clean and orderly in the galley area. By reorganizing frequently and keeping countertops as clear as possible, your service should go very smoothly.

Even though you have prepared carefully and things seem to be in order, problems may still arise, such as turbulence, delays, or illnesses. During turbulence, obtain permission from the cockpit to be out of your seat, and take precautions while walking around. Be honest with passengers when explaining delays in the service, particularly if time is needed to attend to an unexpected emergency.

AFTER A SERVICE

When all passengers have been served, return to where the

service began and pick up food and beverage items from passenger tables. Procedures and staffing are usually designed to avoid making passengers wait a considerable length of time before their trays are cleared. Remember to ask passengers if they are finished before taking their trays away. Upon returning used trays to the buffet units, empty all liquids from cups and glasses. Continue checking the cabin for meal trays until everything is picked up. Carry any refuse to the buffet by use of trays or opaque bags. When the carriers are full, replace the doors and secure their latches.

Prior to landing, clear countertops and secure all storage units. Verify liquor accounting and lock the compartment. If necessary, seal frozen-food units and make one final check of the cabin for remaining glasses, cups, and food items. As always, safety is the underlying responsibility of *any* inflight service.

SANITATION AND HEALTH CONSIDERATIONS

As a flight attendant, you play an important role in food preservation and protection. Maintaining proper storage and temperature levels is the key to preventing spoilage and contamination. Keep carrier doors closed when not in use—this includes hot and cold units. All frozen food should remain in the freezer until needed. Place garbage in proper containers and keep work surfaces clean and organized. Verify that all ovens and refrigerated units are working properly and check · food items for any visible signs of bacteria or mold.

For sanitation purposes, use available tools and utensils in handling all food and beverage items. For instance, use a pair of tongs for putting ice in glasses and lifting rolls and butter pats. Do not handle glasses by their rims and use plate lifters if available. Use only clean utensils and hold silverware by its handles. If you drop a utensil, put it to the side and use a clean one. Discard any food item that drops to the floor, even if a shortage will result from the loss of it. If a passenger's tray table appears dirty or something spills on it, wipe it off with a clean towel as soon as possible.

Pay strict attention to your personal hygiene when involved in food and beverage services. According to appearance standards and health laws, long hair should be secured so as not to fall forward of the face and shoulders. Do not sneeze or cough near passengers and especially around food items. Keep hands clean by washing them with soap and water prior to any services and after using lavatory facilities.

It is vitally important that health is never compromised or jeopardized because of oversights in sanitation concerns. If, after ensuring proper protection and storage, a problem still arises, make a complete report upon return to your home domicile.

QUALITY CONTROL

Communication is an effective part of food and beverage services. You are the one who hears passenger comments regarding the service and it is your responsibility to relate these comments to your airline. Special forms are provided for this purpose and are usually completed by the lead flight attendant or galley attendant. Inflight and food services departments are always interested in your feedback regarding meals, liquor, beverages, supplies, and equipment. An inflight report form can also be used to communicate the same information.

Briefing your company management on problem areas is the best way to effect positive change. Trends are noted so that specific problem areas can be corrected and the high quality of food and supplies can be guaranteed. Be specific and include pertinent information in your description. Offering recommendations and solutions to problems is the most productive method of instituting change.

Certain controls are established for accounting of food and beverage items. Types of forms used for this purpose include frozen food and liquor control forms. The accounting sheets include a tally of used and unused items, as well as the amount of money collected and other pertinent flight information.

One very effective way of communicating service information is to talk to a supervisor. Discuss problems that occurred inflight regarding the service and express your thoughts and ideas. The professional flight attendant is one who is aware that change is needed and then does something about it!

18

APPEARANCE AND HEALTH

When you look good, you feel good. No one could deny the sense of confidence and well-being you acquire when you know you look your best. The image you see in the mirror is indicative of how you regard yourself.

Conversely, when you feel good, you look good. Not all beauty is worn on the outside. It comes from inside and influences your physical appearance and mental outlook. By taking care of yourself through proper diet, rest, and exercise, you display the respect you have for yourself.

As a flight attendant, your overall appearance plays an important role in your job function. Your appearance is judged by many people as a reflection of the airline and also of the attitude you have about your job. Body language—how you carry yourself and the mannerisms you use—is a vital part of the total impression you will make.

During initial training and throughout your career, you develop a certain "look," and this image is projected to others. It is essential to know yourself and your body in order to judge what attributes you have and how to highlight your best features. Also, learn how to recognize conflicting signals in your appearance.

A good, healthy appearance doesn't just happen as a matter of course—it takes a concerted effort to look and feel your best. Just as you set goals in your professional life, you should also set goals for your personal appearance. As a flight attendant, you are an integral part of the business world. Choosing a style of appearance depends on what looks and feels natural for you, as well as what is considered appropriate for the professional atmosphere in which you work.

APPEARANCE STANDARDS

The image you present to passengers and fellow crew members should be a professional one. An attractive, well-groomed flight attendant is preferred by the traveling public. Since the airlines want their flight attendants to project a sense of responsibility and pride, they set certain standards for appearance, which are monitored periodically by inflight management.

CLEANLINESS

Standard: Clean, well-groomed body
              Fresh breath
              Appropriate use of fragrances

The most essential part of your personal grooming begins with general cleanliness. Meticulous attention must be given to the condition of your skin, hair, nails, and clothing, resulting in an exceptionally neat appearance. There is a noticeable difference between a person who takes the time and makes the effort and one who does just enough to get by. Too many health concerns, such as handling food, are involved in the duties of a flight attendant to ignore basic grooming habits.

Proper cleansing is necessary to combat the growth of bacteria and prevent offensive body odor. Since the flight attendant job involves a great deal of physical exertion and mental stress, perspiration can occur just through performing routine duties. A daily bath or shower and the use of a deodorant are imperative to the care of a well-groomed body. Since you often speak with people at close range, it is also necessary to be sure your breath is fresh. Keeping your teeth in good condition, through regular checkups, frequent brushing, and the use of a mouthwash if necessary, helps to control the growth of bacteria in your mouth.

After your body is clean, a fragrance can be applied in the form of after-shaves, cologne, dusting powders, and perfumes. The choice of fragrance is personal—choose a scent that reacts favorably with your body chemistry. It should be light and pleasant to those around you.

SKIN

Standard: Clean, healthy looking
Clear complexion

Whether you are male or female, your skin must be treated correctly to maintain an attractive appearance. Airline standards require that a flight attendant's skin be clean, and that the complexion is clear and natural looking. This is especially difficult when you consider the influences of age, biorhythms, environment, and seasonal changes.

You work in a unique atmosphere. The air inside an airplane is extremely dry. This tends to deplete the moisture in your skin and creates premature aging. Irregular hours and constant changes in environment also contribute to the possibility of skin problems. Therefore, know your skin type (i.e., whether it is normal, dry, or oily), and know how to select skin-care products that will help counteract the conditions under which you work. If imperfections develop in your complexion, you may want to seek the help of a dermatologist, or you may be removed from your flight schedule until the problem is rectified.

Skin care incorporates a variety of treatments. A thorough cleansing should always be the first step through the use of appropriate soaps and cleansing agents. They should be removed by rinsing thoroughly, followed by the application of a moisturizer. Healthy skin has a luster to it through the process of stimulation, such as massages or scrubs.

Your aim should also be to control the oily part of your face and protect exposed skin from the harshness of the sun and wind. If you think of your skin as the shell for your body, you can understand the importance of protecting and preserving it. Avoid excessive sun exposure and use protective lotions and creams year round to maintain your skin's natural elastic tone and healthy glow.

COSMETICS

Standard: Moderate application
Natural looking
Color-coordinated with uniform and complexion

For female flight attendants, cosmetics are used to enhance facial features and as a protection from the elements. They should be applied skillfully to achieve a natural effect. The three basic steps in applying cosmetics are to clean, cover, and color. Wash, rinse, and moisturize your face thoroughly and then use a foundation that blends with your skin tone. For color accents, coordinate your powder, rouges, and lipstick color both to complement the uniform and match your complexion. Check your makeup periodically during a flight and if touchups are necessary, make them out of view of the passengers.

Appearance counselors are available for consultations at flight attendant domiciles. Very often demonstrator products are displayed so that flight attendants can sample the latest in makeup fashions. Occasionally, specialists in cosmetic-related fields conduct seminars for the express purpose of introducing new lines and techniques to flight attendants.

HAIR

Standard: Clean, shiny
Appropriate length and style
Proper hair fasteners and adornments

As a flight attendant, your hairstyle should be attractive, fashionable, and convey a natural look. It should also be neat, well groomed, and in healthy condition. The guidelines set by your airline reflect appropriate lengths and styles to be worn so as to achieve a professional look. The standards for the length and style of your hair are established to coincide with health laws as well as to complement your image and the uniform. Most regulations state that hair should be of a length or properly secured so as not to fall forward, especially during food and beverage services. Accessories such as ribbons and fasteners should be coordinated with the uniform and be the appropriate size, number, and color.

The style you choose should be relatively easy to manage for your work schedule, and at the same time be practical for your life-style outside the job. Additional considerations for deciding upon an appropriate hairstyle include your age, personality, facial structure, and hair texture. If a hat is part of your uniform, also make this a consideration for a suitable hairstyle.

Hair care takes time and energy if hair is to look its best. Establish your own routines for hair grooming according to the type of hair you have and the time available. Depending on whether your hair is dry, normal, or oily, shampoo and condition when necessary. Avoid extremely hot blow dryers and harsh treatments that may damage or break the hair shaft. If hair spray is used, use it sparingly and remember to always brush it out before going to sleep.

If you go to a professional stylist, clearly convey your ideas about how you would like your hair to look. Next to cleanliness, a good cut is the most important factor in healthy, attractive hair. Ask your stylist for an objective opinion, and remember that your hairstyle must complement the uniform.

Should you decide to wear a wig or change the color of your hair, the same standards apply. If you color your hair, be sure to cover up the new growth near the scalp for an overall even look.

Since much of your time as a flight attendant is spent away from home, consider purchasing portable hairstyling equipment that you can pack in your suitcase for use on layovers. Such equipment may include a small blow dryer, electric curlers, curling iron, brush, comb, and an adaptor/converter for electrical appliances if traveling to a foreign country.

If an airline allows their male attendants to wear beards, mustaches, and sideburns, they should be neatly trimmed and of an appropriate length. The growth of facial hair must be coordinated with the person's hairstyle, facial features, and suitable for a professional, business look.

HANDS AND NAILS

Standard: Clean, smooth-textured skin
Manicured nails

Your hands are constantly in view of the passenger, so they should be presentable and meticulously clean at all times. To supplement the loss of moisture due to working in a dry environment, apply lotion or cream to your hands. When flying in and out of cold weather, remember to wear gloves outdoors for further protection from chapping and roughness. Your hands should have a smooth look to them, without cracks on the fingers and around the nails.

Fingernails should be perfectly manicured, regardless of your sex. Keep nails at an even, medium length and never allow dirt to collect under the tips. They should be buffed or polished to give them a finished look. If nail enamel is used, select a color that complements the uniform and your skin tone. Avoid extremes in length and gaudy colors.

WEIGHT

Standard: Proportionate to height and body structure

Your weight should be proportionate to your height and body frame and reflect a trim look. Airlines usually establish minimum and maximum weights for every quarter or half inch of height for male and female attendants. You are to maintain appropriate weight limitations, since any substantial fluctuations alter not only your general appearance, but also the proper fit of your uniform.

APPEARANCE CHECKS

There are means of monitoring compliance with established appearance standards. Ideally you are to maintain a professional look at all times while in uniform, but hectic flights and unexpected adverse weather conditions can take their toll. Time permitting, keep a close watch on your appearance and make the necessary adjustments.

Most flight attendant management departments conduct periodic evaluations of your appearance. Whether these checks are conducted by a supervisor or appearance counselor, you may be evaluated before each trip or during a routine check ride. There may also be a schedule established on a yearly basis during which you must weigh-in and have your appearance scrutinized. If not able to meet required standards, you will most likely receive a negative evaluation or, if warranted, you may be removed from flight status until problems can be corrected. Extreme infractions in appearance may result in ultimate dismissal if your airline deems that your appearance is detrimental to its image. Appearance counseling is more often reinforcement of an attractive look or, if necessary, constructive criticism of minor violations of the accepted guidelines.

THE TOTAL LOOK

It isn't necessary to be the most glamorous, or most appealing one in a group—looking and feeling your best goes beyond surface qualities. An overall appearance is achieved by the interrelation of many factors. The image you portray should be a sum total of all physical features, body movements, and your mental attitude. When all of these work in harmony with each other and a comfortable balance is attained, then you have developed confidence in your actions and pride in your job performance.

UNIFORMS

Flight attendant uniforms are unique to each airline. Airlines employ leading fashion designers to create uniforms for their flight attendants that are durable, practical, and versatile, all the while satisfying current fashion trends. The primary objective of having flight attendants wear uniforms is that they are easily recognized as leaders in an emergency situation. The uniform also sets the flight attendant apart as the individual responsible for providing service and comfort.

A decision on particular uniform design and style is reached after extensive research and testing. Flight attendants are asked their opinions about color, garment pieces, and fabric. Considerations such as cost, durability of fabric, and the coordination with cabin color schemes and other employee uniforms are submitted by the airline to designers. Sample garments are manufactured and subjected to stringent tests. A few flight attendants wear these uniforms on the job to test the fabric and construction under realistic conditions. Once the test results are received, compiled, and discussed, the final choice of fabric and design is selected and the uniforms are produced en masse.

The flight attendant uniform consists of a variety of coordinated garment pieces. Since the uniform is the only apparel worn while working, the flight attendant usually has a choice of several mix and match items so that the same garment is not worn day in and day out. The male and female uniforms are designed to complement each other in color and style. Ensemble components may include any or all of the following: skirt, pants, jacket, trousers, blazer, vest, sweater, blouse, shirt, topcoat, raincoat, scarf, tie, ascot, hat, gloves, serving garment, shoes, boots, purse, wings, and overnight luggage.

On the average, a flight attendant uniform is worn for a period of two to four years before the style is changed. Airlines take great pride in the appearance of their flight attendants; thus every effort is made to replace worn-out pieces, and to change the entire look of the uniform when it appears outdated. There may be a choice of uniform garments for different seasons of the year, or they may be designed for use year round. In either case, certain items are supplied to the flight attendants at the airline's expense, and optional pieces may be purchased. In training, new flight attendants pay for the initial uniform, but subsequent replacements are usually issued free of charge throughout your career.

Standards are also established for the flight attendant uniform. From the time you check in to work a trip, and during the performance of all duties, you are expected to be in full

Male and female uniforms present a coordinated look.
Photo courtesy United Airlines.

Famous fashion designers give flight attendant uniforms a look of sophistication and individuality.
Photo courtesy Braniff International

Some flight attendant uniforms are designed to represent the region that the airline serves.
Photo courtesy Aloha Airlines

Flight attendants may select from a variety of uniform pieces to fit their own personal taste and look.
Photo courtesy Continental Airlines

uniform. Business attire may be substituted while deadheading, but there are no excuses for not having a complete and clean uniform on hand before each trip. Follow the proper cleaning instructions for each piece, taking note whether it is to be dry-cleaned or laundered. Make sure your name and domicile are written in each item and verify that each garment is in good repair. Boots and shoes must be in good condition and polished. Hose should be a color complementary to the uniform, a proper fit, and free of snags and runs. It is advisable to always carry an extra pair in your suitcase. Company-issued wings or insignia must be secured to the appropriate garment any time the uniform is worn.

Any jewelry worn with the uniform must meet appearance standards. Since accessories are the finishing touch to the entire outfit, they should enhance rather than overpower the total uniform look. Guidelines usually include restrictions on number, color, and size. Allowable pieces generally include necklace, bracelet, earrings, rings, and a wristwatch.

It is mandatory for flight attendants to maintain a professional manner and appearance when wearing the uniform. This rule applies not only on the airplane and in the airport terminal, but also while in uniform on public transportation and in layover facilities.

HEALTH

No one word is more important to a flight attendant's well-being than health. However, given the conditions under which you perform, nothing else takes more effort to maintain. The effects of exposure to high-altitude flying and multiple time changes are being studied as they relate to flight crews and frequent air travelers. A discussion of how these factors affect your physiology may or may not be included in flight attendant training programs. You should be aware of some of the health concerns of today's jet travel and what you can do to combat some of the negative, but realistic, aspects of the flight attendant job.

DYSRHYTHMIA

This condition, commonly known as jet lag, is prevalent among people traveling long distances in a short period of time. It is caused by the inability of body rhythms to function properly because of the interruptions of normal time progression. In other words, the more time zones you cross on a flight or a series of flights, the more disrupted your normal body rhythms become. The internal time of the body cannot keep pace with the fast change in external geographic time. For example, let's say that you were traveling on an international flight eastbound from the United States to Europe. If you left New York in the evening, you would arrive in London less than six hours later. However, in England it is already the next morning, but your natural body rhythm says you should be asleep for the night. Unless a gradual change in patterns can take place, your biological and psychological clocks may become unbalanced and upset.

The causes of dysrhythmia include not only distance across a number of time zones, but high-speed travel and environmental conditions as well. Your body is subjected to pressure changes, extremely dry air, and a concentration of undissipated cigarette smoke.

The symptoms of jet lag are often delayed and may not appear until hours after the plane lands. There is abnormal fatigue during which you cannot think clearly or function properly. Until you can get back on some type of schedule, you don't know whether to eat, sleep, or proceed with planned activities. You usually experience pallor of the face, dehydration, eye sensitivity, and a general feeling of malaise and discomfort.

Your body wants to readjust to a normal cycle but it takes time and a concerted effort not to prolong the dysrhythmia. The best recommendation to curb jet lag is to give in to your body's need for sleep. To prevent dehydration, drink plenty of liquids, preferably water. A glass of water consumed once an hour during the flight is recommended, but avoid drinking alcoholic and caffeine-based beverages. When traveling as a passenger, rest frequently and sleep, if possible, on the plane.

Minimize your food intake during and after a flight. Keep your watch on home time and gradually ease into your new environment after proper rest. Keep your activity at a slow pace upon your arrival. If you are working a trip and are scheduled to return home the next day, rest as much as possible to compensate for the imbalance of time.

FATIGUE AND STRESS

The flight attendant job can be quite a strenuous one. At some point rest becomes mandatory to restore a normal state of well-being. Physical fatigue results from manual labor and demanding tasks. For example, pushing a two-hundred-pound cart up an aisle can be very taxing for even the strongest person. Environmental factors such as fluctuations in temperature, intensity of artificial light, loud engine noise, and noticeable vibrations also affect you physically. You begin to notice a decrease in strength and increase in reaction time.

Mental fatigue is a direct result of stress and psychological pressures. Symptoms manifest themselves in the form of irritability and a decrease in attention span. Stress and anxiety take their toll on your appearance and mental attitude, so remain as calm as possible and try not to take accusations and verbal attacks personally. Remember, your comfort and peace of mind are just as important as the passengers'!

If physical and mental fatigue become extreme, the following are common symptoms that may occur: headaches, burning eyes, sweating, insomnia, loss of appetite, and a decrease in performance levels. Errors are made more easily and you become less cooperative. Some people are able to build up a tolerance or resistance to fatigue-causing factors through mental and physical conditioning. For instance, flying the same types of schedules for long periods of time allows your body and mind to become regulated to some sort of routine.

POSTURE AND BALANCE

Flight attendants must not only watch their posture, but must also maintain an acute sense of balance. This is necessary when walking, standing, sitting, reaching, bending, pulling, and pushing. There are certain techniques to learn, not only for the sake of overall appearance, but for maintaining good physical health. For example, a common ailment among flight attendants is back strain caused by improper body movements. When lifting heavy objects from a low level, use flexed knees and leg muscles for support, rather than bending from the waist and applying undue strain on the back.

Develop flexibility in your body posture when the aircraft is in motion so as not to be injured while out of your jump seat. Irregular aircraft movements through pitch, roll, and yaw, as well as turbulent conditions, may test your sense of balance. Distribute your weight evenly in your stance, and maintain an equilibrium in your stride.

FOOT AND LEG CARE

One aspect of your physical health which can have a great effect on your job performance centers around foot care. Flight attendants walk many miles and spend long hours on their feet every working day. Problems can arise as a result of poorly fitted shoes, bad posture, and improper grooming habits. If allowed to persist, these problems can manifest themselves in overwhelming discomfort. Basic care of the feet should be geared to your individual problems and attention should be given whenever necessary. Soaking your feet in bath salts and warm water is an effective means of relaxation. Massaging your feet with your hands and walking on a firm surface help to maintain good muscle tone necessary for the support of your body weight. Ventilate your feet to reduce the growth of bacteria and offensive odors as a result of having shoes on for long periods of time. Don't hesitate to consult a podiatrist if after daily care and proper exercise your foot problems persist.

After being on your feet for long periods of time, it is recommended that you relax your leg muscles at the completion of a day's work. This is most easily accomplished by elevating your legs and doing exercises to improve circulation. Proper leg care also takes into account that flight attendants are prone to develop varicose veins due to multiple changes in cabin pressure. It is for this reason that many flight attendants do proper leg exercises and wear support hose on the job.

EXERCISE

Exercise is necessary for your general appearance and overall body condition. Your objective should be to establish a routine suitable to your individual schedule and capabilities that will maintain good muscle tone and adequate strength. Granted, being a flight attendant involves more physical activity than other occupations, but this form of exertion is sporadic and should be supplemented by a program of regular exercise. Your routine for staying in shape can vary from active participation in organized sports to a simple program done in the privacy of your home or hotel room. Regardless of the form of exercise, your activity should include warming up, the actual program, and a gradual reduction in exertion. Your goal for good physical conditioning is to reduce caloric intake and increase regular exercise.

NUTRITION

An extremely important part of your health picture is maintaining a balanced diet. Your body suffers too many extremes and changes for you to neglect proper nutrition. By eating the right kinds of foods and satisfying vitamin and mineral requirements, you have a better chance of maintaining proper body functions and appearance.

Be attentive to your eating habits. Avoid rushing through meals, gulping your food, and not chewing each mouthful properly. Eat a well-balanced selection of food types (e.g., fruits and vegetables, grains, dairy products, and meats) in moderation, to stay within prescribed weight limitations. Supplement your diet with vitamins when the foods you eat do not contain the recommended daily allowances. Do not, however, rely on pills alone to sustain your physical health—there is no substitute for a well-balanced diet.

Maintaining proper physical and mental health is your responsibility. You were chosen as a flight attendant because of your ability to adapt to changing conditions. Therefore, there is no reason why your health should fail if you make a conscious effort to overcome adversities. Make it a point to have a complete physical examination once a year and periodically monitor your health. Prevention is the key. Through proper diet, rest, and exercise, being a flight attendant can be energy inducing instead of energy reducing.

19

IT'S ALL UP TO YOU!

What makes a job a profession? *You* do by exhibiting pride in your work and in yourself as an individual. As a flight attendant, you are a member of a highly specialized team that offers an important service to the traveling public.

"You only get out of a job what you put into it" applies 100 percent to the flight attendant profession. You can accomplish most of the tasks mechanically but only when you really put yourself into your work do you begin to derive pleasure from it.

As a flight attendant you are an integral part of a service industry. The job you perform for others does not result in a tangible product. People base their satisfaction with and judgment of an airline on the quality of service they receive. It is not as if they can return a product to the place of purchase because it does not measure up to their expectations and standards. Once passengers board an aircraft they depend on the flight attendants to tend to their needs and provide a safe, comfortable trip. You are the airline representative with whom the passenger spends the longest period of time. It is therefore up to you to leave a good impression on which passengers may base a value judgment of the airline.

In dealing with people, you must develop a repertoire of social skills. It's not easy to learn these techniques, and at times dealing with the general public can be puzzling and frustrat-

A courteous presentation enhances the passengers' enjoyment of the meal service.
Photo courtesy Western Airlines

A refresher towel coming from a friendly flight attendant completes the dining experience.
Photo courtesy United Airlines

Modern galley equipment helps the flight attendants deliver an organized, efficient service.
Photo courtesy Air California

ing. If any advice can be offered, it is to expect the unexpected. Look upon difficult situations as challenging and perhaps even enlightening. For the most part, interrelating with people is a rewarding experience. People have so much to give of themselves that you are bound to come away from any communication with some type of knowledge.

Above all, be yourself. You are uniquely different from everyone else. The airline probably hired you for many reasons, but one of them had to do with your personality. Characteristics that might describe a successful flight attendant are: enthusiastic, friendly, positive, genuine, sincere, patient, tactful, empathetic, well motivated.

An important responsibility you have as a flight attendant is to be informed. Keep abreast of current events and be aware of company and government policies that apply to your job. Answer all questions and attempt to solve problems as they arise. Know how to respond and handle yourself in a responsible manner in the face of unfamiliar situations. Maintaining an awareness about your job responsibilities and your behavior can only result in self-improvement. The more experience you gain as a flight attendant, the more confidence you will have. All of these factors—your knowledge, appearance, and attitude—lead to a favorable first, and lasting, impression.

COMMUNICATION TECHNIQUES

The communication that takes place between you, your co-workers, and passengers may be verbal or nonverbal and is as varied as the people you encounter. The mood of the exchange will be based on the purpose and content of the conversation and the attitudes of the persons involved. Effective communication stems from a direct, positive approach to the situation at hand.

CONVERSATIONAL SKILLS

The act of talking to other people requires time and effort to develop proper skills. There must be a genuine interest on the

243

part of the participants in order to have a meaningful exchange. The success of a conversation also depends on an objective evaluation of each person as an individual.

Make an appraisal of the physical environment in which an inflight conversation takes place. Consider the fact that you are in confined quarters. What you are saying might be heard by more people than you had originally intended. The difference between private and public conversations is evident through the appropriateness of the subject matter, the level of your voice, and the way you express yourself.

For more effective communication skills in a conversation there are certain rules of thumb to be followed. Any or all of the suggestions on this list may be employed during a conversation, depending on the circumstances. However, they are all based on one common denominator—respect—not only for all other participants, but for yourself.

Think before speaking
Be considerate
Use appropriate manners
Establish mutual confidence
Try to understand the other speakers' points of view
Be sincere
Show a genuine interest
Encourage others to talk about themselves
Keep personal matters personal
Create a clear image through your choice of words and use
    of body language
Respond intelligently
Speak decisively
Display a sense of humor, if appropriate
Ask questions related to the subject
Know when to speak and when to be quiet

If a situation occurs that may cause embarrassment
    apologize quickly and discreetly
    correct the wrong impression
    maintain poise

To give feedback in a conversation
    restate major points to confirm what you heard
    ask clarifying questions
    show visible reaction through facial expressions and
        mannerisms

One object of a conversation is to allow everyone an equal opportunity to speak. It may be natural for one person to speak more than others, but then this person should lead or guide the conversation rather than monopolize everyone else's time. Whether speaker or listener, as a flight attendant you are often the person responsible for initiating, guiding, or ending a conversation. How well you are able to speak and how effective a listener you are will have a great impact on any conversation.

VERBAL COMMUNICATION

In order to communicate effectively with others you must know how to put your ideas and views into words. You must also have the ability to organize your thoughts before speaking. When you work on airplanes with such a wide variety of people, it is up to you to look for common ground you share with the passengers when engaging in conversation. For instance, consider people's life-styles, experiences, and customs. Be careful in your choice of words so as not to offend anyone and use layman's terms so you will be easily understood. Your passengers are your guests and you want to make them feel at home.

The way you speak can reflect your emotional reactions. You cannot avoid having emotions, but your feelings must be expressed in a controlled, positive manner. Your responses are of the utmost importance since passengers will expect you to display the confidence befitting a leader.

When speaking, your vocal expression should be handled with skill. Be aware of the pitch and tone of your voice while using appropriate rate, projection, and inflection. Remember to enunciate and speak with animation. The proper use of all these skills tends to create a positive mental image of the speaker. Of special importance is your voice quality when speaking over a public address system to passengers or over the interphone to fellow crew members. In these situations, only your voice is going to convey a certain message, since you are only heard and not seen. You will not have the advantage of using body language to aid in the interpretation.

A large part of your conversation with fellow crew members involves supplying information and participating in ensuing discussions. It is imperative that what you say is direct and to the point, since very often time is of the essence. Make every word count.

LISTENING SKILLS

Half of any conversation involves listening to the other persons who are speaking. It is important for you to be a *good* listener in order to achieve effective communication. Over half of the breakdowns in communication are the direct result of poor listening habits. You will not always be the one to initiate a conversation on the plane, but it is your responsibility to listen and respond with interest. Passengers look to you for informal conversation and at times for travel hints and tourist information.

What characterizes a good listener? If you listen with understanding and keep an open mind about the speaker and the subject matter, then you're halfway home. Try to put emotions and feelings "on hold" in order to think more rationally. Be attentive to the person speaking and don't interrupt the conversation before the speaker has a chance to complete a thought.

A good listener also considers the speaker as an individual. As with verbal skills, courtesy and respect play a large part in effective listening. A good indication of a listener's attention to the speaker is the use of direct eye contact.

Sometimes you are not able to listen to passengers when they want to speak to you. For instance, you may be in the middle of a meal service on a short flight when someone stops you to chat about a recent vacation. Offer your apologies if you do not have time to listen. Be honest with passengers, giving a valid reason why you can't listen just then, and offer to come back later, time permitting. It's true that a flight attendant should be sociable, but with all the duties you must perform on any given flight, you must decide what your priorities are as situations arise. Given a chance to understand your position, many passengers respect your honesty and take heed of your obligations.

BODY LANGUAGE

Another dimension is added to conversation through the use of nonverbal communication. Body language reveals a lot about you and plays an important role in the way you are perceived by others. What you do is just as important as what you say. Hand gestures, body movements, and eye contact are visible indicators of your reaction and interest. All body language should be in tune with your verbal communication so as to convey sincerity and help get your point across.

Eye contact is important. Look at people directly as they board and as you walk down the aisle. This not only helps you anticipate their needs but also conveys a sense of confidence and sincerity.

A typical example of body language is the smile. Your airline expects flight attendants to smile frequently to display the

Handing out meal trays with a smile makes the inflight service enjoyable for the flight attendants as well as the passengers.
Photo courtesy Delta Air Lines

favorable image of a warm, friendly crew. Passengers also like you to smile because it gives them a feeling of well-being. Use a smile to enhance the atmosphere on board the aircraft. You are there to attend to passengers in many capacities and are often the focus of attention. Display genuine interest and be aware of your body language at all times.

INTERACTION

The working environment of a flight attendant is one of constant change. To cope with this change and the people involved, you have to understand that interaction between you and the passengers and your co-workers should be dealt with on a mature level. Understand the needs of your flying partners and passengers by being observant and asking questions. Monitor your feelings in stressful situations by showing emotional restraint and accepting your share of the responsibility.

YOU AND YOUR CO-WORKERS

As a flight attendant you are a valuable member of a team. It takes the combined efforts of all crew members on board to see to it that each flight is a success. Approach this team concept in a positive manner and respect the direction of the captain and lead flight attendant. Your work must be coordinated and organized before you can offer any type of service to your passengers. Put personal problems and biases aside. Don't allow personality differences, disillusionments, or fatigue to interfere with your job performance. If problems exist with the presentation of your service, discuss the matter in private with your flying partners. Even if working conditions do not seem up to par, these are none of the passengers' concerns, so do not discuss your problems in front of them.

As a professional flight attendant, try to understand the strengths and weaknesses that your co-workers bring to the job. Keep in mind that in a group of any size there is an intermingling of a wide variety of personalities. As long as they do not reflect a negative image, be tolerant of these differences.

You may encounter a vast range of personal characteristics in your co-workers. For example, some may be passive while others are aggressive. Some flight attendants are lax in completing required duties, yet others strive for a high level of proficiency. You will also find flight attendants who exhibit a preference for the "people" aspect of the job, and those who are strictly task-oriented.

The majority of flight attendants today were chosen because of distinct qualities in their personalities. They are usually cooperative, independent, and concerned. However, a few flight attendants do not display favorable characteristics and it makes working with them that much more difficult. Granted, circumstances are not always ideal, and people's personalities are subject to change. As a flight attendant, you learn a great deal of discipline, and you should exercise control over your thoughts and reactions.

YOU AND YOUR PASSENGERS

For a flight attendant, experience is the best teacher. After dealing with literally thousands of people each month, you acquire a veritable wealth of knowledge and understanding. You learn how to treat people with compassion, realism, and humor. Accept all differences in people related to their physical conditions, mental attitudes, and cultural backgrounds.

Each person is unique and should not be classified into a category, such as Midwesterner or commuter. Where possible, call your passengers by name and offer special recognition if appropriate. People react favorably to your extra consideration and this feeling can make for a pleasurable flight.

In relating to passengers, you may not be taught how to handle specific situations. You were hired because someone perceived in you the ability to apply good judgment and common sense. Rely also on your prior experiences and your acquired knowledge of today's air traveler. Avoid showing favoritism among your passengers—they all deserve your time and attention regardless of who they are or the fare paid for their ticket. A passenger's impression of a flight may be directly dependent on the goodwill you extend to him or her.

Carving a roast at the passenger's seat is one way of satisfying personal taste.
Photo courtesy United Airlines

ETIQUETTE

By now you should know almost every aspect of the flight attendant job as it is today. Now it's time to add the finishing touches that make you what you are—a professional. Because you are so visible and often the center of attention, your manners and behavior must reflect what is socially acceptable and required in public. It takes little or no effort to be thoughtful and considerate to others. Use phrases such as *thank you, please,* and *excuse me* whenever appropriate.

Extend your service to others in a gracious manner. It is always much more professional to address a person by his or her correct title, e.g., doctor or lieutenant. Whenever names are not provided for you by ground services, don't hesitate to approach passengers at the beginning of the flight to introduce yourself. They will usually be glad to offer their names and the flight becomes a much more personal experience.

Off the plane the same etiquette applies. Expect to carry your own luggage. If someone offers to carry it for you, accept graciously and thank the person. If you wish to tip people for their services, do so at your own discretion. Some airlines provide their flight attendants with tipping money but, if not, take it upon yourself to tip for the personal services of hotel valets, limousine drivers, room service, or restaurant personnel. Pay what is appropriate without overpaying.

When flying internationally, you should behave in a manner befitting a guest from America. Accept your surroundings in a foreign country for what they are. Don't compare others' life-styles to those of your homeland. When taking pictures, ask permission, as this is sometimes seen as an offense rather than a compliment. Observe all regulations regarding the amount of luggage you are allowed to bring and don't call undue attention to yourself. When wearing layover clothes, dress according to the custom of the area.

The more you travel, the more knowledge you will acquire regarding what is proper and improper social behavior. Your exposure to regional and cultural differences will make you aware of the appropriate form of etiquette to be used.

ATTITUDE

Job performance is measured not only by your ability to accomplish tasks, but also by the attitude you exhibit toward your work. Your attitude has a direct bearing on your life's work, your home environment, and the goals you establish. Look for the good in people. Everyone has qualities that make him unique. Your behavior and attitudes are reflected back to you through mirrored responses. That is, people tend to treat others as they have themselves been treated. It's the old Golden Rule—if you want to be treated with respect, then you must extend the same attitude to those with whom you come in contact.

A positive attitude is probably the most effective tool in handling any kind of situation. Use it to your advantage on the airplane to turn a negative atmosphere into a good one and to make a good atmosphere even better. Sometimes the negative side of an issue is the most obvious, but challenge yourself to find positive solutions. You come away with a much better

Self-confidence and a positive attitude are the main ingredients for a happy person
and a professional flight attendant.
Photo courtesy Hughes Airwest

feeling and it leaves others with a favorable impression of you
as a person, a flight attendant, and a representative of the
airline in general. A positive attitude about your job stems
from an unselfish desire to please people.

A positive attitude is the key that unlocks the door to being
open-minded, flexible, self-accepting, creative, empathetic,
and motivated. Your work, and life-style in general, for that
matter, become less complicated when you take pleasure in
the things you do and the people you meet. Knowing how to
apply a sense of humor in appropriate situations and a willingness to learn new procedures is a mark of maturity that will
add to your self-esteem.

The zest and excitement that you generate in your professional and personal life have a way of affecting those around
you. Passengers and co-workers like to be associated with a
high achiever and a happy individual. For you, there are the
rewards of self-confidence and a sense of accomplishment. Enthusiasm can become habit forming, thus influencing your
mental and emotional point of view. A positive attitude and
enthusiasm also help you achieve those goals and objectives

you value as most important in your life. Remember, it's all up to you!

YOU ...

... have an unlimited future as a flight attendant. You are among the finest professionals in the airline industry today and can make a valuable contribution to the industry of tomorrow. Be a vital part of the work force through a genuine appreciation of your job—it all comes down to reflecting pride in yourself and your profession.

... have the opportunity to be a part of a very active team of people working together toward a common goal. However, individuality is greatly respected and in turn rewards you with a high degree of self-confidence.

... can make meaningful friendships with co-workers and passengers if you extend yourself and wish to learn from others. Be creative when working in a people-oriented industry and the results will not go unnoticed.

... have something of great value in being able to seek the highest possible standards for yourself as an individual and as a professional flight attendant. Since the industry is constantly changing, so must you. If you regard this change as an opportunity for personal growth, then you have captured one of the greatest benefits of being a flight attendant.

Every facet of the flight attendant profession contributes to your personal character. It offers a view of the world around you and an unsurpassed study of human nature. Value the contribution you make to the traveling public and the business community in general. Most importantly, respect yourself as a hard-working, dedicated professional.

Whether you are just starting out in your career as a flight attendant, or have been one for years, remember that you are carrying on a proud tradition in an industry that could not exist without you.

APPENDIXES

APPENDIX A

HISTORY OF THE FLIGHT ATTENDANT PROFESSION

Now that you have become a member of the flight attendant profession, you may want to learn something about the history of your career. In the early years of the air-transport industry, there were no jet-powered airplanes, five-hour nonstop transcontinental flights, movies, television, or oven-cooked meals. Instead, imagine making thirteen stops on a twenty-two-hour flight from San Francisco to Chicago, in aircraft that often could not withstand hazardous weather conditions. That was air travel in the 1920s.

The first domestic airlines were contracted to carry mail across the United States. It was the dedication and courage of the pilots of those planes that laid the foundation for the acceptance of air travel as a mode of transportation. It took perseverance, ingenuity, skill, luck, and, at times, even the sacrifice of lives to achieve improved safety standards, more reliable schedules, faster, more efficient aircraft, and a route structure that remains virtually unchanged today. The recognition of Charles Lindbergh's achievements also did much to stimulate public interest in the airline industry.

A milestone was reached in the late 1920s when individual air carriers realized the potential of offering their services to the public by carrying passengers as well as the mail. Most air travelers were men. Once they were on board the aircraft, the copilot (on domestic flights) or steward (on over-water operations) looked after the passengers' needs. The service afforded the first passengers was minimal since the flight responsibilities involved the crew in extensive preflight to postflight activities. For example, because of the heavy physical labor involved in operating in and out of airports not manned by ground personnel, Pan American World Airways and Eastern Airlines hired stewards to work on their seaplanes. They moored the aircraft after landing, procured food provisions at local markets, loaded and unloaded cargo, and helped ready the aircraft for flight.

Soon the passenger market not only grew in size, but females became interested in air travel, too. Instead of the original two-seaters, larger planes were manufactured that accommodated twelve people. Airport terminals and facilities were improved, and provisions made for passengers' safety and comfort. All of these changes prompted a redesigning of inflight services and crew responsibilities. One of the commercial airlines to implement a unique approach to passenger service in the United States at that time was Boeing Air Transport. Although some airlines had hired men to attend to their passengers, Boeing Air Transport was the first air carrier to introduce stewardess service to the traveling public through the promotion of its Deluxe Transcontinental Service on May 15, 1930.

STEVE STIMPSON—FATHER OF STEWARDESS SERVICE

At that time, Steve Stimpson was traffic manager for Boeing Air Transport in San Francisco. The traffic department was responsible for encouraging passenger travel and worked closely with the operations department (consisting of pilots) in the safe transporting of not only mail and air freight, but the increasing number of passengers.

In Steve's many travels, he noted that not only was the copilot expected to fly and navigate the aircraft, but it was also his responsibility to see to the needs of passengers in flight. On occasion, Steve assisted the copilot in carrying out these duties, loading provisions on board, setting out maps and sales literature, and greeting passengers as they checked in for their flight. Once the plane became airborne, he distributed box lunches, served coffee from thermos bottles, and administered care—and sympathy, time allowing—to frequently airsick passengers.

With the advent of a new transcontinental service between San Francisco and Chicago, it was becoming increasingly apparent to Steve Stimpson that a more efficient means of providing for the passengers' safety and comfort had to be implemented. The concept of having an additional crew member on board the airplane occurred to Steve as he remembered his prior work with a steamship line, where stewards were hired to see to the needs of passengers. He proposed his idea to the administration of Boeing Air Transport and subsequently six men were selected as possible candidates for the position of steward.

Meanwhile, Steve Stimpson had several visits in his San Francisco office from a petite young nurse named Ellen Church. Miss Church had an avid interest in aviation and air travel, but realized the limited work opportunities at the time for women as pilots. She suggested to Steve Stimpson that he consider hiring a nurse to serve as the additional crew member. Steve agreed and immediately sent a memo to the passenger traffic manager at Boeing headquarters in Cheyenne, Wyoming. It reads, in part, as follows:

A.G. Kinsman, Passenger Traffic Mgr.   San Francisco, California
Cheyenne, Wyoming   February 24, 1930

Subject: YOUNG WOMEN COURIERS

As a suggestion—I was just wondering if you had ever given any serious thought to the subject of young women couriers. It strikes me that there would be a tremendous psychological punch to having young women stewardesses or couriers, or whatever you want to call them, and I am certain that there are some mighty good ones available. I have in mind a couple of graduate nurses that would make exceptional stewardesses. Of course it would be distinctly understood that there would be no reference to their hospital training or nursing experience, but it would be a mighty fine thing to have this available . . . if necessary either for airsickness or perhaps something else worse.

Imagine the psychology of having young women as regular members of the crew. Imagine the national publicity we could get from it, and the tremendous effect it would have on the traveling public.

Also imagine the value that they would be to us not only in the neater and nicer method of serving food and looking out for the passengers' welfare, but also in an emergency.

I am not suggesting at all the flapper type of girl, or one that would go haywire. You know nurses as well as I do, and you know that they are not given to flightiness—I mean, in the head. The average graduate nurse is a girl with some horse sense and is very practical and has seen enough of men to not be inclined to chase them around the block at every opportunity.

. . . The young women that we would select would naturally be intelligent and could handle what traffic work aboard would be necessary, such as keeping of records, filling out reports, issuing tickets, etc., etc. They would probably do this better than the average young fellow.

. . . As to the qualifications of the proposed young women couriers, their first paramount qualification would be that of a graduate nurse . . . and, secondly, young women who have been around and are familiar with general travel—rail, steamer and air. Such young women are available here.

This is just a passing thought and I want to pass it on to you.

S.A. Stimpson
Division Traffic Agent

NO was the answer Steve Stimpson received in the form of a telegram. This reply was indicative of the feeling of many company officials, but it only made Steve more determined than ever to reach his final goal.

Steve then sent a wire to W. A. Patterson, Assistant to the

President of Boeing Air Transport, suggesting a unique approach to protecting passengers' welfare. It was not until Patterson showed the wire to his wife and was convinced by her enthusiasm that he was willing to give it a try. He approved the hiring of eight stewardesses and allowed a three-month trial period in which to prove its success. Steve Stimpson was granted one month to structure the framework for what was later to become one of the most sought-after professions.

A PROFESSION IS BORN

Ellen Church was hired by Steve Stimpson as chief stewardess, and together they were given one month to define the criteria for the hiring of the additional seven crew members and outline their subsequent responsibilities. One month was a very short period of time in which to set down the guidelines for the first stewardess service; therefore, a rigid set of specifications had to be drafted for the type of person who would make the best stewardess. First and foremost, a candidate had to be female and a graduate nurse. This meant that, in addition to being institutionally trained and accustomed to working long hours, she would be intelligent, competent, and able to demonstrate confidence when facing new and unfamiliar situations. Also, she would have to have a likable personality.

Her physical attributes had to be considered as well. According to Steve, "... since weight was an important factor in those little twelve-passenger planes which had narrow aisles and low ceilings, fatties and tall girls were automatically disqualified. I set a weight limit of 115 pounds and a height of 5'4" and I wanted enthusiastic girls, so I set an age limit of twenty-five."

Additional considerations included the development of flight schedules, salaries, the designing and making of a uniform, the writing of a stewardess manual, and the creation of a training program.

The route structures for Boeing Air Transport were centered around its headquarters in Cheyenne, Wyoming. It was decided that the eight stewardesses would be divided into two groups whose home ports would be San Francisco and Chicago, the westernmost and easternmost destinations on Boeing's system. Three nurses, in addition to Miss Church, were hired in San Francisco to work the San Francisco-Oakland to Cheyenne round-trip flights. They would have intermediate stops at Sacramento, Reno, Elko, Salt Lake City, and Rock Springs. Four nurses were hired in Chicago to work the Chicago to Cheyenne round-trip segments, with intermediate stops in North Platte, Lincoln, Omaha, Des Moines, Cedar Rapids, and Iowa City. There would be only one stewardess assigned to work on an airplane at any time. Each stewardess' flight schedule had to be constructed in such a way that her flight time would not exceed one hundred hours per month. She was to be paid $125 per month and allowed an expense account for meals, hotel rooms, and additional land travel when necessary.

When it came to designing a uniform for the girls, not only its appearance but also its function had to be considered. The uniform chosen was a dark green skirt and double-breasted jacket; the material was wool because of the lack of heat on the early planes. It was complemented by a green hat that was shaped like a shower cap, designed to withstand the wind made by the propellers of the early airplanes. The girls also wore flowing green capes with gray collars and silver buttons to give the uniforms a military look. This would, hopefully, make new air travelers feel more confident and secure. Once inflight, the girls were required to change into a stiffly starched gray smock, similar to a nurse's uniform.

Steve Stimpson then began writing a manual that defined the minimum standards of conduct, emphasizing the importance of being "good girls." By the time it was finished, the manual was a four-page set of guidelines stressing specific duties and job responsibilities. It was in the form of a general circular, with supplements added on a continuing basis so that a higher quality of service and working conditions could be maintained.

Since this was a newly created position in the airline industry, a training program was necessary to familiarize the new stewardesses with their jobs. Aside from reviewing materials outlined in their manual, the only other training required would be taking one flight to test the girls for airworthiness. The success of the new inflight program now depended on selection of those girls who best met the qualifications of a stewardess.

THE ORIGINAL EIGHT

On April 24, 1930, a notice was posted at the French Army Hospital in San Francisco, where Ellen Church was once a nursing instructor. It was here that Ellis Crawford, Inez Keller, and Jessie Carter were selected. Ellen Church then proceeded to Chicago, where she hired Harriett Fry, Alva Johnson, Margaret Arnott, and Cornelia Peterman, graduates from the Augustana Hospital School of Nursing. Along with Miss Church, these women were all highly rated in the nursing field and were selected as those who would become pioneers of a brand new profession.

A PROVEN SUCCESS

A new career opportunity for women was launched on May 15, 1930. With positive attitudes and pure determination, these eight women were able to overcome the trials and tribulations of those first flying adventures. They had to deal with preconceived ideas of the passengers and pilots toward a female crew member, unforeseen duties and responsibilities, and a lifestyle unique in that day.

The public had been satisfied with existing railroad services and ground transportation for business and pleasure travel. They found the railroads very accommodating in providing sleepers and dining facilities for long journeys, and they viewed the airlines as primarily carriers of mail. In order to compete with the railway system, the airlines found it necessary to place more emphasis on accommodating passengers. Being attended to by an attractive young lady was an added comfort and convenience. The young lady was trained to cater

The original eight stewardesses were the pioneers of the flight attendant profession.
Photo courtesy United Airlines

to the welfare of each passenger and to answer questions about transportation needs.

The stewardesses initially drew mixed reactions from some "hawk-eyed, weather-beaten pilots" who viewed the presence of women on their airplanes as "just another indication of moral decay of the period." However, copilots began to appreciate that they would have to spend less time away from the cockpit and grew to accept stewardesses as an integral part of the airline operation.

During the three-month trial period, air travel became quite popular. With more people traveling, the first stewardesses realized that providing an effective service would involve not only applying the information written in their manual and company circulars, but using common sense and good judgment when faced with unexpected situations. By sharing experiences with each other and reporting to Ellen Church, they were able to better define their duties and job responsibilities.

Quite often the first stewardesses were responsible for carrying service items on board, such as food in hampers, medical supplies, and passenger reading material. Once inflight, their duties were those previously delegated to the copilot, including everything from serving coffee in hot thermos jugs to offering expert care to the airsick passenger. At times they also found themselves swatting flies in the cabin; supplying ashtrays to passengers and warning them not to throw their cigarettes out the windows (especially over populated areas and farm fields); making sure that the airplane was properly ventilated and heated; and keeping the washroom clean and orderly at all times. In addition, they were also required to carry railroad schedules for the areas over which they flew, supply passengers with current magazines such as *Life, Judge,* and *Redbook,* learn the names of their passengers, and treat everyone to equal service.

"Stewardess" was selected as the name for these young ladies, and it was a title that was to last until the early 1970s. That is not to say that throughout the years it would remain unchallenged. In Steve Stimpson's own words:

> as to the name *stewardess:* for a long time it was felt that this name or title left something lacking, and through the years, many names were suggested to replace *stewardess* such as: cadet, attendant, courier, courierette, agent, airette, purserette, airess, page, attaché, escorte, hostess, skipper, airmaid, airaide, aidette, etc., etc. But it looks like *stewardess* and the stewardesses will be with us for a long time to come.

PROGRESS THROUGH THE YEARS

Steve was right. Stewardesses were here to stay. In less than six months other air carriers saw the advantage of instituting a similar service to their passengers. In a little more than thirty years, the job of a stewardess gradually changed to keep pace with newer aircraft and a steady increase in passenger travel. But the standards established by Steve Stimpson and Ellen Church were maintained as stewardesses grew in numbers.

The qualifications and requirements changed to reflect society's attitudes and life-style. At the onset of World War II, the requirement of being a registered nurse was lifted because nurses' services were more urgently needed in hospitals abroad. This crucial time in American history, however, did not curtail commercial passenger travel, nor did it dissuade girls from seeking jobs as stewardesses.

The stewardesses were to take on a different look. Due to a textile shortage created by the war, their uniforms lacked certain detail, such as lapels, cuffs, and collars, yet maintained a military appearance. World War II was not the only influence in uniform fashion, however. In the peaceful years that followed the war, the stewardess uniform was predominantly blue in color to reflect the public's new interest in the "wild blue yonder." The military look of the past was replaced in the early 1960s by a refreshing change in style and color created by the designers of the day. Many airlines competed with one another to be represented by stewardesses dressed in the latest fashion.

Working conditions also changed. The airlines began acquiring a larger fleet of aircraft designed to accommodate more passengers over an expanded route structure. People were flying more places more often for business and pleasure. For competitive reasons the airlines began creating more elaborate inflight services, thus requiring a larger number of stewardesses per flight. To ensure a high quality of passenger service, airlines opened their own training schools to instruct their stewardesses on the latest procedures and serving techniques.

Changes occurred rapidly and often for the better. Planes were equipped with built-in modern conveniences (ovens, serving carts, etc.) to make the job easier. This was a far cry from the original eight stewardesses who previously carried cold box lunches and coffee on board for their passengers. In addition, as newer planes were designed, space was allotted on board for the storage of reading material and first aid supplies, now considered permanent parts of the aircraft.

Inasmuch as changes did occur, it is important to realize that certain aspects of the stewardess profession remained the same for almost four decades. Stewardesses were required to maintain specified weight restrictions and to agree to stop flying when they reached the maximum age dictated by their airline. Also, until legislation was passed in the late 1960s, the girls were to be single when hired and had to resign when they married. Due to these restraints, the average length of a stewardess' service was about a year and a half.

The success of an idea can best be illustrated by time. Steve Stimpson, before his death in 1974, was able to see the merit of a thought expressed in 1930. The flight attendants of today owe the principles and standards of the profession to the perseverance, courage, and adventuresome spirit of Steve and the "Original Eight" who saw to it that the career got off the ground.

APPENDIX B

JOB REFORM

The demands of the changing airline world have produced tremendous transformations in the flight attendant's job and life-style. These changes are due to social influences, union pressures, and issues stemming from the Civil Rights Act of 1964.

THE NEED FOR ORGANIZATION

As years went by, the work force of stewardesses began to grow in size, and eventually organization and a representative body were necessary. Unions began to make the needs of their members known to the individual airlines through negotiations and bargaining sessions. Today, flight attendants for the majority of U.S.-based air carriers are represented by a union.

Flight attendant unions differ in size and name, but their purpose and structure remain relatively similar. The choice of union affiliation is not an arbitrary decision for the individual flight attendant. As a group, all flight attendants for one airline belong to the same union. Among the unions operating for flight attendants today are: Association of Flight Attendants; Transport Workers Union, AFL-CIO; International Brotherhood of Teamsters; Southwest Independent Stewardesses Association; Union of Flight Attendants; Local Service

Employee's Union; Independent Federation of Flight Attendants; Association of Professional Flight Attendants; and Independent Union of Flight Attendants.

Flight attendants may have a choice in deciding whether or not they wish to join the flight attendant union representing their airline. If given the option, a flight attendant should make the decision based on a careful examination of the contractual agreement between the union and the airline. Most unions require that flight attendants become members upon completion of their probationary period following training. Members are encouraged to remain active participants in union activities throughout their professional career.

The goal of every flight attendant union is to determine pay and working conditions through the process of contract negotiations. Unions also strive for better benefits relating to insurance, medical programs, pass privileges, and retirement. Other negotiable items include scheduling restrictions and legalities, and improvements in hotel accommodations. The main objective is always to improve overall working conditions and strengthen the flight attendant's status as a professional.

Unions represent the thoughts, feelings, and attitudes of flight attendants in national affairs pertinent to their position and have an ever-increasing voice in safety matters. As issues involving discrimination began to arise, unions supported individuals fighting for their human rights.

PROGRESS THROUGH LEGAL RIGHTS AND ISSUES

The Civil Rights Act of 1964 had a significant impact on the course of human rights in the United States. It was designed to prevent discrimination on the basis of age, sex, race, religion, or national origin. It also provided flight attendants with a legal basis for challenging and eliminating discriminatory hiring practices and work stipulations. Flight attendants have come a long way since the 1930s. Working conditions have improved and discrimination has been virtually eliminated.

Issues such as maximum age, marital status, and the hiring of male attendants became the basis for precedent-setting cases that virtually changed the image of the flight attendant.

AGE

The original eight stewardesses were hired with the understanding that they had to retire at age twenty-five. As the years progressed, stewardesses for most major air carriers had to sign an agreement upon employment that they would quit their jobs when reaching a specified age—usually in their mid-thirties. This restriction was not placed on males.

As the industry continued to grow, stewardesses were hired in very large numbers. It was becoming quite costly for the airlines to sustain the high price of recruitment and training. Allowing women to stay in the job longer also proved to the airlines the value of having experienced, efficient flight attendants, who made it unnecessary to waste the time and money in perpetually training new personnel. It became evident that a stewardess' increasing age produced a maturity and sense of job commitment rather than a loss of interest.

MARRIAGE

The early stewardesses were also required to remain single as long as they flew. No other employees, including stewards, were subjected to the same ruling. As women became more interested in having both a career and a family, they were less satisfied with the marital restrictions under which they were hired. Having no precedent-setting decisions on which to base their complaints, some stewardesses chose to wed secretly, while others complied with airline policy and quit flying when they married.

Within a few years of the passage of the Civil Rights Act, lawsuits began pouring into the courts proclaiming discrimination against stewardesses because of their marital status. The airlines considered their no-marriage rule a bona-fide occupational qualification. However, when stewardesses began to contest this ruling, the airlines could not substantiate their claim that married women could not offer the same service to passengers as single women. The airlines finally realized that a person's ability to provide safety, comfort, and a feeling of security to passengers was not related to marital status.

The courts ruled that even though the airlines claimed that

single stewardesses were preferred by the traveling public, passenger preference was not a valid reason for enforcing the no-marriage rule. By 1968, the airlines started lifting their ban on married stewardesses. As this policy was later accepted and practiced by all airlines, restrictions on marital status were ended.

MALE ATTENDANTS

In the 1960s no U.S. domestic carrier was hiring males for the position of steward; however, males began to contest the hiring practice as it became illegal to discriminate against any individual on the basis of sex. It was soon judged discriminatory to refuse a male the opportunity to apply for the steward position. Employing only female attendants would have been allowed if an employer could have shown that hiring a particular sex was necessary to the operation of the business. Airlines contended that females had the attributes of poise and charm and the ability to exude warmth and compassion while serving their passengers. However, they could not prove that hiring a male for the position of flight attendant would be detrimental to the business of running an airline.

Today there are substantial percentages of male attendants working for domestic and international air carriers. This issue became the basis for establishing the title of "flight attendant" as the universal term for stewards and stewardesses.

MATERNITY

Another issue involving discrimination against females resulted when female flight attendants decided to become mothers. As soon as a female attendant discovered she was pregnant, her employment was terminated. On the other hand, male attendants who became parents were allowed to continue their flying status. As it stands today for most air carriers, female attendants must report a pregnancy immediately to the airline and are given the option of continuing their flight status up until the last trimester of pregnancy, or go on a maternity leave of absence until after delivery of the baby.

271

APPENDIX C

REGULATORY AGENCIES

FEDERAL AVIATION ADMINISTRATION

The extent of the role that the FAA plays in aviation safety can best be illustrated by reviewing some of its foremost responsibilities:

To regulate air commerce and ensure its safe and proper development

To ensure the safe and efficient use of the nation's air space under the direction of the Air Traffic Control

To develop and operate a common system of air navigation and air traffic control for both civil and military aviation

To regulate airport safety

To assist in the development of an effective national airport system

To certify individuals, schools, aircraft, and aircraft components according to government safety standards

To provide for development and improvement of aircraft

To conduct research to improve air traffic control and environmental procedures

To sponsor aviation safety programs on a nationwide basis

To discourage and detect acts of air piracy through the implementation of security screening measures

To ensure and enforce safety regulations for the protection of passengers and crew

To do all the above with due regard for the safety, environmental, and economic factors involved

CIVIL AERONAUTICS BOARD

An economic regulatory agency, the duties of the CAB are as follows:

To monitor the fare structure for passenger transportation
To issue certificates and permits for U.S. and foreign carriers
To approve and/or disapprove airline mergers
To take part in the negotiation process concerning the exchange of air rights between governments
To monitor financial standings of air carriers through established accounting procedures
To ensure service to smaller communities through payment of federal subsidies

AIRLINE DEREGULATION ACT OF 1978

On October 24, 1978, President Carter signed into law the Airline Deregulation Act of 1978. The act was designed to:

Give the CAB a new scope of authority over domestic air transportation during the transition to total domestic deregulation
Prevent any deterioration in established levels of safety
Increase competition among carriers in order that they might profit through capital gain to improve passenger service and to lower fares
Allow carriers more freedom in establishing airfares and choosing new routes and markets
Encourage entry into air-commerce service by new carriers
Ensure service to smaller communities through payment of federal subsidies

APPENDIX D

AIRPORT/CITY CODES

THE UNITED STATES

HONOLULU TIME ZONE

Hawaii
HNL   Honolulu

PACIFIC TIME ZONE

Washington
SEA   Seattle/Tacoma
GEG   Spokane
Oregon
PDX   Portland
SLE   Salem
EUG   Eugene
MFR   Medford
PDT   Pendleton
California
SFO   San Francisco
OAK   Oakland
SMF   Sacramento
SCK   Stockton
MOD   Modesto
FAT   Fresno
VIS   Visalia
BFL   Bakersfield
LAX   Los Angeles

SAN   San Diego
Nevada
RNO   Reno
LAS   Las Vegas

MOUNTAIN TIME ZONE

Idaho
BOI   Boise
Utah
SLC   Salt Lake City
Colorado
GJT   Grand Junction
DEN   Denver
Arizona
PHX   Phoenix
TUS   Tucson
New Mexico
ABQ   Albuquerque

CENTRAL TIME ZONE

Nebraska
OMA   Omaha

LNK   Lincoln
Oklahoma
OKC   Oklahoma City
Texas
DAL   Dallas
SAT   San Antonio
IAH   Houston
Minnesota
MSP   Minneapolis/St. Paul
Iowa
CID   Cedar Rapids
DSM   Des Moines
Missouri
MKC   Kansas City
Louisiana
MSY   New Orleans
Wisconsin
MKE   Milwaukee
Illinois
ORD   Chicago
MLI   Moline/Rock
       Island/Davenport
Tennessee
MEM   Memphis
Alabama
HSV   Huntsville
BHM   Birmingham
MOB   Mobile

EASTERN TIME ZONE

Michigan
MKG   Muskegon
GRR   Grand Rapids
LAN   Lansing
DTW   Detroit
FNT   Flint
MBS   Midland/Bay
       City/Saginaw
Indiana
SBN   South Bend
FWA   Fort Wayne
IND   Indianapolis
Ohio
CLE   Cleveland
YNG   Youngstown/
       Warren/Sharon
CAK   Akron/Canton
CMH   Columbus
DAY   Dayton
TOL   Toledo

Tennessee
TYS   Knoxville
CHA   Chattanooga
Georgia
ATL   Atlanta
Florida
JAX   Jacksonville
TPA   Tampa/St. Petersburg/
       Clearwater
PBI   West Palm Beach
MIA   Miami
North Carolina
GSO   Greensboro/High
       Point/Winston-Salem
RDU   Raleigh/Durham
CLT   Charlotte
AVL   Asheville
Virginia
RIC   Richmond
PHF   Newport News
ORF   Norfolk
West Virginia
CRW   Charleston
Maryland
BAL   Baltimore
Washington, D.C.
IAD   Washington, D.C. (Dulles
       International)
Pennsylvania
PIT   Pittsburgh
ABE   Allentown/
       Bethlehem/Easton
PHL   Philadelphia
New Jersey
EWR   Newark
New York
BUF   Buffalo
ROC   Rochester
SYR   Syracuse
ALB   Albany
JFK   New York (John F.
       Kennedy
       International)
LGA   New York (La Guardia
       Airport)
Connecticut
BDL   Hartford/Springfield
Rhode Island
PVD   Providence
Massachusetts
BOS   Boston

THE CARIBBEAN

Bermuda
BDA Bermuda
Jamaica
KIN Kingston
Haiti
PAP Port-au-Prince
Dominican Republic
SDQ Santo Domingo
Puerto Rico
SJU San Juan
Virgin Islands
STT St. Thomas
STX St. Croix
Barbados
BGI Barbados

CANADA

British Columbia
YVR Vancouver
Alberta
YYC Calgary
Manitoba
YWG Winnipeg
Ontario
YYZ Toronto
YOW Ottawa
Quebec
YUL Montreal
YQB Quebec

MEXICO AND CENTRAL AMERICA

Mexico
ACA Acapulco
GDL Guadalajara
MEX Mexico City
Guatemala
GUA Guatemala City
El Salvador

SAL San Salvador
Honduras
SAP San Pedro Sula
Nicaragua
MGA Managua
Costa Rica
SJO San José
Panama
PTY Panama City

SOUTH AMERICA

Venezuela
CCS Caracas
Colombia
BOG Bogota
Ecuador
UIO Quito
Peru
LIM Lima
Bolivia
LPB La Paz
Brazil
GIG Rio de Janeiro
CGJ São Paulo
Paraguay
ASU Asunción
Uruguay
MVD Montevideo
Argentina
EZE Buenos Aires
Chile
SCL Santiago

EUROPE

Finland
HEL Helsinki
Sweden
ARN Stockholm
Norway
OSL Oslo
Scotland
PIK Glasgow

Ireland
DUB   Dublin
England
LHR   London
Denmark
CPH   Copenhagen
Holland (Netherlands)
AMS   Amsterdam
Belgium
BRU   Brussels
Poland
WAW   Warsaw
Germany
HAM   Hamburg
TXL   Berlin
FRA   Frankfurt
Czechoslovakia
PRG   Prague
Hungary
BUD   Budapest
Austria
VIE   Vienna
Switzerland
GVA   Geneva
France
ORY   Paris
Italy
FCO   Rome
NAP   Naples
Romania
OTP   Bucharest
Yugoslavia
BEG   Belgrade
Bulgaria
SOF   Sofia
Greece
ATH   Athens
Spain
MAD   Madrid
BCN   Barcelona
AGP   Málaga
Portugal
LIS   Lisbon

AFRICA

Morocco
RBA   Rabat

Algeria
ALG   Algiers
Tunisia
TUN   Tunis
Egypt
CAI   Cairo
Senegal
DKR   Dakar
Gambia
BTH   Banjul
Sierra Leone
FNA   Freetown
Liberia
ROB   Monrovia
Ivory Coast
ABJ   Abidjan
Ghana
ACC   Accra
Nigeria
LOS   Lagos
Cameroon
DLA   Douala
Gabon
LBV   Libreville
Zaire
FIH   Kinshasa
Ethiopia
ADD   Addis Ababa
Uganda
EBB   Entebbe/Kampala
Kenya
NBO   Nairobi
MBA   Mombasa
Tanzania
DAR   Dar es Salaam
Rhodesia
SAY   Salisbury
Republic of South Africa
JNB   Johannesburg
DUR   Durban
CPT   Cape Town

U.S.S.R.—ASIA

U.S.S.R.
LED   Leningrad
SVO   Moscow
Turkey

IST   Istanbul
Syria
Dam   Damascus
Iraq
BGW Baghdad
Iran
THR Tehran
Afghanistan
KBL   Kabul
India
BOM Bombay
DEL   New Delhi
Burma
MDL Mandalay
Japan
HND Tokyo
OSA Osaka
Korea
SEL   Seoul
Hong Kong
HKG Hong Kong
Philippines
MNL Manila
Thailand
BKK Bangkok

Indonesia
HLP Djakarta

AUSTRALIA—NEW ZEALAND

Western Australia
PER Perth
Northern Territory
DRW Darwin
South Australia
ADL Adelaide
Queensland
BNE Brisbane
New South Wales
SYD Sydney
Victoria
MEL Melbourne
New Zealand
AKL Auckland

GLOSSARY

The definitions found in the Glossary are meant to supplement the text. For more complete descriptions, refer to the subject listing in the Index.

Aborted Takeoff/Landing The interruption of an aircraft's normal takeoff or landing procedure resulting from a mechanical malfunction or potential safety hazard.

Actual Time See BLOCK TO BLOCK.

Aerodynamics The science used in the designing of aircraft so that it functions by the effects of air in motion.

Aero-stretcher Apparatus installed in the passenger cabin to carry or hold persons physically unable to ride in a passenger seat.

Aerotitis Irritation to the eardrum during descent caused by congestion in the Eustachian tube.

Aft The rear part of an aircraft.

Agent Ground service personnel who provide specialized services for the traveling public, e.g., reservations agent, ticket agent, passenger agent.

Aileron Movable part on the trailing edge of the wing surface that controls the roll of an aircraft.

Airborne Refers to that period of time when an aircraft is free of any contact with the ground.

Air Carrier An airline authorized by the government to engage in the transportation of passengers and cargo.

Aircraft The vehicle used to transport persons and cargo by air.

Air Foil Any surface of an aircraft, movable or fixed, designed to aid in the craft's maneuverability through its relative position to the passing air.

Airline A commercial organization that engages in the business of providing air transportation.

Air Piracy Crimes punishable by federal law in which person(s) attempt to or do in fact seize or control by force or violence the command of an aircraft, e.g., hijacking.

Airplane See AIRCRAFT.

Airport The facilities used for the landing and takeoff of aircraft engaged in the receiving or discharging of passengers and cargo.

Air Route Path of air space that an aircraft occupies while operating between one airport and another.

Airsickness Motion sickness suffered by air travelers; characterized by nausea and light-headedness.

Air Space The space above the earth's surface allotted by the Federal Aviation Administration for safe travel of commercial, private, and military aircraft.

Air Speed The velocity at which an airplane travels through the atmosphere relative to the ambient air, rather than on the ground.

Airstairs Means of entry or exit on certain types of aircraft where a set of stairs is a permanent feature of the aircraft design and can be raised or lowered for use.

Air Traffic Control The vast network of radio communication facilities responsible for the safe guidance of aircraft through the nation's air space and on airport taxiways and runways.

Aisle Chair A narrow, straight-back wheelchair used by ground personnel to assist physically disabled persons to and from their seats during boarding and deplaning.

Altitude Distance above sea level, measured in feet; inside an aircraft, the elevation to which the cabin is pressurized.

Anticollision Lights Rotating lights on the top and bottom of the fuselage used to indicate position to other aircraft flying in the vicinity.

Arm The act of preparing a cabin door so that the slide housed within is ready for use in the event an emergency evacuation becomes necessary.

Arming Device Mechanism for arming and disarming cabin doors.

Arrival When an aircraft has come to a complete stop at a gate.

Artificial Respiration Life-sustaining technique in which mouth-to-mouth resuscitation is applied to a victim who has stopped breathing.

Ascent The upward motion of an aircraft.

Aspirator Part of a life raft that allows for the intake of a stream of high-pressured surrounding air in order to achieve full inflation.

Assess Conditions Under normal flight operations, the practice of monitoring the passenger cabin; during emergency situations, the practice of evaluating potential threats to the health and safety of passengers and crew.

ATC See AIR TRAFFIC CONTROL.

Attitude The position of an aircraft around one or all of its axes in relation to a fixed point of reference.

Axis An imaginary line around which an aircraft rotates to achieve roll, pitch, and yaw.

Baggage Claim An airport facility where baggage may be retrieved after having been delivered from an arriving aircraft.

Bank To turn an aircraft laterally, causing one wing to be higher than the other.

Base See DOMICILE.

Base Salary A minimum rate of pay guaranteed for a specified period of time; usually on a monthly basis.

Bassinet A portable bed used by infants during flight.

Beacon A device used for transmitting a one-way distress signal from an aircraft or raft to ships or aircraft monitoring frequency 121.5 MHz.

Belly The lower lobe of an aircraft, designed to hold cargo containers, landing gear and, in some cases, a galley.

Bidding A process of choosing a work schedule on a seniority basis for a specific period of time.

Blocks Wooden or metal blocks placed in front of and behind the wheels of an airplane to prevent its movement.

Block to Block The period of time commencing with the removal of the blocks at departure and ending when blocks are once again in place at the aircraft's arrival point; used to determine actual flight time when an aircraft is moving under its own power.

Boarding The act of entering an aircraft.

Boarding Area Departure lounge used by passengers who are waiting to board an aircraft.

Boarding Pass A card given to a passenger that authorizes his or her entry to an aircraft.

Boarding Ramp Means of access to an aircraft.

Briefing A meeting of inflight crew prior to the departure of a flight to discuss pertinent information relevant to that trip.

Buffet The area of an aircraft used to store catering supplies; becomes the center of operation from which food and beverage services are organized and delivered to passengers inflight.

Bulkhead A wall or partition dividing the passenger cabin.

CAB See CIVIL AERONAUTICS BOARD.

Cabin Interior portion of an aircraft accommodating passengers and inflight crew; extends from the cockpit entry door to the rear of the aircraft.

Call Light Visual indicator used to locate the source of a call from within the passenger cabin or cockpit.

Canopy Removable protective covering on a life raft.

Capacity Maximum number of passengers and crew that can be accommodated on board an aircraft.

Captain The pilot-in-command, who is responsible for the safety of the passengers, crew, and aircraft; sits on the left side of the cockpit.

Cardiopulmonary Resuscitation Life-sustaining technique used to revive an unconscious victim through the use of external heart stimulation and artificial respiration.

Carrier Unit Removable buffet compartments used for storing food, beverages, and catering supplies.

CAT See CLEAR AIR TURBULENCE.

Ceiling The distance from the base of the lowest cloud to the earth's surface, measured in feet.

Charter A nonscheduled flight contracted for the express purpose of carrying special interest group(s) that have entered into mutual agreement regarding cost and services with the airline.

Check-In Scheduled report time prior to the departure of a flight; commencement of duty period.

Civil Aeronautics Board Federal regulatory agency established for economic control of air commerce.

Clear Air Turbulence A disturbance of air currents encountered by an aircraft when flying through an area free from clouds.

Coach Main cabin of an aircraft designed to accommodate high-density passenger loads.

Cockpit Compartment forward of the passenger cabin from which the flight crew navigate and operate the aircraft.

Codes Three-letter abbreviations for airports and cities served by airlines; two-letter abbreviations for airline companies.

Concourse Open passageway between the main terminal lobby facilities and flight departure gates.

Configuration The arrangement of seats and other cabin features of the interior of an aircraft.

Contract Negotiated agreement between airline management and a faction of the labor force.

Control Panel Call- and light-switch panel near a flight attendant jump seat.

Control Tower An airport structure above the airport complex from which Federal Aviation Administration personnel monitor and direct arriving and departing aircraft.

Copilot See FIRST OFFICER.

Cover Letter Letter of introduction that accompanies a résumé stating an applicant's occupational objective and request for an interview.

Cowling The aircraft structure that aerodynamically encloses the engine to reduce drag; nose section of cowling provides the duct that directs air into the engine.

CPR See CARDIOPULMONARY RESUSCITATION.

Crack The slight opening of a cabin entry door as an indication to ground service personnel that the slide is not attached and the door may be opened fully.

Credited Time Amount of time for which a flight attendant receives a prorated amount of pay based on the combination of duty time and actual flight time.

Crew Complement Number of working inflight crew members assigned to any given flight.

Crew Desk Center of operations where personnel arrange the staffing of aircraft to meet the requirements established by the Federal Aviation Administration and the airline.

Crew Member Person(s) designated to perform specialized duties on board an aircraft, e.g., flight officers and flight attendants.

Crew Scheduler Person responsible for the assignment and monitoring of flight attendant work sequences.

Cruise Period of flight between ascent and descent during which an aircraft travels at a steady altitude and speed.

Customs Federal agency responsible for levying taxes against imported and exported items that exceed prescribed duty-free allowances.

Daylight Savings Time A method by which clocks in the U.S. are set one hour ahead of standard time during the summer months to allow for longer daylight hours.

Deadhead Transport of a nonworking crew member on an airplane or ground transportation for the purpose of protecting or returning from a flight assignment.

Debriefing Meeting of crew members following the termination of a flight for the purpose of discussing said flight.

Declaration A formal statement made to customs officials regarding the amount of imported or exported items liable to be taxed.

Decompression Sudden loss of cabin pressurization resulting in an equalization of inside and outside air pressure.

Departure Commencement of a flight; when the plane taxis from the terminal facilities.

Deplane To leave an aircraft at the termination of a flight.

Deploy The act of inflating an emergency evacuation slide.

Desalting Kit Set of charcoal/silver zeolite briquettes and a pouch; used on a life raft to convert seawater to potable water.

Descent The downward motion of an aircraft.

Destination Predetermined arrival point.

Discrepancy Log Book Written record of permanent cabin features requiring repair or replacement; recorded on a trip-by-trip basis.

Disembarkation See DEPLANE.

Dispatcher Person responsible for the routing and scheduling of an aircraft.

Ditching An emergency landing on water.

Domestic Flight operating within the boundaries of the continental United States and its territories.

Domicile Major airport location that serves as a center of operation for the dispatch of flight attendants and/or pilots.

Drafting Enlistment of a working crew member for the purpose of covering a flight that becomes understaffed just prior to departure.

Drag The backward-acting force on a plane inflight.

Duty Time Period of time for which a flight attendant is paid, commencing with the report time and continuing to the termination of debriefing responsibilities.

Dye Marker Chemical found on board a life raft that when placed in the sea changes the color of the water and serves as a visual identifier from the air.

Economy Standard class of service offered at a reduced fare.

Elevator Movable surface of a horizontal stabilizer used to control the pitch of an aircraft.

Embarkation See BOARDING.

Emergency Unexpected situation that poses a potential threat to health and safety.

Empennage Tail section of a plane.

Engine Power source of an aircraft of the turboprop or turbojet variety.

Engineer See SECOND OFFICER.

Enplane See BOARDING.

Entrée Main course served during a food/beverage service on board an aircraft.

Equipment All types and model series of aircraft.

Escape Hatch Means of emergency egress from an enclosed compartment.

Escape System An arrangement of evacuation routes to aircraft door and window exits that serves to expedite an emergency evacuation.

ETA Estimated time of arrival.

Evacuation Process of leaving an aircraft immediately under emergency conditions.

Extinguisher An apparatus used to fight a fire.

FAA See FEDERAL AVIATION ADMINISTRATION.

FAR See FEDERAL AIR REGULATIONS.

Fare Price paid by a passenger for air transportation.

Federal Air Regulations Rules established for the airlines by the Federal Aviation Administration to guard against potential safety hazards.

Federal Aviation Administration Federal regulatory agency responsible for the safety of the U.S. air-transportation system.

First Aid Immediate care

First Class Deluxe standard of service available to a small percentage of passengers on a given aircraft.

First Officer Pilot who is second in command and sits to the right of the captain; also known as the copilot.

Flaps Movable surfaces on the trailing and leading edges of the wing; they control the lift of an aircraft.

Flares Day or night signaling devices found on board a life raft.

Flight Movement of an aircraft from takeoff to landing.

Flight Attendant Crew member working in the passenger cabin whose prime responsibility on board is for the safety and welfare of those passengers.

Flight Crew See PILOT.

Flight Deck See COCKPIT.

Flight Number Numerical designator assigned to each flight or series of flights.

Flight Operations Center of activity for the assignment and monitoring of cockpit crews.

Flight Plan Written or oral statement of intended route of flight filed with Air Traffic Control.

Flight Station Flight officer or flight attendant jump-seat area.

Flight Time Period of time commencing with an aircraft's departure from one gate, the duration of the flight, and ending with the aircraft's arrival at the next gate.

Flotation Device Portable life-saving flotation equipment found on board an aircraft for possible use on over-water flights.

Flow Plan Organized system for distribution of inflight services.

Forward Front part of an aircraft.

Fuselage Main body of an aircraft excluding wings, tail, and landing gear.

Galley Part of an aircraft where food is stored and from which food and beverage services are prepared and distributed inflight.

Gate Departure or arrival waiting area in a terminal building.

Gateway The last U.S. city from which an international flight departs or the first to which it arrives.

Gear Hydraulically operated landing-wheel structure that supports an aircraft on the ground.

Girt Bar Long steel rod at the aircraft end of an evacuation slide that secures the slide pack to the doorsill.

GMT See GREENWICH MEAN TIME.

Greenwich Mean Time Reference local time at the Prime Meridian in Greenwich, England, which serves as the basis for calculating times around the world.

Grievance Procedure used by labor unions for filing a formal complaint with the company.

Headset Earphone apparatus used on board an aircraft for listening to audio entertainment programs piped to each passenger seat.

Head Winds Winds that move in the opposite direction of the aircraft, thus slowing its rate of speed.

Hearing Formal session conducted for the purpose of investigating both sides of an issue in a labor dispute.

Heaving Line Rope, attached to a life raft, that is thrown overboard to aid persons who enter the raft from the water.

Heimlich Maneuver First aid procedure used to dislodge an obstruction in the throat of a choking victim.

Holding Time Period of time an aircraft must wait in a traffic pattern while awaiting clearance from Air Traffic Control; prorated amount of credited time a flight attendant is allotted for remaining on board with passengers at a gate.

Home Port See DOMICILE.

Horizontal Stabilizer Fixed winglike structures on the tail of an aircraft used to stabilize the aircraft vertically.

Hydraulics Science of producing pressure by forcing liquids through a narrow opening; means by which some aircraft systems operate.

Hyperventilation A physical condition, caused by an excess of air in the lungs and a loss of carbon dioxide from the blood, resulting in rapid breathing.

Hypoxia Lack of oxygen in the blood, most prevalent after a decompression.

Immigration Federal agency responsible for entry into a country of persons who are not native residents of that country.

Inboard Toward the center of an aircraft.

Inbound Arriving aircraft, personnel, and/or equipment.

Inertia Reel Type of device with a built-in slowing mechanism.

Inflation Pump Apparatus found on board a life raft; used for manual inflation.

Inflight See AIRBORNE.

Inflight Crew See FLIGHT ATTENDANT.

Inflight Services Department responsible for the quality and type of care administered to passengers on board an aircraft.

International Refers to countries outside the boundaries of the U.S. and its territories.

International Dateline Imaginary line at 180° longitude, at which point one day ends and the next begins.

Intrastate Pertaining to travel within the boundaries of one state.

Jet Common term for a turbojet-engine aircraft.

Jet Escape Door Emergency exit door used only in the event of an evacuation.

Jet Stream A high-speed wind path high above the earth's surface that moves in a west-to-east direction.

Jetway Enclosed elevated passageway from the terminal to an aircraft used for boarding and deplaning.

Jumbo Aircraft See WIDE-BODIED.

Jump Seat Seat, located by emergency exits, in which a flight attendant sits during takeoff and landing.

Junior Crewing See DRAFTING.

Landing The act of bringing an airborne aircraft back in contact with a ground surface.

Landing Cards Admittance cards distributed to passengers before deplaning from an international flight.

Landing Gear Support wheel structure for an aircraft.

Lanyard A short wire loop used to secure a slide pack to the girt bar.

Latitude Distance measured in degrees north and south of the equator.

Layover Crew rest break between flight assignments.

Lead Flight Attendant Crew member in charge of inflight services and staff, and usually compensated with additional pay.

Leading Edge The front part of an airfoil that first meets the air.

Left The left side of an aircraft when facing the cockpit from the cabin.

Leg One flight from takeoff to landing. See SEGMENT.

Legalities Those scheduling rules and work provisions as established in a negotiated contract agreement.

Legal Rest Minimum mandatory rest period for crew members between work assignments.

Lift Personnel or cart elevator found on wide-bodied aircraft; also the upward-acting force on an aircraft.

Lightning Rods Static lightning diverters found on aircraft exteriors.

Line of Flying Crew member's schedule of trips in a specified work period.

Load Total number of passengers and crew on board an aircraft.

Longitude Distance measured in degrees east and west of the Prime Meridian.

Lower-Lobe Galley Kitchen facilities found one story below main passenger cabin on wide-bodied aircraft.

Main Cabin Door An aircraft door used for entry and exit under normal conditions and for evacuation under emergency conditions.

Maintenance Upkeep and repair operation of an aircraft.

Manager Person who supervises an inflight services office at a flight attendant domicile.

Manifest See TRIP ADVISORY.

Manual Reference book that outlines policies and procedures and must accompany each working flight attendant on every trip.

Marketing The process of selling an airline service to the public.

Mechanic Person who maintains and repairs the mechanical features of an aircraft.

Meridian Imaginary line encircling the circumference of the earth, passing through both North and South Poles; line of longitude.

Mobile Lounge Enclosed vehicle used to transport passengers between the terminal and an aircraft.

Mock-Up Replica of cabin interiors and exteriors used for training purposes.

Module See CARRIER UNIT.

Narrow-Bodied Term used to describe an aircraft that has one aisle dividing the passenger seats.

Navigational Lights Colored lights on the wing tips that aid one aircraft in identifying another aircraft's direction.

Negative Panic Behavioral reaction demonstrated during an emergency; characterized by passiveness.

Nonstop A flight without intermediate stops.

Nose Gear Landing-gear structure forward of the main landing gear.

Nose-Up Position of an aircraft when the nose is higher than the tail.

OAG See OFFICIAL AIRLINE GUIDE.

Observation Trip Flight on which a flight attendant-in-training rides as an observer and performs duties as requested by the working crew members.

Official Airline Guide Reference book that lists the schedules for all flights on commercial airlines within the U.S. and abroad except in the U.S.S.R.

On-The-Line Term denoting a flight attendant's active work status.

Operations See FLIGHT OPERATIONS.

Outboard Away from the center of an aircraft.

Outbound Departing aircraft, personnel, and/or equipment.

Oxygen Mask Facial apparatus connected to a supplemental oxygen supply that enables a person to breathe pure oxygen.

Oxygen Systems Emergency and first aid supplemental oxygen supplies.

Passenger Airline customer who books passage on an aircraft.

Passenger Service Unit Panel, within reach of the passenger seat, that houses an air vent, call button, reading light, and supplemental oxygen supply.

Passport Official document showing proof of citizenship, required for international travel.

Pilot Crew member responsible for flying an aircraft.

Pitch An aircraft's movement up or down on its lateral axis.

Pod Housing for an aircraft engine.

Pool See RESERVE.

Positive Panic Behavioral reaction demonstrated during an emergency; characterized by an outward display of emotion.

Positive Space Travel classification whereby airline employees flying at reduced fare may reserve a seat.

Pressurized The condition of aircraft cabins when air pressure is increased inflight to make breathing comfortable at high altitudes.

Prime Meridian First line of longitude used as point of reference; located at Greenwich, England.

Propeller Type of power source on aircraft that functions by air passing through revolving blades.

Propeller Wash Disturbance of air currents produced by the movement of propeller blades.

Protective Position Ideal body position to protect against injury in anticipation of an abnormal landing.

Purser Supervisor of inflight crew and services on international flights.

Pylon The aircraft structure attached to the wing or the fuselage that supports the weight of the engine and transmits the engine thrust to the airplane.

Qualification Sheet Listing of airline eligibility requirements for a specific position and general airline information.

Radar Unit located in the nose of an aircraft used to detect distant objects and their relative positions, height, and speed through high-frequency radio waves.

Radome Dome-shaped protective covering for an aircraft's radar unit.

Raft Inflatable oval- or rectangular-shaped flotation device for over-water evacuations; accommodates a group of passengers and crew.

Ramp Paved surface area adjacent to the hangar and terminal facilities; passenger stairway from the ground to the aircraft entry door.

Range Distance that can be flown by an aircraft; determined by its fuel capacity and influenced by speed and altitude.

Relief Line Scheduled line of flying comprised of trips vacated by flight attendants on sick list, vacation, or leave of absence.

Remain Overnight Legal rest at hotel accommodations away from home domicile.

Reserve A percentage of a domicile required to be "on call" to the company to cover open trips; a flight attendant who is aware of scheduled days off and is available to the company for the remainder of the days.

Résumé Written statement of a job applicant's history and qualifications.

Right The right side of the aircraft when facing the cockpit from the cabin.

Roll Movement of an aircraft around its horizontal axis.

RON See REMAIN OVERNIGHT.

Round-Trip A trip to a destination and back.

Route Predetermined path of travel.

Rudder Movable surface on the vertical stabilizer that controls the yaw of the aircraft.

Runway A narrow, long strip of paved land adjacent to the airport for the takeoff and landing of airplanes.

Safety Card Information card at each passenger seat that highlights emergency-exit locations, oxygen use, seat-belt operation, protective position, and flotation equipment.

St. Elmo's Fire Visible bluish corona resulting from the buildup of electrical charges.

Scheduling Process of devising and assigning work schedules.

Sea Anchor A conical, canvas-covered frame found on a life raft, that, when thrown overboard, reduces drift.

Seat Belt A restraining strap attached to each passenger and crew seat that buckles across a person's lap to prevent injury from sudden aircraft movements.

Second Officer Member of flight crew who sits behind the copilot and monitors the operation of aircraft systems; also known as an engineer.

Security System of screening all persons entering an aircraft departure area to discourage and detect acts of air piracy or unlawful intent.

Segment One flight from takeoff to landing; may be a portion of a complete flight sequence. See LEG.

Seniority Priority system based on longevity with the company.

Seniority Number In the training academy it is determined by age or social security number; on the line it is determined by the length of service as a flight attendant.

Service Center Main galley on a wide-bodied aircraft.

Shoulder Harness Restraining strap, worn by crew members on a jump seat, that passes over the shoulders to the lap and attaches to a seat belt.

Sidewall The vertical surface of the cabin interior wall.

Skycap A porter at the entry of an airport terminal who assists passengers with baggage.

Slats Movable flaplike surfaces on the leading edge of the wing.

Slide Inflatable rectangular chute

deployed during emergency evacuations for egress of passengers and crew from the aircraft to the ground.

Space Available Travel classification whereby airline employees flying at reduced fare cannot reserve a seat, but may stand by if one is available.

Spoilers Movable flaps on a wing's surface to decrease lift and increase drag.

Stabilizer Airfoil on the horizontal tail surface of the airplane to increase stability.

Standard Time Local time of any given time zone in the United States.

Standby A type of reserve availability whereby a flight attendant may be called for immediate trip coverage; type of passenger who does not possess a confirmed reservation for a flight; a method of travel by company personnel who are in possession of a reduced fare ticket or a pass.

Stewardess See FLIGHT ATTENDANT.

Stow The securing of baggage and aircraft equipment for takeoff and landing.

Stratosphere Atmospheric layer six to fifteen miles above the earth's surface.

Supervisor Management person responsible for evaluating flight attendant job performance; may work in an office or on board an aircraft.

Supplemental An air carrier authorized to operate charter flights to supplement scheduled service.

System Board A panel of company and union officials who hear and decide grievance cases on an appeals level.

System Timetable A booklet or brochure listing all scheduled flights operated by an airline.

Tail Winds Winds blowing in the same direction as the aircraft, thus increasing its speed.

Takeoff Commencement of a flight; when the aircraft is free of contact with the runway.

Taxi Slow movement of an aircraft under its own power from the terminal building to the point of takeoff, or from the landing of an aircraft to the terminal building.

Terminal Airport facilities utilized by airlines for arriving and departing flights.

Through Term used to describe a flight, crew, or passengers continuing on the same trip route after an intermediate stop.

Thrust The forward-acting force on an aircraft.

Ticket Counter Location where passengers purchase tickets, check luggage, obtain seat assignments, or make future reservations.

Ticket Coupon Printed document issued to passengers demonstrating proof of purchase for passage on a flight and the conditions of liability for such travel.

Ticket Wallet Container that holds the passenger's ticket coupon and baggage claim checks.

Tie-Down Locking devices built into the floor of the aircraft to secure serving carts inflight.

Time Zone A 15-percent segment of the earth's circumference.

Toggle Switch Lever which moves back and forth to open or close a power system.

Trailing Edge Last part of an airfoil to go through the air.

Transceiver Device on a life raft, much like a walkie-talkie, that transmits a distress signal over frequencies 121.5 MHz and 123.1 MHz.

Transcontinental That which travels across the continental U.S.

Trip A flight or series of flights.

Trip Advisory A briefing sheet that lists passenger and flight information.

Trip Pairing Combination of flights to be staffed by flight attendants that meets with contractual legalities.

Trip Sequence Combination of trip pairings for a given time period.

Trip Trade An exchange of trips between two consenting flight attendants.

Troposphere Atmospheric layer extending from the earth's surface to twelve miles high at the poles and six miles high at the equator.

Turbojet A type of engine using a gas turbine and turbine-driven compressor.

Turboprop An engine powered by a gas-turbine-driven propeller.

Turbulence Jolts or sudden movements of an aircraft caused by changes in atmospheric conditions.

Turnaround Type of work assignment whereby a crew member originates from an airport and returns to the same location in the period of one day.

Twenty-Four-Hour Clock Clock used in the airline industry in which each hour of the day has an assigned number from one to twenty-four.

Union A labor organization whose membership consists of one faction of the work force in a company.

Vertical Stabilizer Finlike fixed structure on the tail of an aircraft; used to stabilize the aircraft horizontally.

Visa Endorsement on a passport that entry to a country is authorized.

Visibility Distance from a given point to the horizon that indicates a clear view.

Vortex Generator Small metal tabs on an aircraft's wing surface used to break the airflow.

Weight Manifest Record of total aircraft weight prior to takeoff.

Wide-Bodied Term used to describe an aircraft that has two aisles dividing the passenger section.

Wing Horizontal airfoil attached to an aircraft's fuselage to provide lift.

Yaw An aircraft's movement around its vertical axis.

Zone Portion of a passenger cabin interior.

BIBLIOGRAPHY

BOOKS

Abernathy, Dr. C. Cecil. *You and Success in the Working World.* Downey, California: Abernathy Enterprises, 1976.

American National Red Cross. *Advanced First Aid and Emergency Care.* Garden City, New York: Doubleday and Co., 1972.

Banaka, William H. *Training Indepth Interview.* New York: Harper & Row Publishers, Inc., 1971.

Bernardo, James V. *Aviation in the Modern World.* New York: E. P. Dutton and Co., Inc., 1960.

Bilgeleisen, J. I. *Job Résumé.* New York: Grosset, 1969.

Black, James M. *How to Get Results from Interviewing.* New York: McGraw-Hill, 1970.

The Boeing Company. *Pedigree of Champions.* 1977.

Bolles, Richard N. *What Color Is Your Parachute?* Berkeley, California: Ten Speed Press, 1972.

Caves, Richard. *Air Transport and Its Regulators.* Cambridge, Massachusetts: Harvard University Press, 1962.

Chapman, Elwood N. *Career Search, A Personal Pursuit.* Chicago, Illinois: Science Research Associates, Inc., 1976.

Department of Transportation. *FAA Historical Fact Book—A Chronology, 1926–1971.* Washington, D.C.: Federal Aviation Administration, 1974.

Donaho, Melvin W., and Meyer, John L. *How to Get the Job You Want.* Englewood Cliffs, New Jersey: Prentice-Hall, 1976.

Edlund, Sidney W. *Pick Your Job and Land It.* Santa Barbara, California: Sandollar Press, 1973.

Gentle, Ernest J. *Aviation and Space Dictionary.* Los Angeles: Aero Publishers, 1974.

Glines, Carroll V. *Saga of the Air Mail.* Princeton, New Jersey: D. Van Nostrand Co., Inc., 1968.

Grant, Harvey, and Murray, Robert. *Emergency Care.* Bowie, Maryland: Robert J. Brady Co., 1971.

Haldane, Bernard. *Job Power Now.* Washington, D.C.: Acropolis Books, Ltd., 1976.

Hix, Charles. *Looking Good.* New York: Pocket Books, 1977.

Irish, Richard K. *Go Hire Yourself an Employer.* New York: Anchor Books, 1973.

Kane, Robert M., and Vose, Allen D. *Air Transportation.* Dubuque: Kendall/ Hunt Publishing Co., 1976.

Keefe, John. *The Teenager and the Interview.* New York: Richards Rosen Press, 1971.

Lathrop, Richard. *Who's Hiring Who?* Berkeley: Ten Speed Press, 1977.

Rothenberg, Robert E., M.D., F.A.C.S. *First Aid—What to Do in an Emergency.* New York: Medbook Publishing, Inc., 1967.

Taylor, Phoebe. *How to Succeed in the Business of Finding a Job.* Chicago: Nelson-Hall Publishers, 1975.

Van Sickle, Neil D. *Modern Airmanship.* New York: Van Nostrand-Reinhold Company, 1971.

Ware, Kay, and Sutherland, Lucille. *Let's Read About Time.* New York: Webster Publishing Company, 1960.

Whitcomb, Helen, and Lang, Rosalind. *Today's Woman.* New York: McGraw-Hill, 1976.

PERIODICALS

AFA Flightlog. "Deregulation." Association of Flight Attendants, Vol. 16, #1, March, 1978, pp. 8–9.

Airfair. "Something New in the Air? Not Exactly!!" May, 1975, pp. 18–19.

Airfair. "Cut Rate Fares: Stimulation or Strangulation?" March, 1978, p. 14.

Airfair. "Eastern Airlines Turns 50." July, 1978, p. 18.

Airline Pilot. "Supplementals: Repositioning for the Future." January, 1978.

Airline Pilot. "The Passenger's Perspective." February, 1978.

Business Week. "Carry-on Luggage Worries the FAA," p. 80, and "Pan Am: In the Black—For Now," September 5, 1977, pp. 52–53.

Business Week. "A Commanding Voice in Airline Reform." November 14, 1977.

Clips. "Aviation Pathfinder Recalls Hiring First Stewardess." United Airlines Public Relations, February 13, 1974.

Mainliner Magazine. "30 Years of Stewardesses." United Airlines Publicity Department, Chicago: Vol. 4, #5, May, 1960, pp. 1–2.

Mainliner Magazine. "How it all began." United Airlines Public Relations Department, Chicago: Vol. 9, #5, May, 1965.

Time. "Airlines: All's War in Fares." February 13, 1978, pp. 74–75.

NEWSPAPERS

Denver Post. "Airline Stewardess 'Inventor' Reminisces." December 26, 1962, p. 27.
Independent-Press-Telegram. "Once They Checked Floor Bolts, Flying Cigar Butts." Long Beach, California, May 15, 1955.
Los Angeles Times. "Originator of Radical Idea." March 19, 1972.
Los Angeles Times. "Flight Attendants Now Less Ornamental, More Militant." September 12, 1976, Part VI, p. 1.
New York Times. "The Airlines Try to Cope With Freedom." April 23, 1978, Section 3, p. 1.
Oakland Tribune. "Carter OKs Low Air Fares." September 27, 1977.
Palo Alto Times. "CAB chief offers approach to airline 'bumping.'" July 26, 1977.
Palo Alto Times. "Traveling through the air fare." September 28, 1977.
Palo Alto Times. "Airline rivalry is a boon to passengers." November 19, 1977.
San Francisco Chronicle. "Service in the Sky." May 15, 1965.
San Francisco Chronicle. "Air Waves Jolt Jet—11 Hurt." April 20, 1978, p. 2.
Star-Ledger. "Checks show increase in airport guns." April 12, 1978.

BROCHURES AND BOOKLETS

"The Airport—Its Influence on the Community Economy." Systems Planning Division, Airports Service, Federal Aviation Administration, 1967.
"Air Traffic Control." Department of Transportation, Federal Aviation Administration, 1978.
"Career Opportunities for Attorneys with the CAB." Civil Aeronautics Board, Revised, July, 1975.
"Explanation of a Miracle." McDonnell Douglas, Long Beach.
"Federal Aviation Administration." Department of Transportation, Washington, D.C., 1978.
"How to Do It: A Guide for Preparing Your Résumé." State of California Health and Welfare Agency, Employment Development Department, June, 1971.
"Information Guide for Training Programs and Manual Requirements in the Air Transportation of Hazardous Materials." Advisory Circular, 121–21, July 30, 1976; Department of Transportation, Federal Aviation Administration.
"L-1011 Flight Crew Familiarization." Lockheed Company.
"McDonnell Douglas' DC-10 Family, Technical Summary." Douglas Aircraft Company.
"The McDonnell Douglas DC-9 Super 80." Douglas Aircraft Company.
"Review of Federal Aviation Administration Activities." Fiscal Year 1975, U.S. Department of Transportation, Federal Aviation Administration.
"Standard Time in the U.S." Department of Transportation, July, 1970.

MISCELLANEOUS

Capricorn Television Enterprises, Inc., July 3, 1962, script from "Who in the World."

Collier's Encyclopedia. 031, MacMillan Educational Corporation, P. F. Collier. Inc., New York, 1978.

Fair Employment Practice Cases. Bureau of National Affairs, Inc. Washington, D.C., 1975; Vol. 9.

Federal Supplement. "Cases Argued and Determined with U.S. District Courts, U.S. Customs Court and Rulings of the Judicial Panel on Multidistrict Litigation." St. Paul, Minnesota, West Publishing Company, 1970; Vol. 308 (Sprogis), pp. 1057–1060, and Vol. 311 (Diaz), pp. 559–569.

The Lore of Flight. New York: Crescent Books, 1976.

Original Memo, Steve Stimpson, "Reminiscing." Los Angeles, May 12, 1955.

Original and Revised Stewardess Manuals, Boeing Air Transport, Steve Stimpson, 1930.

Pilot's Handbook of Aeronautical Knowledge. New York: Arco Publishing Company.

INDEX

A

J

Jet engines, 87
Jet lag, 236–37
Jet streams, 89
Job-hunting technique, 9–10
Job interview. *See* Interviews
Judgment, 64
Jump seats, 122

L

Landing, 169
  abnormal, 186–87
  on water, 195–97
Landing gear, 86–87
Lavatories, 124–25, 162–63, 165
Layover, 174
Leadership role of flight attendant, 176–78
Lead flight attendant, briefing and, 151–52
Leading edge, 83
Leading edge devices, 84
Leaves of absence, 21
Leg care, 238–39
Legal rest, 141
Life rafts, 188–89
Life vests, 188
Lift, 77
Lightning, 91
Lights, 164–65
  emergency, 189
  exterior (navigational), 87–88
  passenger cabin, 123
Liquor. *See* Alcoholic beverages;
  Food and beverage services
Listening skills, 246–47
Living quarters during training, 46
L-188, 114–15
L-1011, 116–17

M

Male attendants, 271
Manual, 51
Marital status, 18
Marriage, 270–71
Maternity, 271
Meal services, 216–19
  See also Food and beverage
    services
Megaphone, 187–88
Mentally handicapped passengers, 134
Money, 55
  See also Accounting procedures
Movies, 165

N

Nails, 239
Night flights, 166–67
Nonambulatory passengers, 133
Nutrition, 239–40

O

Orientation, 50–51
Oxygen, first aid, 200–3
Oxygenated passengers, 132
Oxygen bottle, portable, 200–1
Oxygen masks, 122
  in a decompression, 181

P

Panel interview, 34–35
Passenger briefing card, 121
Passenger cabin. *See* Cabin
Passenger convenience items, 121, 125